# Business Metadata

**Praise for Business Metadata**

"Despite the presence of some excellent books on what is essentially "technical" metadata, up until now there has been a dearth of well-presented material to help address the growing need for interaction at the conceptual and semantic levels between data professionals and the business clients they support. In **Business Metadata,** Bill, Bonnie, and Lowell provide the means for bridging the gap between the sometimes "fuzzy" human perception of data that fuels business processes and the rigid information management models used by business applications. Look to the future: next generation business intelligence, enterprise content management and search, the semantic web all will depend on business metadata. Read this book!"

—David Loshin, President, Knowledge Integrity Incorporated

These authors have written a book that ventures into new territory for data and information management. There are several books about metadata, but this is the first to offer in-depth discussion of the important topic of business metadata.

Business metadata is really about understanding the business – something that IT people have struggled with since the dawn of information technology. I see this as a "must read" book for for anyone with a role in data strategy, data architecture, data governance data stewardship, IT compliance and audit, or improving data quality.

Not just theory, but rich with experience-based examples, this book dives deep into the why, what, how, when, where, and who of business metadata. It is sure to be a valuable contribution to the field of data management.

—David L. Wells, Director of Education, TDWI: The Data Warehousing Institute

# Business Metadata
## Capturing Enterprise Knowledge

W.H. Inmon
Bonnie O'Neil
Lowell Fryman

AMSTERDAM · BOSTON · HEIDELBERG · LONDON
NEW YORK · OXFORD · PARIS · SAN DIEGO
SAN FRANCISCO · SINGAPORE · SYDNEY · TOKYO

Morgan Kaufmann Publishers is an imprint of Elsevier

| | |
|---|---|
| Publisher | Denise E.M. Penrose |
| Publishing Services Manager | George Morrison |
| Senior Project Manager | Brandy Lilly |
| Assistant Editor | Mary James |
| Cover Design | Joanne Blank |
| Composition | SPI |
| Copyeditor | Betty Pessagno |
| Proofreader | Phyllis Coyne et al. |
| Interior printer | Sheridan Books |
| Cover printer | Phoenix Color |

Morgan Kaufmann Publishers is an imprint of Elsevier.
30 Corporate Drive, Suite 400, Burlington, MA 01803, USA

This book is printed on acid-free paper.

**Library of Congress Cataloging-in-Publication Data**
Inmon, William H.
    Business metadata : the quest for business clarity / W.H. Inmon, Bonnie O'Neil, Lowell Fryman.
        p. cm.
    Includes bibliographical references and index.
    ISBN 978-0-12-373726-7 (pbk. : alk. paper) 1. Database management. 2. Metadata. 3. Management information systems. I. O'Neil, Bonnie K. II. Fryman, Lowell. III. Title.

    QA76.9.D3I53744 2007
    005.74–dc22

                                                                            2007015136
ISBN: 978-0-12-373726-7

Printed in the United States of America
07  08  09  10  11  5  4  3  2  1

# Brief Table of Contents

# Complete Table of Contents

Chapter 9

**Business Metadata Infrastructure** 157

Chapter 10

**Data and Information Quality as Business Metadata** **175**

Chapter 11

**Semantics and Business Metadata** **195**

Chapter 12

**Unstructured Business Metadata**                                    **219**

Chapter 13

**Business Rules**                                                   **235**

# Preface

## Purpose of this Book

Data without context is worthless. We as IT professionals have seen countless times where people misunderstood the data—and the consequences were not pretty. On the flip side, when presented with context behind the data (the background, history, assumptions, business rules, definitions of terms, etc.) things became clearer, people understood each other better, and decisions were easier, with better results. We have a name for this business context behind data: it's called Business Metadata.

There are a bunch of books on the market which talk about metadata in general; one of which was written by Adrienne Tannenbaum, our reviewer. It is not our intention to replicate what has already been said in these books. The purpose of this book is to educate IT professionals, specifically data experts, to the problem of delivering the context behind data to businesspeople directly. It is our experience that the current literature on metadata stresses its value to IT. This book is about serving the business directly.

## Intended Audience

This book is geared mainly for IT professionals and data practitioners. It is written for the lowest common denominator in that segment, however; there are no code fragments in this book and you don't have to be an Oracle DBA to read it. It is geared for business analysts, IT managers, data and enterprise architects, and all sorts of IT positions that do not necessarily "cut code" for a living. However, developers can also glean a lot from the book, because it provides valuable perspective for adding value to our customers: the businesspeople.

Speaking of businesspeople, we are hoping that they will catch the vision of business metadata, and not only read the book but encourage their IT departments to read it and provide them with the needed motivation by saying: "This is what I want you to do!" Then they should turn around and fund it!

## How Technical is this Book?

This book provides an overview of issues surrounding business metadata. It covers both technical and non-technical topics, mainly from an architectural perspective. It is not intended as a technical reference but in many cases will point the reader to the appropriate reference if more technical depth is required.

## Book Organization

The book is organized into four sections:

Rationale and Planning: Why go to all the trouble of capturing and delivering business metadata? These four chapters provide lots of ammunition for funding business metadata initiatives.

How To: This section provides practical ideas for implementing business metadata, from its capture, from both people and technical sources, to its delivery. There are also chapters on how to initiate a business metadata project and the infrastructure required.

Special Categories of Business Metadata: This chapter highlights special types of metadata that have their own particular care and feeding, such as data quality, compliance, business rules and unstructured data.

Putting it All Together: This is the summary and conclusion of the book, reiterating why business metadata is so important, why your business people should be demanding it, and what you need to do about it.

## Acknowledgements

Obviously, the ideas in this book represent what we have learned and tested in the "school of hard knocks". We are extremely grateful to have had the privilege of assisting many clients over the years with their data problems, and it is that combined wisdom that has been jointly acquired in partnership with them that has formed the basis of this book. In particular, we would like to thank Bonnie's company, Project Performance Corporation, who gave her the opportunity and time to write this book and contributed several successful case studies and screen shots that are in the book; Dave Neitz and Bryan Stroble of Dex Media; Phillip Slater; Dean Murphy of Fed Ex Freight; EPA Quality Staff; Patrick Heinig for all kinds of wonderful insights; Rajeev Kumar, Jordan Rose, Zach Wahl, Mike Fleckenstein and Dale Tuttle of PPC; Earl Russell, Lucas Aimes, Alison

Case and Yazmin Rowe of ATF; Theresa Fresquez, Melanie Rhinehart and Leslie Cone of BLM; Ken Chomic, who with Bonnie O'Neil was often known as the "Bonnie and Ken" show due to our successful projects. We are sure we are forgetting some, so for all those who we have worked with in the past and who have contributed to this body of knowledge, we are thankful.

Vendors have been really helpful, especially with supplying screen shots of their new products, and some on extremely short notice. We would like to thank Ajay Gandhi from BEA, Steven Totman from IBM, and James Taylor from Fair Isaac.

We also wish to thank everyone we have quoted in the book, who are too numerous to list here. They represent the body of knowledge that served as the springboard for the ideas in this book.

We were indebted to the great quality of reviewers we had, all knowledgeable in one or more specialty areas covered in this book, and all authors in their own right, with at least one book to their credit. They are: Sid Adelman, Adrienne Tannenbaum, Dave Hay and Dave McComb. Thanks to David Loshin, who reviewed one chapter with so many ideas and thought-provoking comments that we were sad to lose him; he ditched us to go write a book of his own! We wish him much success in that endeavor.

We are very privileged to have such a great editor, Diane Cerra and assistant editors Asma P and Mary James. Diane was extremely responsive and helpful, guiding us through the process and helping us figure out delivery dates that would work for everyone.

On a personal note, this has been an extremely hectic time in the O'Neil household, with the delivery of final manuscript due around the same time as Chris O'Neil's movie was released, The Last Mimzy. Tyler O'Neil has also been very busy, visiting colleges and finishing up his Eagle Scout requirements. Tyler is now a published author too; one of his poems got accepted in an anthology. We are celebrating the completion of these things! We are thankful that we survived the birthing of this book during these frantic times.

Lowell and Bonnie are grateful for our friendship with Bill Inmon, who was very instrumental in getting this book off the ground. Each of us did our share, and Bill helped us get up the initiative to do this project. We deeply appreciate Bill's knowledge of the industry and his encouragement that we really did have an important idea that can make a difference in an ever-changing landscape of IT.

Thanks to all.

**W.H. Inmon**
Castle Rock, CO

**Bonnie K. O'Neil**
Golden, CO

**Lowell Fryman**
Thornton, CO

# Introducing
# Business Metadata

## 1.1 Introduction

Business metadata has existed since man formed the first business. Then all business metadata existed in the heads of the business owner and employees. Over time some of the business metadata was recorded on the writing instruments that were available. While much of our business metadata today also exists in the heads of the business's employees, a significant amount of it has been captured in the form of documents, pictures or illustrations, e-mails, spreadsheets, or in databases and technology tools.

This book explores the often neglected role of business metadata in today's world. It is not merely a technology book, though we envision that the main audience will be made up of technology practitioners. It touches upon many trends evident in the use of technology today, by businesspeople and technical people alike. Although we will discuss traditional metadata technology, we will also venture into technology subjects such as:

✦ Web 2.0

✦ "The Semantic Web"

✦ Collaboration and Groupware

✦ "The Wisdom of Crowds"

✦ Data Management and Governance

The proper exploitation of business metadata, by both technologists and businesspeople, can revolutionize the use of technology, making it the facilitator of enterprise knowledge that it was always meant to be. Technology can lend assistance to how business metadata can enable business to be conducted on many levels, from facilitating communication and fostering true understanding to providing background information so that appropriate decisions can be made.

Technical metadata has been around since the invention of computers; it has had various incarnations based on the requirements of the technology, but technical metadata has always been found in one form or another. The first section of this chapter covers a brief history of information technology, highlighting where business and technical metadata in general has surfaced and what role it has played over the years.

Metadata can be broken down into two major categories, based on the audience that it serves: business and technical. Commercial off-the-shelf software products (COTS) have in the past focused on technical metadata, which serves the technical practitioner, programmer, or DBA (database administrator). Technical metadata has been seen as important to managing the technical environment, especially as these environments get increasingly more complex.

Business metadata concerns itself with assisting businesspeople, nontechnical users, in understanding the data. It adds context to the data. It is meant to communicate with businesspeople and not the technicians.

This chapter provides examples of what simple, common, everyday business metadata looks like and traditionally where it is stored. Today a lot of attention is being given to business reference data or Master Data Management, and this subject will be discussed briefly in the context of business metadata.

This chapter also discusses how business metadata changes over time. It is important to consider exactly what is changing: is it just the instance of the data, or is it the meaning of the field (metadata)? If it is the metadata, then the business metadata is changing, and it is important that the business is aware of this because it affects the interpretation of the data. Business metadata is all about the correct interpretation of the data and how this affects the business as a whole. And this book examines all the facets of business data, demonstrating its overall role and importance. The diligent management of business metadata can greatly enhance the running of the business and its efficient and effective use of information throughout the enterprise.

The rest of the book will discuss topic such as:

- ✦ Where business metadata comes from
- ✦ How you capture it when it lives in people's heads
- ✦ How you would implement a business metadata initiative
- ✦ Who funds such an initiative
- ✦ Where you would store the business metadata
- ✦ How you would integrate business metadata with technical metadata
- ✦ How you would deliver it to the business community in such a way as to be useful

In addition, special classes of business metadata will be introduced, such as:

- ✦ Unstructured business metadata (also covered briefly in this chapter)
- ✦ Business rules
- ✦ Data/information quality
- ✦ Semantics
- ✦ Governance and compliance

# 1.2 A Brief History of Metadata

Business metadata can be traced back to the very earliest information systems. In order to identify the roots of business metadata, it is necessary to go back to the beginning. We will not review all of the forms of its technological lineage, such as networks or online applications; rather, we will just cover some of those technologies that impact our discussion of business metadata.

### *1.2.1   In the Beginning*

In the beginning were early forms of storage and technology. There were paper tape and punched cards. These early storage media operated on the basis of punches (chads) made in paper, which represented text or numbers. The languages that operated on these early forms of storage were assembler, COBOL, and Fortran (see Figure 1.1). The storage media was good for small amounts of data to be used in a short amount of time. But when a lot of data appeared or when the data had to be used over a long period of time, these storage media were not adequate.

Soon magnetic tape appeared and much more data could be stored much more reliably. Magnetic tape was a lot faster to access than punched cards and magnetic tape could handle a lot more data (see Figure 1.2).

A structure of data called the "master file" grew up with the magnetic tapes of the day. The master file was the place where applications stored data that was central to the processing of the application. But magnetic tapes were not without their limitations. On the occasion that a magnetic tape shredded or lost its oxide, the tape and all its data were rendered useless. And with a magnetic tape it was often necessary to spin the entire tape in order to look at 5% or less of the data.

### *1.2.2   Disk Storage*

Soon another storage medium appeared (see Figure 1.3). This medium was called the disk store, or DASD (direct access storage device). With disk storage, data could be accessed directly. And with disk storage lots of data could be stored (relative to the amount of data that could be stored on punched cards).

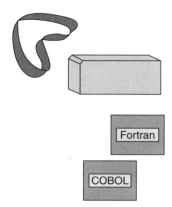

**Figure 1.1**   Paper Tape, Punched Cards, COBOL, and Fortran.

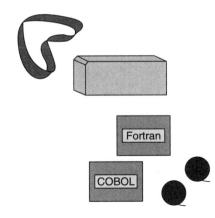

**Figure 1.2**   Magnetic Tape Is Invented.

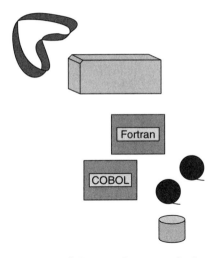

**Figure 1.3**   Disk Storage Comes on the Scene.

Soon applications built on disk storage began to appear. With the advent of disk storage began a class of system software known as a database management system (DBMS), and soon after the DBMS came online database applications (see Figure 1.4). Online database applications opened up computing to the corporate world in a way that nothing previously had approached. With online systems came transaction processing. And with transaction processing, the clerical community of the corporation was exposed to the computer.

Soon there were bank teller systems, ATM systems, airline reservation systems, manufacturing control systems, retailing systems, and many more.

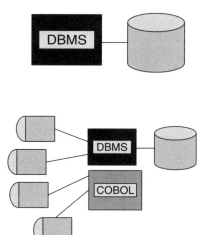

**Figure 1.4** DBMSs and Online Database Applications.

Prior to online processing, if the computer went down, the business hardly knew it. But with online processing, if the computer went down or the computer slowed, the business was affected negatively in many ways. With the power rendered by online processing and disk storage came even more applications.

### 1.2.3 Access to Data

Soon lots of applications were springing up, and with the applications came the realization that entire large groups of people who needed data from the applications could not access the data. The applications that were built were designed for the specific requirements of a few users. If you were one of these users, you were fine. But if you were not, then you were unable to use the data that coursed through the veins of the applications. Much of the inability to use those applications was due to the lack of business metadata. There was no capability developed with the application that communicated what the application functions were and how to use them. In particular, the marketing, accounting, sales, and finance organizations felt left in the cold when it came to gaining access to the data flowing through the applications.

Into this environment came 4GL (Fourth Generation Language) technology, which enabled somewhat technically savvy mere mortals (nonprogrammers) to create reports (see Figure 1.5).

Access to data was enabled for all sorts of people! The problem was that the data the reports requested were in different systems and not integrated. The applications had been built to satisfy immediate requirements, not to be integrated with other applications.

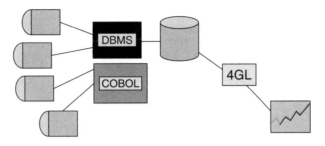

**Figure 1.5**   4GL and User-Created Reports.

### 1.2.4   The Personal Computer

In the same time frame came the personal computer. The appeal of the personal computer in the context of corporate systems was that corporate data could be stripped from the large mainframes holding applications, and it could be made available to anyone having a personal computer. Indeed, many sorts of interfaces to the personal computer were beginning to spring up.

But it was noticed that merely throwing corporate data off to a personal computer or off to a 4GL was no solution. Several problems were endemic to the access and usage of corporate applications data, notably:

+ No integration. Each application captured, stored, and organized data in its own way.

+ No place for historical data. Applications—especially online applications – stripped historical data out of the environment as quickly as possible in the name of high performance,

+ No granular foundation of data from which data could be looked at in different ways and still have a single point of reference.

Figure 1.6 illustrates the proliferation of 4GL reports and PCs.

### 1.2.5   Data Warehousing

Soon the concept of a data warehouse developed, and there appeared a place where integrated, historical data and a granular level could be stored. Now there was a place where the difficulties of multiple applications could be resolved (see Figure 1.7).

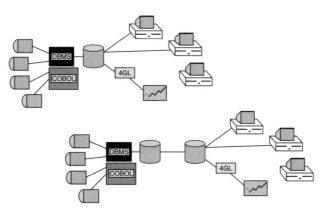

**Figure 1.6** Proliferation of PCs and 4GL Reports.

Around the data warehouse grew up different architectural constructs such as the Corporate Information Factory, all for the purpose of accessing and analyzing data for better management decisions. Some of the architectural constructs that surrounded the data warehouse were:

✦ Data marts, where different departmental organizations could look at data in their own unique way

✦ Exploration warehouses, where statistical processing could be done with no interference from the regular users of the data warehouse

✦ The ODS (operational data store), where online real-time access of data could be done

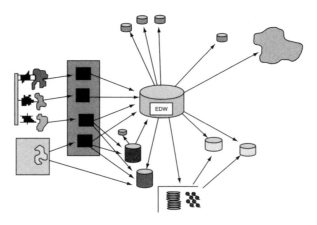

**Figure 1.7** The Data Warehouse and Corporate Information Factory.

✦ Near-line storage, where overflow processing could occur when the data warehouse became very large

✦ Adaptive project marts, where temporary analytical files could be created

✦ DSS applications, where applications were created using the data found in the data warehouse

✦ ETL, where data was read from the operational environment and transformed into corporate integrated data in the data warehouse; and so forth

## 1.2.6  Metadata in Systems Evolution

Throughout the evolution that has been described in Figures 1.1 through 1.7, metadata has existed. The classical definition of metadata is "data about data." But this simple definition belies the complexity that inevitably comes with business and technical metadata.

Some simple examples of metadata are:

✦ The business term or name of the field

✦ The business definition of the field

✦ The business application and organization responsible for the creation and management of the field

✦ The business understanding of the rules around the usage of the field

✦ The business-valid values or domain for the field

✦ The technical length, precision, and data type of the field in a table

✦ The technical name of a table

✦ The technical name of a field

✦ The layout of data within a record, and so forth

Indeed, from the first assembler program onward there has been metadata. The metadata has sometimes been very obvious, but at other times it has been hidden and not obvious at all.

As an example of metadata in early technology, metadata is found in paper tape and punched cards. Figure 1.8 shows this paper-based metadata.

This figure shows that a punched card is organized into fields. Columns 2 through 13, shown as area Abc, represent the place where the key of the card

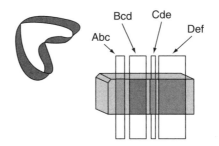

**Figure 1.8**   Metadata in Punched Cards.

will be found; columns 16 through 35, area Bcd, represent the place where the name of the person will be found; columns 40 through 50, area Cde, the amount of the transaction that is being recorded; columns 51 through 58, area Def, the place where the date of the transaction is found; and so forth. All of these specifications about field placement are forms of metadata.

Over time punched cards became obsolete. Next came magnetic tape-based master files that were read and processed by languages such as COBOL and Fortran. Figure 1.9 shows the usage of these early languages to read data found on a magnetic tape.

The language specification indicates the layouts of data. The program contains statements such as:

01 record_layout

02 record_key                    varchar(35)

02 record_name                   varchar(35)

02 record_address                varchar(150)

02 record_telephone              char(10)

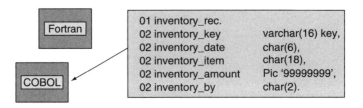

**Figure 1.9**   Languages Use Metadata to Read Magnetic Tape.

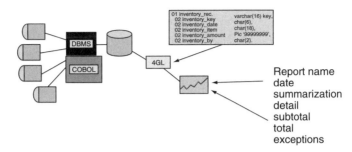

**Figure 1.10**    Metadata in the 4GL and PC Environment.

These statements tie the program to the data being read or written and are classical forms of metadata. This metadata tells the program how to interpret a record found on a magnetic file master file.

As time passed and technology became more sophisticated, metadata continued to be part of the environment. When database management systems arrived, metadata described such things as the indexes that had been created, the tables, the contents of the tables, the number of records in the tables, the relationships of one table to another table, and so forth.

When reports, 4GL processing, and personal computer access to corporate data began to be a reality, metadata accompanied the data in the report itself. Figure 1.10 shows metadata in the 4GL and personal computer environment.

The 4GL personal computer environment contained interface specifications, table names, report names, report fields, table layouts, data definitions, and the like.

The world of the data warehouse contained metadata in many different places: metadata in the data warehouse, in the operational environment, in the ETL tools, in the data marts, and so forth. Figure 1.11 shows the widespread proliferation of metadata.

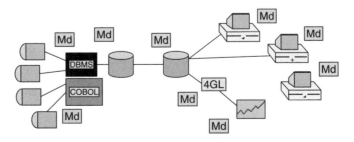

**Figure 1.11**    A Lot of Metadata in a Lot of Places.

# 1.3    Types of Metadata

### 1.3.1    Business Metadata versus Technical Metadata

The progression as seen beginning in Figure 1.1 has been accompanied by metadata as each new technological advancement occurred. In some cases, metadata was very obvious and easy to find; in others, metadata was not easy to find at all. In the early part of the progression, metadata was fairly straightforward and simple. As the progression continued, however, and as the architecture became more complex and varied, metadata became much more difficult to fathom.

One of the early distinctions made between different types of metadata is that between technical metadata and business metadata. The technician uses technical metadata for design, development, maintenance, and other functions. Typical technical metadata includes:

- Database table name
- Database index name
- Database table layout
- Database field name
- Field physical characteristic
- Field constraints
- Inter-record or intertable relationships, and so forth

Technical metadata is therefore that metadata which is useful to the technician. Often technical metadata has a strange name. A field may be known as "rec_temp_fld_a," or a table may be known as "236IN_TAB." These cryptic names have meaning only within the halls of technology. Tell an end-user these names and all you will get is a blank stare.

### 1.3.2    Business Metadata

Business metadata, in contrast, is the metadata that is useful to the businessperson in the day-to-day conduct of business. Business metadata therefore must be in the language of the businessperson. The businessperson is normally not interested in record lengths and internal field names. Instead, he or she is interested in such things as

- Customers
- Accounts
- Account balances
- Due dates
- Sales amount
- Product identification

## 1.4   Where Can You Find Business Metadata?

Business metadata is found everywhere:

- On reports
- Screens
- The newspapers
- Documents
- Contracts
- Proposals
- Statements of work
- Letters of understanding
- Bank statements
- Spreadsheets
- Application software, and so forth

Wherever there is a business user you also find business metadata. Business metadata provides the businessperson with the context and meaning of the data represented by the computer, so it can be accurately used by the enterprise.

### 1.4.1   Business Metadata on a Screen

Figure 1.12 shows a simple screen from the airline industry.

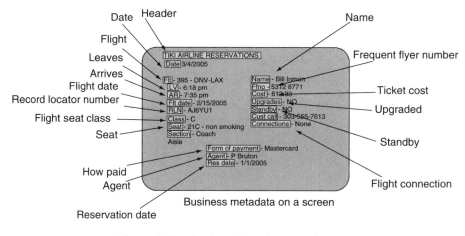

**Figure 1.12**   Business Metadata on a Screen.

The airlines screen shows a lot of business metadata, such as frequent flyer number, flight seat class, flight, arrival time, and departure time. Each of these terms and their abbreviations that are shown on the screen are forms of business metadata.

### 1.4.2   Reports and Business Metadata

Business metadata is not found just on screens; it is also found on reports. Figure 1.13 shows a simple report for inventory.

On the report in Figure 1.13 are found these words:

- ✦ Inventory by
- ✦ Totals
- ✦ Retail price
- ✦ Item
- ✦ Qty (short for "quantity")

It is the business metadata that allows the businessperson to perceive the business context to understand what is being communicated by the computer. Put another way, the computer could spew forth all sorts of things, but without business metadata whatever the computer was saying would have no meaning (or limited meaning at best).

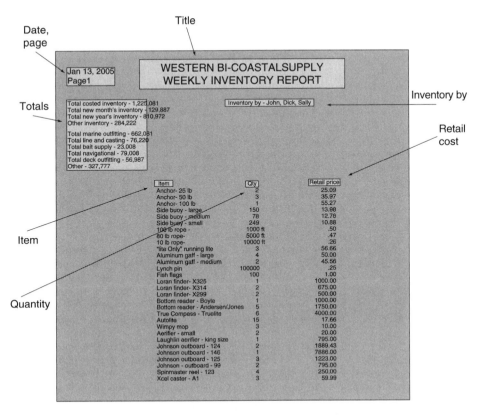

**Figure 1.13** Report with Business Metadata.

### *1.4.3 Corporate Forms and Business Metadata*

Business metadata is also found in a corporation's forms. Figure 1.14 shows the forms used for job applicants.

This figure shows that the job application form is filled with business metadata. On the form are found such terms as:

- ✦ Name
- ✦ Address
- ✦ Phone
- ✦ Education
- ✦ E-mail
- ✦ Degree
- ✦ University
- ✦ GPA

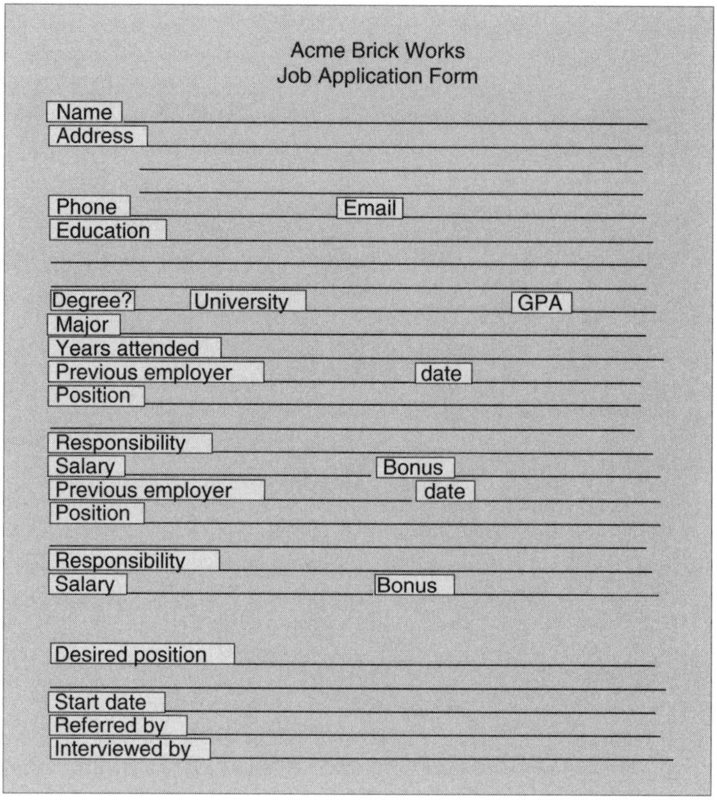

Acme Brick Works
Job Application Form

Name
Address

Phone
Email
Education

Degree?
University
GPA
Major
Years attended
Previous employer
date
Position

Responsibility
Salary
Bonus
Previous employer
date
Position

Responsibility
Salary
Bonus

Desired position

Start date
Referred by
Interviewed by

**Figure 1.14** Application Form with Business Metadata.

As you can see, the label tells what should be supplied in the input area. It provides context for what the person supplies. This is the function of business metadata.

# 1.5 Structured and Unstructured Metadata

One of the most basic ways to divide the world of metadata is by technical metadata versus business metadata. But it is also possible to divide along the lines of unstructured versus unstructured metadata. The form shown in Figure 1.4 is a classical example of structured metadata. The metadata that occurs in that form is uniform. Everyone who fills out a job application is asked the same information. If the person has the information, it is placed in the appropriate place. Structured metadata, then, is metadata that has a regular occurrence in a prescribed location.

The other form of metadata is unstructured metadata. Unstructured metadata occurs in an unpredictable and irregular manner, and occurs even more frequently than structured metadata. As an example of unstructured metadata, refer to Figure 1.15.

This agreement is between Tom Wilson, contractor, and Asbestos Products, Inc, a division of the XYZ Company, of Duluth, Minnesota, 76330. This agreement is for work to be performed by Tom Wilson as a subcontractor to XYZ for the property found on 1255 Tonka Place, Bloomberg, Minnesota. Tom agrees to survey the property and to not harm the wildlife and greenery, especially the shrubs found on the east side of the property abutting the Minnetonka Creek, which runs from east to west except for a small stretch on the Minneapolis city line, just south of the Miller brewery and plant. Part of a contract is shown in Figure 1.15. The contract contains these words:

- ✦ Agreement
- ✦ Contractor
- ✦ Division
- ✦ Work
- ✦ Subcontractor
- ✦ Property

In the figure, unstructured metadata is found scattered throughout the contract. The business metadata is in random places, appearing as descriptive text. There is no regularity or no apparent order to the data or to the business metadata terms that are found in the contract in Figure 1.15. Stated differently, if there were ten contracts laid side by side, there would be no uniformity of the business metadata found in those contracts. It would be impossible to tell at

This agreement is between Tom Wilson, contractor, and Asbestos Products, Inc, a division of the XYZ Company, of Duluth, Minnesota, 76330. This agreement is for work to be performed by Tom Wilson as a subcontractor to XYZ for the property found on 1255 Tonka Place, Bloomberg, Minnesota. Tom agrees to survey the property and to not harm the wildlife and greenery, especially the shrubs found on the east side of the property abutting the Minnetonka Creek, which runs from east to west except for a small stretch on the Minneapolis city line, just south of the Miller brewery and plant....

**Figure 1.15**  A Contract: Example of Unstructured Data.

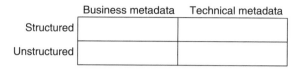

**Figure 1.16**  Grid with Business/Technical and Structured/Unstructured.

a glance if all contracts contained the same types of metadata. Some contracts would have some business metadata terms, whereas other contracts would not. Some contracts would have business metadata terms in a different order, and others would refer to the same type of business metadata using a different term than other contracts. In a word, there is no order, no predictability of business metadata terms from one contract to another. It is for this reason that this business metadata is called unstructured.

### 1.5.1   A Grid for Metadata

A grid can then be created for divisions of metadata. Figure 1.16 shows the grid.

As shown in the figure, the grid has four basic quadrants:

✦ Structured business metadata

✦ Structured technical metadata

✦ Unstructured business metadata

✦ Unstructured technical metadata

The grid is useful for classifying different forms of metadata. Different classifications of metadata will have different characteristics.

## 1.6   Where Business Metadata Is Stored

Although the classification of different forms of metadata is an interesting subject, where metadata actually resides and is stored is also of great interest. In fact, metadata can reside in many places; some of the more common places are seen in Figure 1.17.

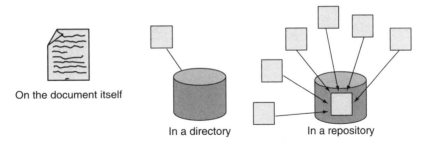

On the document itself

In a directory

In a repository

**Figure 1.17**   Where Metadata Is Stored.

The figure shows that metadata can reside on:

✦ A document

✦ In a file directory

✦ In a database repository.

As an example of metadata residing in a document, consider the job application form shown in Figure 1.14. The business metadata resides on the form itself.

Now consider a database management system (DBMS). Data resides in the DBMS. The internals of the DBMS contain system tables that have all of the specifications and structures about the data, such as column information, data types, indexes, and primary and foreign keys. Even though these system tables reside within the DBMS, they are still separate from the data.

In some cases, organizations have created a metadata repository, which contains metadata about all kinds of tables found in all kinds of places. A repository serves a similar purpose as system tables in a DBMS, except that it can contain information about data in different systems and different databases; the DBMS's system tables only contain information about the data stored within the immediate confines of the DBMS.

## 1.7   When Does Business Data Become Business Metadata?

When does business data become business metadata? Figure 1.18 illustrates business data; or is it metadata?

"This is an ⬚agreement⬚ between Bill Inmon and Guy Hildebrand, ⬚owners⬚ of Inmon Data Systems, a ⬚company⬚ founded in 2003..."

**Figure 1.18** Is This Data or Metadata?

As a rule, business data becomes business metadata when the data is be abstracted to a broader enterprise context. For example, Joe Foster is the name of a person. As such, Joe Foster is not business metadata. But when Joe Foster is referred to as an "employee," then the employee, such as Joe, can be considered as business metadata. Remember that metadata provides context to the data; it tells you what the data is about; it describes the data. In this context, Joe serves as an example of an employee, and hence, serves as business metadata.

As we explore business metadata throughout this book, we will see all sorts of different kinds of business metadata, for example, taxonomies and other business metadata that facilitate enterprise search. We will see how measuring the quality of data involves both business and technical metadata. We will also discover the challenges of capturing business metadata and how to do a "Vulcan mind meld" to get it out of people's heads.

As in the case of data quality measures, we will discover along the way that sometimes "data" will become metadata, and sometimes this data will need to be transformed and translated in order to become business metadata. We have dedicated one chapter to the discussion of business metadata capture from existing data. Then two chapters deal with the presentation or delivery of business metadata.

# 1.8 Business Metadata over Time

One of the interesting aspects of business metadata is that sometimes it needs to be tracked over time. Because business metadata is an abstraction of other data, in some cases what the actual data refers to can change over time. Therefore, an abstract reference to one thing one day may be a reference to something entirely different the next.

For example, consider a field called Shipping ID. Suppose one day they get the idea to nest the source location identifier as a prefix to the Shipping ID. Then later an astute technical data modeler notices this, and says this data should be separate from the Shipping ID. So in this case the actual definition of the field (which is metadata) has changed. Shipping ID starts out as representing a unique identifier of the shipment assigned by the system. Next it becomes the unique identifier of the shipment with the source location added; then it again becomes the identifier of the shipment alone. The metadata itself has changed, which of course will affect the data.

```
Company - Prism Solutions - 1990 - 1997
    Company - Ardent Technology - 1997 -1998
        Company - Informix- 1998 - 1999
            Company - IBM -1999 - 2000
                Company - Ascential-2000 - to the present
```

**Figure 1.19**   Changes over Time.

This is different from the actual data changing, which does not affect the metadata at all. Consider the reference to a company. Over time reference is made to the "company." But over time that company, for any given instance in the real world, may change. As an example, consider the company Prism Solutions. Prism Solutions began in 1990, and then in 1995 it was acquired by Ardent Software. Figure 1.19 shows the different changes of the "company" over time.

At different moments in time, the value of the company name for an instance may change, but the metadata is "company" and the abstraction is still the same. Time changes things, and it is very important that it is clear what is changing over time. The meaning of a field may morph over time; for example, users may not have a place to store a new piece of data that they think is critical, so they "overload" an existing field. In this case, the meaning of the field changes and takes on additional meaning. The meaning of the field is business metadata, and the metadata has indeed changed.

## 1.9 Reference Files: Master Data Management (MDM) and Business Metadata

One place in the corporation that is full of business metadata is the reference file, otherwise known as a reference table. Reference files are used for decoding abbreviations and acronyms. For example, a corporation may keep a reference file for customers that might look like this:

✦ KO – Coca Cola

✦ GM – General Mills

✦ PEP – Pepsi Cola

✦ ATT – ATT Corporation

✦ QW – Qwest

It is much more convenient for the corporation to refer to these abbreviations if they are used every day many times than it is to spell the abbreviations out. In this sense reference files are a form of corporate shorthand.

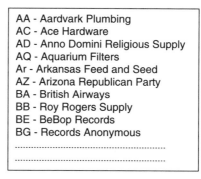

```
AA - Aardvark Plumbing
AC - Ace Hardware
AD - Anno Domini Religious Supply
AQ - Aquarium Filters
Ar - Arkansas Feed and Seed
AZ - Arizona Republican Party
BA - British Airways
BB - Roy Rogers Supply
BE - BeBop Records
BG - Records Anonymous
................................................
................................................
```

**Figure 1.20** Reference File/Table.

Figure 1.20 shows a simple corporate reference file.

The reference files are a form of business metadata because the abbreviations are aliases and at times they are abstractions (or codes) of something else.

Today, reference files are considered part of an overall discipline area known as Master Data Management (MDM). MDM concerns itself with managing the Master Data: that data that runs the corporation, which is referenced all over the enterprise, in multiple systems. The main areas of master data are Customer and Product, but geography and corporate structure (Divisions, Branches, etc.) are often also considered master data.

Master data reference files have their own set of issues. One issue is that the same reference files needs to be used across the corporation. If one department thinks that GM means General Motors and another department thinks that GM stands for General Mills, then the potential for misunderstanding exists. This is one of the challenges that MDM as a discipline seeks to solve; it has become a hot topic for contemporary data management.

Another challenge associated with MDM concerns keeping the master data (reference files) up to date. Consider a reference entry that is changed in July 2004. Prior to July 2004, the term "KN" refers to Knightsbridge Consulting. After July the term "KN" refers to Kildare and Noble. If data before July 2004 is matched with a reference to the reference file that is current, confusion will arise as to the meaning of "KN." The reference files need to be made time-variant, just as the data they refer to is time variant.

# 1.10 Summary

There has been a progression of technological advances throughout the history of the computer profession. Throughout the progression metadata has played a role, albeit a somewhat passive one.

Metadata can be classified into one of two categories—business metadata and technical metadata. Business metadata is that metadata that is useful to the businessperson.

Business metadata is found everywhere—on screens, in spreadsheets, on reports, on corporate forms, and so forth. Another way of categorizing metadata is in terms of structured and unstructured metadata. Structured metadata is descriptive information that has a consistent layout. Unstructured metadata is metadata that can appear anywhere at any time.

It may be very important to the business to track metadata over time as both the data and the reference data (abstractions) change. As change becomes more frequent, the role of metadata becomes more active.

Metadata is very valuable to the business and helps facilitate proper understanding of the enterprise data assets. Without this understanding, the data would be relatively useless.

# The Value of Business Metadata Management

## 2.1 Introduction

This chapter provides an overview of the value of metadata in general and business metadata in particular. Later in the book, we provide more detailed descriptions of many of the value components touched lightly on in this chapter. For instance, one of the values of business metadata is that it helps businesspeople find documents such as policy and procedure manuals. We devote an entire chapter to Search in Chapter 4. Thus, the present chapter serves as a short introduction to more detailed material.

# 2.2 **Background**

For years information technology has been about processes and data. The focus and energy have been on the building of systems and the business operation of those systems. But after a lot of systems have been built and the case for integration of information is made, it becomes apparent that another important element of information has been neglected—metadata.

As long as there were only a few systems, programs, and databases, metadata was a subject that could be shuffled to the side. In this case, the people involved are often able to manage the metadata through formal or informal social groups. How many times have you heard "George is the only one that understands how that process works, please call him now."? Or "Mary knows how that system works. Find out from her what needs to be input to get that invoice generated correctly." But now that there are many systems, programs, and databases, metadata management has become increasingly important. This is especially true with regard to aging systems that are undocumented and to the daily disappearance of the people who built and understood those older systems.

# 2.3 **Definition of Metadata Revisited**

Chapter 1 took us on a historical journey in which we explored the roots and evolution of metadata. The classical definition of metadata is data about data, but that definition hardly tells us what metadata really is and why it is important. Metadata is important because it supplies the context to the data. Therefore, without metadata supplying the context, the data in the enterprise cannot be understood properly. Perhaps its importance should be stated even more clearly: Without metadata, the data is totally meaningless.

For example, think of the number "42." What is the first thing that comes to mind?

If you are a fan of a certain science fiction writer, you will giggle; 42 means (extremely tongue and cheek) "The Answer to Life, the Universe and Everything": the culmination of Douglas Adams's series *The Hitchhiker's Guide to the Galaxy*. However, if you haven't read the books or seen the movie, you won't "get" the significance of this number. If you mention the number 42 in a crowd, you can instantly find the Douglas Adams fans; everyone else has a blank stare. Without any context, 42 is just a number.

Here's another example, starting out with no context and gradually adding it. Look at the data found in Figure 2.1.

7

**Figure 2.1**    The Number 7.

Figure 2.1 shows the number 7. What does this number tell you? By itself it doesn't say very much. It could mean almost anything. It could mean the age of your child. It could refer to the number of days in the week. It could tell you how many runs your baseball team scored last night. In a word, the number 7 standing by itself really doesn't say anything at all; it's meaningless. In order to be meaningful the raw number 7 needs context.

Suppose we added some metadata so that we now have a value of $7-NYSE.

Now we can see that the number 7 refers to dollars and that furthermore those dollars relate in some way to the New York Stock Exchange. Now we have a slightly clearer vision of what the number means. Unfortunately, even though we have added some context, we still aren't sure what the number 7 means, exactly. It could mean that the NYSE is only valued at $7 or that a given stock on the NYSE is trading at $7. So we need to add some more context. Now consider the following in Figure 2.2.

This now says that on November 17, 1998, Oracle stock went up 7 dollars on the New York Stock Exchange. Now that we have added more context, we have a very clear view of what is meant by the number 7. Without context, data is raw and is of questionable value. With context we are able to understand what fact in the real world the data pertains to.

### 2.3.1  Library Card Catalog

Consider going to a local library. In the library you will find lots of books. How do you find what you are looking for? One way is to start walking up and down the stacks of books, randomly encountering all sorts of books in an order that may be incomprehensible to you. It will probably take you a long time to find what you entered the library for. But if you go to the card catalog, you can efficiently search for what is of interest to you. After having searched the card catalog, you can go directly to what your topic is and find what you need right away.

↑ $7-NYSE — Oracle, November 17,1998

**Figure 2.2**    Stock Price Change.

Metadata is like the card catalog. Without metadata or a card catalog, the contents of your information system are almost inaccessible, or at best very inefficiently accessible.

See Figure 2.3 for a picture of a card catalog.

Notice that a card catalog contains lots of information about a book, such as:

✦ The Dewey Decimal System reference number, which tells the person where it can be physically found in the library (located at the top left)

✦ The author

✦ The title

✦ The subject

✦ The publisher, the date it was published, and the like

✦ The number of pages

✦ Sometimes a description of the book (The example in the figure instead shows subject access points.)

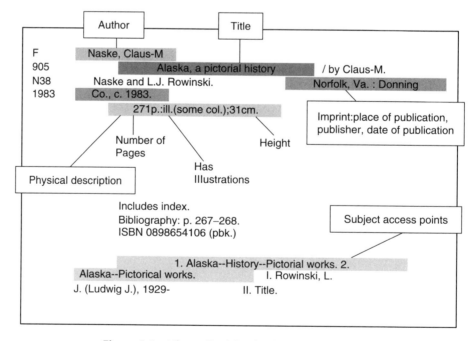

**Figure 2.3**   Library Card Catalog [University of Alaska].

In short, a card catalog provides a context for the book: it shows what the book is about, and it also gives general bibliographic information. The card catalog helps the researcher identify the right book to check out and where to find it. Furthermore, each book has three (or more) cards referencing it, because each card is in alphabetical order according to one of three different sort orders: Title, Author, and Subject.

Here is what Todd Stephens, metadata expert and holder of many metadata patents, has to say about the card catalog analogy:

> For every system, interface, application, component, metric or whatever asset you can define within the technology community. … locating, loading and delivering quality meta data is the hard part. Building neat, functional and creative utilities for the data is the easy part. It's really too bad that most people fail to see or acknowledge the utility of tracking the inventory of the greatest asset we have. Next time you get a chance to visit your local library, take a look around. Imagine all of those books are data components, entities, attributes or tables. To the left is the current system and inventory map. Back in the right is the data access room filled wall to wall with common components.

> And at the center of it all is your enterprise metadata catalog. Every entity, table attribute, field, transformation, business rule, steward, component, etc., will be catalogued with a solid description, keywords, owner, location, business meaning and all of the other normal meta-model constructs. Wow, wouldn't that be nirvana? (Stephens, 2003)

## 2.4    Business Metadata's Importance in a Report

Figure 2.4 shows a typical report.

Let's look at some of the metadata existing on this report. This report is a Sales Analysis report. Looking at the Header of the report we can find valuable metadata, "Sales Analysis by Year, Region and City." In addition, the Header has a brief description explaining how the ranking is computed; "This report uses the rank function to show the rank of cities based upon sales figures." The Header of this report is an exceptional example of the business metadata that is appropriate for understanding and using this report. Suppose this report did not have this description in the report Header? We would have sales numbers and ranking without the complete context. How would we know what the ranking was based upon? We would be left to guess, leading to potentially incorrect usage of the report and incorrect business decisions.

Even with the very good metadata in the Heading of this report, we are still missing context of the definition of Sales. Does everyone in the enterprise who will view this report have the same understanding of what is included in "Sales"? Where is the definition of Sales? Does it include or exclude the following:

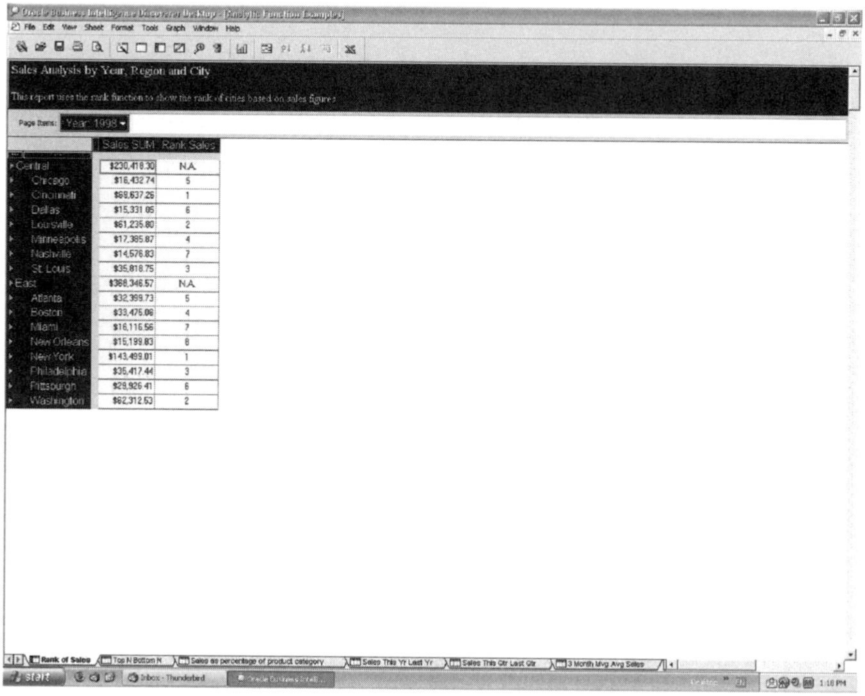

**Figure 2.4**    Reports and Screens Contain Metadata.

✦ Sales taxes

✦ Shipping charges

✦ Commissions

✦ Discounts

✦ Promotions

✦ Disputes and damaged goods

✦ Returns

✦ Noncollectables and write-offs

✦ Partner sales (packaged in our products)

Looking at the bottom of the report in Figure 2.4, you can see a number of associated workbooks or reports. Each of those may provide more or less business metadata context to help the enterprise. Let's look at the report "Sales as Percentage of Product Category" in Figure 2.5.

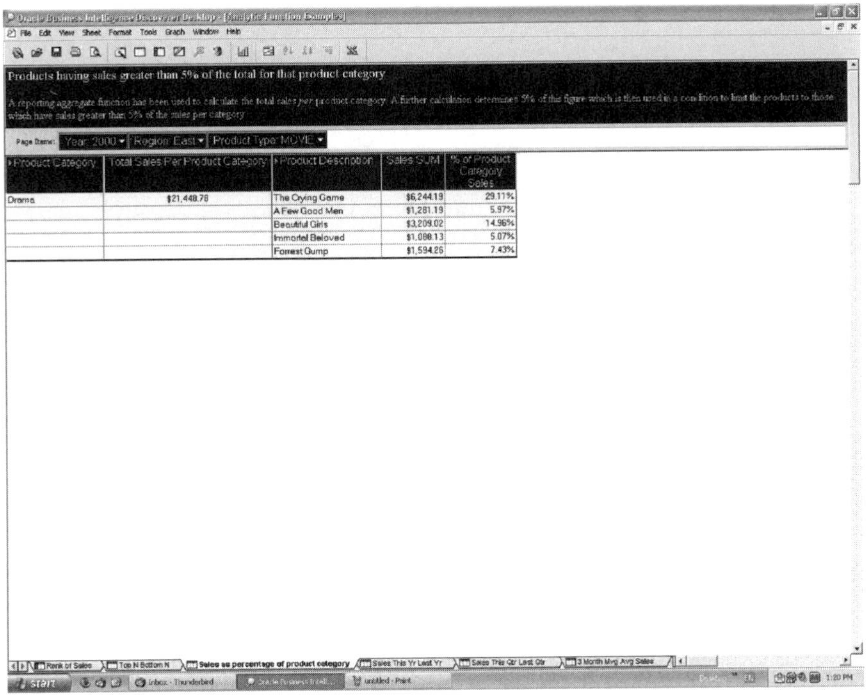

**Figure 2.5**   Reports and Screens Contain Metadata.

Again the Header of this report provides great metadata, "Products having sales greater than 5% of the total for that product category." In this case we have additional metadata in a sub-Header, "Page Items," which defines some of the filtering used to produce this report. The report is filtered by Year, Region, and Product Type. Yet we are still missing metadata and have to infer that the Product hierarchy is Product Type, Product Category, and then Product. Our point here is that great metadata exists in many of the enterprise's reports and spreadsheet. However, only a portion of the metadata necessary for complete business understanding can be embedded in the body of a report, a spreadsheet, or a screen. Additional business metadata may be required in order to understand the report. Business metadata should be found everywhere people need to look at and use information.

## 2.5  Metadata Chaos

As we discussed in Chapter 1, the problem with metadata is that it is found everywhere and that there is no coordination from one pool of metadata to another. Not only is there no connection between the different pools of metadata, but there is no language consistency. One metadata word in one place may mean something entirely different in another place; and the same thing may be called many different names. There simply is no cohesiveness or integration among metadata found in different places.

Actually, an interesting observation can be made about metadata: It is in essence another data warehouse. Just as the enterprise needs a data warehouse to gather together and harmonize all the data from the diverse departments and divisions from the enterprise and bring it to one place so that it can be analyzed together, so the same thing needs to be done with the metadata.

A typical response to the distribution and lack of integration of data across the enterprise is the creation of an enterprise metadata repository. An enterprise metadata repository can be the collection point for metadata from different places in the organization. Once it is gathered or integrated and stored in one place, there is an opportunity to examine and "rationalize" the metadata across the enterprise.

### 2.5.1 So Why Is Metadata Management Important?

Metadata management is important for many reasons. It is important first because of the time required to find a piece of information. Chapter 4 details the cost to the organization of personnel looking for documents — and not being able to find things fast and easily. In order to illustrate this point, suppose that you get a request from the IRS to document a claim you have made on a past income tax return. How long does it take you to find the data to do the verification? The real problem lies not in verifying the amount or the date of the transaction in question, but in finding the check or the checkbook where the date and the amount are written down. Finding where to look is the biggest problem in understanding far-flung and disparate pieces of data. Once you find where to look, everything else is fairly straightforward. But finding where to look in the first place can be a real challenge. Through metadata we can find where to go when we are challenged with finding information. All the wonderful search engines that all of us have become dependent on use metadata to answer our search requests. Without metadata, what you are looking for could be anywhere. It is metadata that saves you enormous amounts of time when you are trying to find a particular piece of information.

### 2.5.2 Reusing Data

A second very important way in which metadata helps the organization to run more efficiently is by cataloging what reports and analyses have already been created. In order to appreciate this advantage, consider an organization that needs a new report or analysis. The organization's analysts sit down and plan how they are going to write programs in order to get the analysis done. If they had a good metadata repository, they could ask the simple question: Has someone in this organization already addressed this problem or a very similar problem? And if the problem has already been addressed, wouldn't it be much faster and more efficient to use reports and analyses that already exist than to have to write a new set of reports? When there is no metadata directory, the organization is faced with building everything from scratch every time a new request for information arrives. But with metadata the organization can have reusability of information, which in the long run is a tremendous factor in the efficient gathering and usage of information.

### 2.5.3  Accuracy of Information

Yet another very important aspect of metadata is that of making sure you know what you have. Suppose an organization is looking for revenue on a monthly basis coming from a particular source. If all the organization has to go on is the term *revenue*, then they are going to be doing a lot of guessing as to what it means and the validity and consistency of revenue. Maybe the revenue figures they are using are valid, and maybe they are not. Typically, an enterprise's organizational business unit report has conflicting numbers for "monthly revenue" numbers. It is also typical that personnel functioning as business analysts spend 80% of their time gathering and validating data owing to a void of good metadata around the quality and context of the data accessed by the analysts. Quality, accuracy, and timeliness of the data in reports are often missing metadata that would help business analysts. Thus, adding metadata context about data quality gives the organization reasonable assurance that the figures accurately represent the correct values.

Let's look at another report as an example. Figure 2.6 shows Total Sales by Year, by Quarter, and by Region.

The Total Sales are shown in their absolute numbers as well as color coded against the parameters described in the report Heading; where ($<$ \$50000) = Red and ($>$ = \$90000) = Green. The context of Red, Normal, and Green coloring seems fully understandable. Now, let's look at the Margin columns that are also reported here.

There is metadata in the report Heading that will help us. According to the metadata in the report Heading, the coloring for Margin is based on Red = ($<$ = 0.645), Yellow = (0.645 to 0.69), and Green = ($>$ = 0.69). As a business analyst, one would have to question the quality of the data and the coloring values of this report. No absolute values are shown. Are the values for Margin missing due to a processing problem? Do we normally not show the values of Margin, and why? How is Margin computed? What dates were used to compute

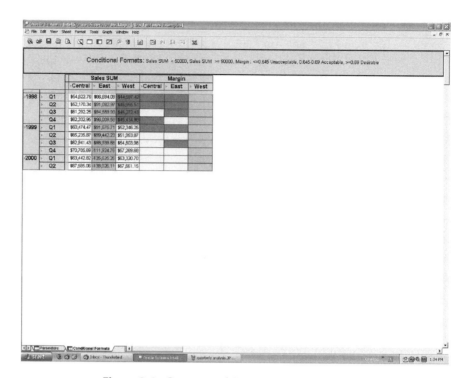

**Figure 2.6**  Reports and Screens Contain Metadata.

the values showing these colors since there are no dates attached to the report? If the quality of the data and its values are questioned, then the coloring of the Margin cells must be questioned, leading to business analyst research efforts that could be avoided if more robust business metadata were available.

## 2.6 Summary

This chapter has shown that business metadata is very valuable for assisting the enterprise in the understanding of what data means and its practical ramifications, and the value of this metadata is emphasized when it is missing.

There are many reasons metadata plays such an important role in a corporation's information management. As long as there are only a few systems and lots of people who are familiar with the system, then metadata is not all that important. But in the world where lots of complex systems are in place and where people come and go frequently, metadata is absolutely essential. It adds clarity and meaning to data; it helps businesspeople find what they are looking for in the way of information assets; and it helps prevent the organization from reinventing reports that have already been written. Much of the rest of this book will be about adding examples and statistics to build a business case for the value of business metadata in particular.

## 2.7 References

+ Stephens, R. Todd. "Knowledge: The Essence of Meta Data: Is the Library Card Catalog Analogy Good or Bad for Meta Data?" *DMReview*, July 17, 2003: http://www.dmreview.com/article_sub.cfm?articleID = 7095

+ University of Alaska Fairbanks, Card catalog image: http://www.uaf.edu/library/instruction/ls101/images/CatBibRec1.jpg

# Who Is Responsible for Business Metadata: Business Metadata Stewardship

**CHAPTER 3**

# 3.1 Introduction

Chapters 1 and 2 have established that business metadata is much broader than, and quite different from, the structured technical metadata that we have historically captured in our technical application implementations. Now that we have presented the definition of business metadata and discussed its value to the enterprise, this chapter will introduce some of the organizational options and challenges for managing business metadata.

The objective of this book is not to discuss the content and complexity of the structured metadata that could be maintained by an enterprise; there are many technical publications that currently address this subject. However, many of the concepts and management functions of technical metadata such as data stewardship are applicable to business metadata as well.

Certain business metadata has been defined as an attribute of structured technical metadata since the techniques of data modeling became popular in the early 1980s. Since that time we have been asking the data modelers to define the "attribute business definition" in our data models. This business definition can be captured in our logical modeling tools and then transferred to the database catalog or structured metadata repository. Yet, should a member of the IT group, in this case the data modeler, be responsible for formulating a business definition of the data in the enterprise? While this one metadata attribute is valuable, the larger question is, "Who will be responsible for defining, maintaining, and communicating business metadata of the enterprise?"

# 3.2 Who Is Responsible for Business Metadata?

The quick and simple answer to this question is everyone who functions in a business capacity. Of course, metadata is not a simple enterprise challenge, and so it does not have a simple solution. Historically, the Information Technology (IT) organization has been considered as being "responsible for managing" all of the data, as well as the structured metadata of the enterprise.

Yet, business metadata exists in the heads of every person working in a business function. In fact, a significant amount of business metadata is not written down and only exists in people's heads.

Enterprises now commonly recognize that the various business organizations have the ultimate responsibility for the data content and that the IT organization functions as a custodian or caretaker only and is responsible for the management of the physical implementation of the data and the associated structured metadata. Many publications and conferences have discussed the issues of whether IT is actually responsible for managing the data or is just a steward of the physical implementation. Some of the confusion in the past over what is meant by data stewardship is also reflected in this caretaker issue. Is a steward a caretaker only or an owner? That discussion is not within the scope of this book; instead our focus is on how to assign responsibility for business metadata.

Only a small quantity of the business metadata is generally represented in the structured metadata defined and managed within the organization. Much of the overall quantity of business metadata has historically been recorded within

- ✦ Business policy and procedures manuals
- ✦ Business workflow processes
- ✦ Technical application user documents
- ✦ E-mails
- ✦ Verbal communications between individuals
- ✦ General business documents
- ✦ The heads (gray matter) of the individuals working in the business organization
- ✦ Technology implementations of business applications (such as business rules)

Certain business metadata may only have significant value to one business unit and thus may be considered a local or departmental responsibility. This is an important consideration. For example, the Marketing Department could be responsible for the definition, execution, and monitoring of a marketing campaign. In this case it is logical that Marketing could be responsible for all of the business metadata associated with the marketing campaign. However, most business metadata will be used by more than one business unit. In this case many business units may provide input; therefore, the metadata should be considered an enterprise responsibility. For example, most processes dealing with the life cycle of Customers will require the involvement of many business organizations, as well as IT. One business unit should not be responsible for the "ownership" of all the challenges in managing the enterprise business metadata around Customers. Enterprise-level challenges and concerns have helped to popularize the concept of stewardship rather than organizational ownership.

# 3.3 Business Metadata Stewardship Concepts

Over the last decade *ownership versus stewardship* has been a topic for discussion within the data management community. Thus, a significant number of publications exist that discuss the concepts of stewardship around data. The same concepts of stewardship can be applied to business metadata and metadata in general. First, let's define some of the critical terms of stewardship and ownership.

## 3.3.1 Ownership Definition

Often business managers desire full control over all resources necessary to maintain and monitor the business processes, as well as the data and metadata for the IT applications. The potential exists that a business unit can "own" the processes, procedures, and IT applications used only within their organization. Ownership, therefore, is defined as the process of exercising sole authority over the resources being governed. However, ownership is not possible for enterprise-level business processes, data, applications, or metadata. As enterprises mature, it seems natural that more business applications develop into enterprise-level applications. Ownership of enterprise processes, procedures, data, and business metadata by one business unit is not achievable in most organizations; it requires the coordination of resources from many business units. In these cases, corporations look to the concepts of stewardship.

## 3.3.2 Stewardship Definition

The concept of stewardship for enterprise responsibilities is not new; in fact, the stewardship of processes and procedures has been in existence for many decades. Consider the definition and management of the people or money of your organization. Does the Chief Financial Officer or even the finance organization own the actual funds of the enterprise? Of course not. However, what the CFO and Finance organization are responsible for is to define, maintain, monitor, and communicate the practices and procedures that everyone in the enterprise will use to manage the money that flows through the organization.

The following are a few definitions of stewardship from dictionary sources.

✦ A person who manages another's property or financial affairs; one who administers anything as the agent of another or others.[1]

✦ One who manages another's property, finances, or other affairs.[2]

From these definitions, then, a "steward" fits well into the preceding example as to how we use the Finance organization to manage the challenges of money in the enterprise.

Data stewardship has been recognized as a way to manage enterprise data. The following is from DAMA-International, the internationally recognized data management organization:

> Data management is a shared responsibility between the Information Technology (IT) organization supporting the enterprise and the data consumers within the enterprise. Data Stewards are the trustees of enterprise data. IT data management professionals are the custodians of enterprise data. Effective data management depends on an effective partnership between data stewards and data professionals, especially in data governance. Data stewardship is the non-technical portion of responsibilities for the partnership in data management. These responsibilities address data strategy, data policies, data quality, data meaning, and data requirements.[3]

# 3.4 Organizational Options for Business Metadata Stewardship

Many of us in the IT industry can recall organizations that attempted to initiate data stewardship more than a decade ago. Many of these early efforts were technology focused, managed under the IT organization, and did not last more than a few years. Let's learn from history. Many positive lessons were learned from those attempts that can be applied to establishing an organization for managing business metadata.

The first experiments at data stewardship were attempted in the early 1990s. At that time, many corporations established formal data stewardship organizations and allocated budgets, resources, and responsibilities. While some

---

[1]stewardship. (n.d.). *Dictionary.com Unabridged (v 1.1)*. Retrieved May 15, 2007, from Dictionary. com Web site: http://dictionary.reference.com/browse/stewardship

[2]stewardship. (n.d.). *The American Heritage® Dictionary of the English Language, Fourth Edition*. Retrieved May 15, 2007, from Dictionary.com Web site: http://dictionary.reference. com/browse/stewardship

[3]Data Management Association, Guidelines to Implementing Data Resource Management, Version 4, © 2002.

corporations established stewardship teams in business units, the overwhelming majority established the teams within the IT organization. The stewardship teams generally focused on the major data subjects or enterprise data model in the corporation. For example, these subjects could be

✦ Product (the infrastructure for creation and delivery of products and services)

✦ Customer (the definition and management of the corporation's customers)

✦ Network (the infrastructure and management of the network of a telecommunications firm)

✦ Finance (the definition and management of the financial policies)

✦ Engineering (the processes and policies for developing products)

Most of these early attempts were not integrated into business unit implementations. They most often seemed to deliver excellent technical work products but were of little value to the business. Great models for Customer data integration and management may have been defined, but little integration and alignment with business unit goals and objectives took place.

Figure 3.1 is an example of the early organization view of these data stewardship organizations:

Fortunately, we learned a great deal from these early attempts. Today, successful data stewardship organizations are committees comprised of individuals from both business units and IT. We find that the business staff is more familiar with the data issues and can work effectively with an IT partner on the stewardship team to formulate solutions rapidly.

### 3.4.1   The Data Governance Council

Today there are many examples of extremely well-run and valuable data stewardship programs. We now recognize that data stewardship has formal,

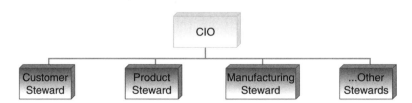

**Figure 3.1**   Original Data Stewardship Organization.

nontechnical accountability for effective control and use of enterprise data assets. This requires active involvement from the business, because they understand the proper use of and expectations for the data. Data stewards are appointed to represent the business interests of the organization, ensuring the definition, quality, and effective, appropriate use of enterprise data. In addition, there must be an effective partnership between the business and technology organizations. The Data Governance Council responsibilities usually encompass all aspects of data use and management, including strategic, tactical, and operational. Strategy and tactics of data use involve the business and how data supports business planning and execution, and how operational data management is accomplished by database administrators (DBAs) working in concert to support business requirements. The Data Architect is also a vital member of the team, ensuring that data management supports the entire enterprise and is not biased toward any single view of the data.

Many corporations today have established a cross-functional committee as the data stewardship organization. A member of a business unit or IT can be the chairperson of this committee. Such a committee is often titled the Data Stewardship or Governance Council and is an organization that may look like the organization outlined in Figure 3.2. The main differences between Figures 3.1 and 3.2 are:

✦ The appearance of IT as another business unit with representation

✦ Each business unit is represented by someone in their group and not an IT person not familiar with their specific requirements.

The responsibilities of the Data Stewardship Council organization include:

✦ Planning activities such as data quality, data standards, data capture, and data usage policies

✦ Definition and monitoring of data governance policies

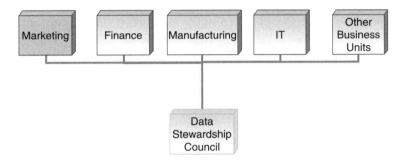

**Figure 3.2** Data Stewardship Council.

✦ Definition and monitoring of business rules in business practices as well as technology implementations

✦ Tactical activities such as monitoring of data quality, standards, and policies

✦ Resolution of conflicts between data creation and data usage business rules. For example, the data capture rules used to create a customer address on an individual order may be driven by the Sales organization's metric to "get the order from the customer in less than 3 minutes." Meeting this metric may force the personnel taking the order to capture less data than the Marketing organization wanted for their usage.

### 3.4.1.1   Data Stewardship Artifacts Are Business Metadata

Many of the artifacts created by any data stewardship initiative, including those created by a Data Stewardship Council, are all considered business metadata. For example, the data definitions and business rules are business metadata; the list of personnel serving on the Council is business metadata; and if the organization appoints line-of-business data stewards, the data steward for that line of business becomes business metadata. This information can be extrapolated and inferred for every data element. For example, if someone had a question about a specific data element, he or she could look up who the steward was for that element and direct his or her question to the right person.

## 3.4.2   Approaches to Business Metadata Stewardship

There is not just one approach that will lead all organizations toward business metadata success. If that were the case, we would likely not need a discussion in this book. That said, we should also leverage the history and experiences we have with data and data stewardship. In fact, many of the data stewardship councils in existence today are dealing with a limited amount of business metadata. Data Stewardship Councils that have significant membership from the business community are far better positioned to deal with the issues and challenges of business metadata then those that have primarily a technology focus. Organizations that have a Data Stewardship Council that can deal with business challenges should consider leveraging this organization for business metadata. For those organizations that have a Data Stewardship Council comprised solely of IT resources or dealing solely with IT related issues, then a Metadata Stewardship Council should be established in addition to a Data Stewardship Council, as shown in Figure 3.3. Although Figure 3.3 shows the Data Stewardship and Business Metadata Stewardship Councils as two separate

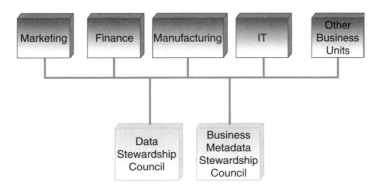

**Figure 3.3** Data Stewardship and Business Metadata Stewardship Councils.

organizations, we firmly recommend that these be organized as one team, with both IT and business representatives.

The responsibilities of the Metadata Stewardship Council may include the following.

+ Define vision and objectives for business metadata.

+ Define the standards and practices for the capture and management (life cycle) of business metadata.

+ Align business data capture and processes and all of the diverse data usages across the enterprise.

+ Define and monitor the quality parameters of business metadata.

+ Document the roles and responsibilities involved with the business metadata life cycle.

+ Establish the metrics to monitor compliance to standards and quality.

+ Establish and communicate the process to manage the life cycle of metadata.

+ Conduct issue resolution and escalation.

+ Work with business units and IT to fund business metadata implementations.

# 3.5 Metadata Life Cycle and Governance

Business or technical metadata projects often suffer the same fate as Data Stewardship initiatives: They are successful for only a very short period of time, and then they fizzle. Metadata and governance go hand in hand. The root cause of metadata failures can often be traced to ignoring metadata governance and life-cycle issues. For metadata to be valuable and sustainable over time, the enterprise must recognize and define solutions to metadata governance. Consequently, effective and comprehensive data governance requires metadata to prove its effectiveness.

Metadata governance is concerned with the metadata life cycle. and how time affects data and metadata, for example:

✦ Metadata changes

✦ Business definitions

✦ Security and regulatory compliance

✦ Business rules

✦ Usage requirements and presentation of the metadata.

Many initial business or technical implementations end up just capturing the metadata. We recognize that capturing the metadata is often an extremely difficult job, but just getting the metadata into a database or spreadsheet is akin to building what we refer to as a "roach motel" (data goes in but does not come out). Your metadata requirements must address the issues relating to the usage and presentation of the metadata, as well as the life cycle necessary to govern and keep the metadata valuable to the audience.

Although governance and maintenance life cycles are distinct and separate concerns, they are so closely related that we can address the issues and requirements as one. Many metadata repository tool vendors discuss the requirements and functionality for governance and life cycle as metadata administration functionality, but the requirements associated with metadata governance and the metadata life cycle are not merely administration functions.

Let's define what we mean by the life cycle of metadata:

> The metadata lifecycle is defined as the organization, processes, and technology that must occur from the initial identification of a metadata object through the retirement of that object.

Some common life cycle processes are as follows.

✦ The identification of a metadata object (for example, a business term definition)

✦ The definition of the System of Record, stewardship responsibility, physical location, and in what technology the metadata object exists

✦ The capture of the metadata object so that it can be validated and consolidated for local or global usage

✦ The processes to apply quality assurance to the metadata object and then approval and recognition that the metadata object is acceptable for publication and usage

✦ The processes and technology for the communications, publication, and reporting of the metadata object

✦ The processes and procedures for maintaining the metadata object. This includes the repetitive capture, QA, approval, and publication of a new version for the metadata object

✦ The processes and technology for retiring the values for the metadata object, as well as retiring the metadata object itself

Figure 3.4 illustrates a sample metadata lifecycle. Here is an explanation of the acronyms used in the figure:

✦ MD: Metadata

✦ SOR: Source of record, the place where the occurrence of the metadata instance is accurate for a specific point in time (usually current moment)

✦ QA/QC: Quality assurance, quality control

Metadata governance requirements should include a definition of the stewardship, System of record (SOR) management, quality management, and security management. Identification of the system of record and keeping this

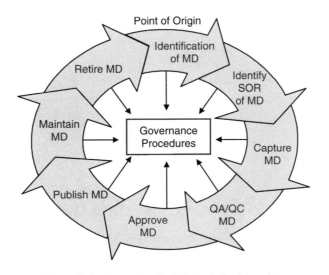

**Figure 3.4**  Example of a Life Cycle for Metadata.

| Meta Object | Strategic Modeling Tool | Tactical Modeling Tool | DBMS Tool | Data Integration Tool | Reporting Tool |
|---|---|---|---|---|---|
| Entity Name | C | | | | |
| Entity Type | C | | | | |
| Entity Definition | C | U | | | R |
| Entity Scope | C | | | | |
| Entity Active Ind | C | U | | | |
| Entity Logical Business Rule | C | U | | U | R |

**Figure 3.5**   Metadata System of Record Example.

accurate over time is a very good way to begin recording the metadata life cycle. Each metadata object should have one, and only one, process and organization responsible for its creation. It is valid to have optional means for creating the object, but the creation and maintenance processes should be established when requirements are being defined.

Figure 3.5 presents an example of a system of record and maintenance matrix for a small number of metadata objects. Symbols used indicate the database operation performed on the metadata element specified (CRUD):

✦ C- Create

✦ R- Read

✦ U- Update

✦ D- Delete

We have included a file entitled "Metadata SOR table example" on the Web site for this book, www.mkp.com/businessmetadata, as an example of a table that can be used to define the creation and maintenance life-cycle processes and tools for a set of metadata objects.

## 3.6   Business Metadata Data Quality Considerations

Data quality may be the greatest challenge that enterprises face in managing the life cycle of business metadata. Not surprisingly, many enterprises have not yet considered defining what they consider to be the quality component for business metadata; this is mostly because business metadata is just now being recognized as a distinct category of metadata, deserving of attention and management in its own right. Metadata data quality components are very similar to those of data. Defining metadata quality should be one of the early activities of the Business Metadata Stewardship Council. The level of data quality can be different for local departmental metadata, for example, Employee Annual Reviews, versus enterprise metadata, such as Customer Call Management. In addition, the level of data quality for metadata may differ based on the importance of the business processes supported by that metadata.

The Data Warehousing Institute has published a data quality report[4] that many organizations follow when defining their data quality programs. Organizations considering the following quality components for data should also be considering these conditions for each metadata object.

1. Accuracy: Does the metadata represent the current business condition, and is it from a verifiable source?

2. Integrity: Does the metadata conform to appropriate business and data structural rules?

3. Timeliness: Is the metadata available when personnel are attempting to access or use the data that it describes? Is it up to date with business processes, or is it outdated?

4. Consistency: Is the metadata consistent throughout, or does it conflict with other metadata descriptions?

5. Completeness: Is all the metadata populated to the defined standard for completeness, or is some portion of it missing? For example, the metadata may have a title/name defined but not have a description.

6. Validity: Are the values for business metadata (such as definitions) populated with correct and current values expected for the specific type of metadata? For example, if the business metadata in question is a definition, does it meet your standards for a definition? Does it make sense as a definition? Is it a valid definition for that specific metadata object?

7. Accessibility: Is the metadata easily accessible, understandable, and usable for the business user?

One of the many metadata challenges is that all seven components of metadata quality are important and are worthy of consideration. Although data has similar quality components, some of those components are often ignored in

---

[4]Eckerson, Wayne W., Data Quality and the Bottom Line. TDWI Report Series, © 2002.

favor of others, depending on business emphasis. Data accuracy can be less of an issue for certain less critical data. This is not the case for metadata, however. No metadata component can be ignored. The purpose of metadata is to describe the data. It is vital that the description of the data is current, accurate, accessible, complete, and consistent (with the data itself as well as with the processes that created the data) and that it has integrity. In short, the metadata must be of such high quality that business and technical users can rely on it. If any component of the metadata does not meet the user's quality expectations, then the user will quickly deem the metadata data to be "completely unusable," which will put your metadata program in jeopardy.

# 3.7 Funding Business Metadata

The approaches that an enterprise will take are likely to align with the funding options chosen. Funding options, discussed in greater detail later in this chapter, can be summarized as

✦ Local business metadata within one business unit or one business function

✦ Enterprise business metadata considered along with data stewardship

✦ Centralized Enterprise Metadata Repository implementations

Although we have implemented a number of business metadata projects as "stealth projects on a shoestring," one of the most important aspects of business metadata revolves around who is going to pay for it.

Several factors influence business metadata and who pays for it. Easily the most important factor relating to who pays for business metadata has to do with its packaging or delivery. Specifically, business metadata can be packaged as

1. A part of a larger infrastructure project, where business metadata exists as a part of a centralized metadata infrastructure package. In this case probably a lot of technical metadata components will be mixed in with business metadata in a centralized metadata implementation. This often occurs as a comprehensive enterprise metadata project and is implemented with a technical centralized metadata repository product.

2. A separate component, where the business metadata is packaged as a separate application or as part of a separate application. In this case, the business users are likely to be heavily involved. This is often the case if the project effort is to implement a business policy or a categorization such as a taxonomy or ontology. We often find that this option garners strong business support and long-term funding.

3. Business metadata is packaged as a combination of the above choices. This can be the case when a business terms and definitions dictionary is built and integrated with technical metadata. This is a less intense effort than the one outlined in (1). Fewer business organizations may be involved, and less technical metadata integration activities have to occur. However, we have found that longer term funding is often not supported when this option is selected.

### 3.7.1   The Centralized Implementation

Business metadata can be packaged as part of a technical metadata repository effort. In this case, business metadata is merely just one part of a larger infrastructure. The business metadata and the technical metadata are freely intermixed. There is a common infrastructure that supports all the metadata needs of the organization. In this case the metadata is collected and managed by a central group of people—administrators. The metadata infrastructure works closely with different standard database technologies, such as DBMS (database management systems) and BI (business intelligence) tools. The centralized metadata infrastructure has many components, only one of which is business metadata.

When business metadata is closely aligned with or attached to a centralized product, the payment for business metadata is done along with the product itself. In other words, the cost justification is based on the need for support of metadata, both technical and business. In this case, business metadata is funded by a centralized means, often through the IT organization. Some business units pool together and fund the centralized metadata repository, but this method is not common. Most organizations have a need for metadata support long before formal funding takes place.

Business metadata funding can occur as part of a large ramp-up for a specific business project. Occasionally, some large business infrastructure needs to be built, and it is recognized that metadata needs to be part of the ramp-up. Much more frequently, however, it takes a long time to achieve funding for the metadata effort and it may be a localized effort by a few business analysts.

### 3.7.2   The Localized Implementation

The opposite approach to the funding and implementation of business metadata is to effect the implementation on an individual business unit or to pool multiple business units together. In this case the business metadata is implemented one user, or one application, at a time, as in the case of a Business

Terms Dictionary. Individual end-users probably do not know that it is actually business metadata that is being implemented. The user merely knows that the implementation allows him or her to be more productive or that it permits greater analysis and discovery. Stated differently, with an implementation of business metadata, the end-user merely sees a much broader perspective of data. Only when someone mentions that the application is rich with business metadata does the end-user even know that there is something different about his or her application. However, to the user, business metadata merely appears to be a natural extension of the application and nothing more.

When business metadata is implemented in this way, the business unit pays for the business metadata. Usually the cost of the business metadata is minimal, compared to the cost of a centralized enterprise metadata repository infrastructure. In addition, the business metadata is closely aligned with an application or a group of applications managed within one business unit. Some organizations will consider localized business metadata as "end-user documentation." We would consider that a very myopic view of business metadata.

### 3.7.3   Advantages and Disadvantages of Funding Models

There are both advantages and disadvantages to funding business metadata as a centralized function or as an individual end-user function.

Advantages of centralized funding:

✦ Business metadata represents only a marginal cost, compared to the entire infrastructure.

✦ The business case for metadata includes business metadata as well.

Disadvantages of centralized funding:

✦ The cost of a centralized metadata infrastructure is high.

✦ The centralized metadata infrastructure is usually years late.

✦ Business metadata may get lost along with the other forms of metadata.

Advantages of end-user funding:

✦ The end-user sees a direct benefit.

✦ The end-user probably doesn't even know that business metadata is in fact business metadata.

✦ There is no competition with other metadata at implementation time.

- The cost of business metadata in this form is minimal.

- The implementation can be done according to the end-user's schedule.

Disadvantages of end-user funding:

- The relationship between business metadata and technical metadata may be lost.

- There may not be an awareness that business metadata is part of a larger framework.

# 3.8  Summary

This chapter has discussed how to set up data stewardship organizations within an enterprise for the purpose of governing business metadata, and highlighted the idea that such efforts can piggyback onto traditional data stewardship programs if they revolve around participants representing the business and not IT only. Data stewardship must involve the business or it will fail.

In addition, this chapter presented several funding models for business metadata: centralized, separate (usually localized, for delivery to one main business area), and a combination of these two. The advantages and disadvantages of each model have been presented. Although there is no perfect way to implement business metadata, we can learn from the efforts of others and hopefully have a plan in place that will mitigate any problems that occur and make up for some of the shortcomings of the implementation method chosen.

# 3.9  References

- Data Administration Management Association, (DAMA) International. Guidelines to Implementing Data Resource Management, Version 4, © 2002, ISBN: 0-9676674-0-2

- Eckerson, Wayne W. "Data Quality and the Bottom Line." TDWI Report Series, © 2002.

# Business Metadata, Communication, and Search

## 4.1 Introduction

This chapter discusses the role that business metadata plays in communications, both people-to-people and between people and computers. Communication between a person and the computer also comes into play with enterprise search. How we define our terms, using the precise terms we mean, and how we classify information are all included in business metadata. This chapter illustrates how business metadata facilitates our work lives, allowing us to find the information we need when we need it, and also allowing us to understand and be understood by others.

# 4.2 The Basic Problem in Information Management

The number one problem today in making data useful to the enterprise is the failure to understand that data, both its meaning on a fundamental level and its context. Here are a few examples familiar to all of us:

✦ Mars Climate Orbiter problem: The data was assumed to represent one unit of measure, but it was actually stored as another (miles versus meters); hence millions of dollars of equipment were lost (Isbell, Hardin, and Underwood, 1999).

✦ Bombing of the Chinese Embassy in Belgrade, Yugoslavia, in 1999: The map that was used was out of date (Wikipedia, 2006).

## 4.2.1 Lack of Communication Clarity

Public corporations and government agencies must produce an annual report, which is filled with counts and statistics. The assumptions behind these counts can be misunderstood and easily misconstrued. For example, consider the simple problem of counting how many customers you have. What is the definition of a customer? You can easily arrive at different counts based on different definitions of a customer. Since the way Customer is defined can affect so many Key Performance Indicators (KPIs), it is important to figure out exactly what a customer is. For example, consider the following questions:

✦ Is a Customer an individual or an organization, or neither? Could an individual be a customer himself, a member of a family, and also represent a larger organization? Would this situation involve two separate customers?

✦ Is anyone who has purchased anything a customer? Is there a minimum order amount?

✦ If someone has placed an order but the transaction has not completed yet, is the party placing the order considered a customer?

✦ What if the party purchased something from you over ten years ago; are they still considered a customer?

### 4.2.1.1 Everyday Communications

Have you ever been in a meeting and you thought you understood the topic of discussion but then someone used a business term in a way that you had never heard before? Suddenly you realize that you may not have understood what was being discussed after all. Most people are afraid to ask for clarification in a meeting, for fear of looking stupid. However, if terms are not well understood, people will not be communicating, and meanings will be misconstrued. Bad business decisions can often result from this miscommunication. Figure 4.1 shows how this miscommunication can occur.

### 4.2.1.2   Result: Bad Business Decisions

Extrapolate even further: Consider business people using a BI (business intelligence) tool to make financial decisions. Multidimensional cubes are used to look at various levels of summaries and details. It is highly likely that at least one cube has hidden assumptions about the meanings of business terms that the analyst may not be aware of, or he may have different assumptions than the individual who constructed the cube. Misunderstood data may unwittingly cause many errors in judgment, because the business terms used are not clarified and their definitions are not made readily available.

### 4.2.1.3   Do Your Rollups Really Roll Up?

One area in which we can readily see the results of faulty understanding is in the drill-downs and rollups that are part of BI reports. Faulty rollups are semantically diverse items (apples and oranges) improperly classified into the same

**Figure 4.1**   Miscommunication Due to Different Meanings of the Same Word.

larger category and summarized in error. Faulty rollups can be very insidious, and usually don't get identified until they have done major damage. Figure 4.2 illustrates how a count of apples can be wrong if it includes an orange. Figure 4.3 shows a questionable rollup based on classification of a tomato as a fruit.

Large enterprises are particularly prone to problems with accounting roll-ups. "Revenue" without any modifier might be very confusing and might be the cause of faulty rollups. For example, does it refer to Net Revenue or Gross Revenue? Obviously, if different organizations within the company report on revenue differently, a rollup of total revenue will not be correct for all points of view. If the underlying formula that was used is different in each division, then you don't have a rollup; you have a mess. It is the apples and oranges problem again.

This is a taxonomy problem. A taxonomy is a hierarchical classification scheme. We will discuss taxonomies later in the chapter.

**Figure 4.2**   Apples and Oranges.

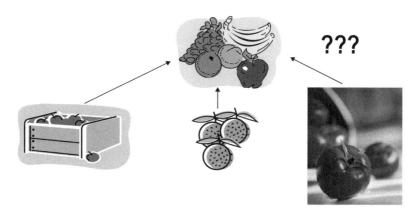

**Figure 4.3**   Is a Tomato a Fruit?

### 4.2.1.4   Units of Measure Differences

Another way that formulas can appear to be all apples but have oranges hiding in their midst is when you have different units of measure. This is a very insidious problem because all looks normal on the surface, and indeed it may go undetected for a long period of time.

The classic example is the Mars orbiter problem back in 1999, which we introduced in the beginning of this chapter. Here is a quote from CNN concerning this data screw-up:

> NASA lost a $125 million Mars orbiter because a Lockheed Martin engineering team used English units of measurement while the agency's team used the more conventional metric system for a key spacecraft operation. (Lloyd, 1999)

Unfortunately, the communication problem is very widespread. We as humans do not communicate well; in fact, we are downright sloppy communicators.

### 4.2.1.5   Is Our Language to Blame?

Part of the problem is our language itself. English is filled with lots of opportunities for ambiguity. For example, many words are spelled the same and pronounced the same but mean different things. Consider the word "book": based on the context in which it is used, it can mean:

+ An object containing published reading matter (example: what you are holding in your hands now)—a noun

+ The action of making a reservation such as an airline seat—a verb

The two uses of the same word are referred to as homonyms. This is also called "word sense"—a different sense of the word.

Most of the time, we are smart enough to discern from the context of the sentence which meaning is implied. But what if the context is hidden somehow, or ambiguous, and cannot be gleaned from the context?

## 4.2.2   The Importance of Definitions

As we have seen, many business decisions are made (and later regretted) due to a misunderstanding of the data and what the data element used in a report is signifying. Context is everything. Business metadata is all about adding context to data. A dictionary or glossary is part of business metadata, and it is all about making meaning explicit and providing definitions to business terms, data elements, acronyms, and abbreviations.

### 4.2.2.1 Business Function of a Glossary

In the normal flow of business, a dictionary or glossary is useful for the following functions:

✦ <u>Orientation and indoctrination of new employees.</u> The corporate culture of any business is filled with both industry-specific and company-specific terms that baffle new employees. A dictionary helps these new employees get up to speed quickly.

✦ <u>For personal clarification.</u> An employee is using an application or reading a document and comes across a word or phrase that is confusing. The glossary can be accessed immediately to clarify the material.

✦ <u>"Linguistic Arbitration."</u> This is a wonderful term coined by my friend James McQuade from Giant Eagle. Two or more individuals or groups have different definitions for the same business term. A dictionary can assist in clarification of meanings and as an authoritative source can help resolve disputes.

✦ <u>Data harmonization.</u> The process of creating and maintaining a corporate glossary can help the enterprise arrive at terms that everyone can agree on as to the meanings and everyone can use these terms with a common understanding. The analogy of "singing off of the same sheet of music" is apt so we call this function "data harmonization." It is critical for any type of data integration work, including data warehouses and data migration projects.

## 4.3 The Definition

What is the definition of a definition?

A definition is a description of the meaning of a term, formally stated (Carliner, 2002). For our purposes here, "term" is defined as a word or phrase that has a definite meaning to the business and is significant enough to be managed by the business. Specifically, a definition consists of describing the general class of things that the object of the term is a member of, as well as the characteristics that distinguish it from other members of the class.

ISO 11179 standard for vocabulary management asserts some basic guidelines of a good definition, as follows:

✦ A definition should always be stated in the singular.

✦ A definition should state what the concept is, not just what it is not.

✦ A definition should be stated as a descriptive phrase or sentence.

✦ A definition should contain only *very* common abbreviations or acronyms; these should be avoided if at all possible.

✦ A definition should not contain definitions of other concepts embedded in it. (In other words, if you don't understand what a term means that is used in a definition, you look it up.)

### 4.3.1 Components of a Definition

Use of controlled vocabulary and thesaurus concepts helps software manage glossaries and can also empower enterprise search capabilities. They can also assist us in writing more complete and comprehensive definitions. Acronyms and specialized terms are indicated in italics and parentheses. For more information about controlled vocabularies and thesauri, see Chapter 11, Semantics.

Here are the components of a well-written definition. Not all components are required for every definition, but the more you have, the more precise the definition.

1. **Name of the Term** being defined.

2. **Part of Speech** (optional; can be helpful). Examples: noun, verb.

3. **Broader Term** (*BT*): General class to which the thing belongs; sometimes this is implied. In object modeling parlance, this is called an "IS-A" relationship. Example: "A spoon is a utensil." Note that some definitions may be explaining things in the past, as in "a ladle was a utensil."

4. **Distinguishing Characteristics**, otherwise known as pertinent attributes with specific values. In object modeling parlance, this is called a "HAS-A" relationship. Example: "A spoon has a small bowl attached to the end."

5. **Function**: A description of how the thing being defined is used; this usually involves one or more verbs. For example, a spoon is a utensil with a small bowl attached to the end, used for bringing food to the mouth. The controlled vocabulary structure should probably be extended to include USED-FOR, but this term is not to be confused with USE-FOR, described below.

6. **Narrower Term** (*NT*): The classes below the term being defined. For example, if the term that is being defined as Spoon, then pertinent narrow terms of interest could be Soup, Tea, Serving.

7. **Related Term** (*RT*): A term that has relevance to the term being defined but is not a synonym. For example: Can opener is related to can but is not a synonym. Dictionaries, indexes, and search engines often have a "SEE ALSO" section that lists related terms.

8. **Synonyms:** Terms that mean nearly the same thing as the term being defined. Controlled vocabularies often handle synonyms using a synonym ring, defining one term as the Preferred Term *(PT)*. The language "USE FOR" is indicated in a controlled vocabulary when preferred terms are used. Example: Suppose Division and Department mean the same thing in an organization; they are synonyms, but suppose Division was the Preferred Term. When you look up Department, the glossary will state "Division: USE FOR Department." Glossaries, indexes, and search engines display synonyms in the "SEE..." section of the search results.

9. **Examples:** Example of the term; an instance of the term as it is seen in everyday life. Example (of the example!): An example of an employee is Mary Jones.

10. **Usage:** Refers to using the term in a sentence. The example can incorporate sentence usage, but it doesn't have to. Definition example: A Spoon is defined as an eating utensil that has a small bowl at the end. Usage: Mary gracefully lifted her spoon to her mouth to sample the soup.

11. **Source:** Where the definition came from. If it came from a document or manual, pertinent reference information may be important (date of the document, author, etc.).

12. **Dates:** At a minimum, the date that the term was created or added into the glossary, and also the date that it was last modified should always be recorded, which track glossary history. In addition, sometimes dates that indicate the governance status of the definition may be necessary such as Effective Date and Expiry Date.

13. **Replaced by:** Sometimes you may want to keep "legacy" terms in your glossary, especially if reengineering or a migration to a different system that uses different terms has occurred. You may want to indicate that the term is legacy and has been replaced by some other term. Alternatively, you can use Synonyms, but Replaced by indicates that you should not use the legacy term in common usage.

14. **Approval Information** can be added to track the governance trail, for such things as when the definition was approved, by whom, etc.

### 4.3.2  Definition Usage Notes

#### 4.3.2.1  Definition Text Structure

The three major parts of the definition text are indicated in 3, 4, and 5 above. They are:

+ Broader Term: IS-A, what class does it belong to?

+ Distinguishing Characteristics: HAS-A, how is this distinguished from other members of the class?

+ Function: USED-FOR, what is it used for?

A good, sound definition must make explicit two out of three of these components. The following example incorporates IS-A and USED-FOR:
IS-A:
A spoon is a utensil that
USED-FOR:
Is used for eating, specifically foods with more liquid concentration.
Note that "is a" indicates the broader term or class: Utensil. "Eating" illustrates a function or use of the spoon. More detail is added for the function, so it is eating a specific type of food that the spoon is used for. If we add "that has a small bowl at the end" to the definition, we have added a distinguishing characteristic and all three parts of the definition are used.
PART-OF and TYPE-OF are examples of terms that indicate a broader class relationship. Often the class relationship denoted by IS-A is implied. Sometimes these types of implications can be important to make explicit, sometimes not.

### 4.3.2.2 Enumerated, Multiple Meanings

Sometimes a definition can include more than one meaning, as in the homonym discussed above. This is common in a typical dictionary, and our language is full of such cases. The meaning in which the term is used must be derived from the context of the sentence. The multiple meanings are enumerated in a definition description as follows:

1- < definition text >

2- < definition text >

Different communities of interest within the same enterprise may have perfectly valid differences in meaning for the same term. Both meanings should be listed in the glossary, so if someone from one division is reading a report produced by another division, the reader can look up the term in the corporate glossary and see both definitions.

### 4.3.2.3 Broader/Narrower

Broad term and narrow term distinctions can get tricky. Sometimes a broader term or class is implied and is not important to the scope of the controlled vocabulary. For example, the formal definition of "definition" might be "a group of words that expresses the meaning of a term." A rule of thumb is that all terms used in definition text should be defined in the glossary. However, it is possible to get into a cyclic dependency with either broader terms or terms used in the definition. Do you really need to define the broader term "word"? You obviously get to the place where there are classes (generalizations) that are not useful and are certainly not worth the effort of defining. As always, the Law of Diminishing Returns applies; this means that more work applied at a certain point will yield less and less value.

There are some common, building block words that do not need to be defined, which are "atomic" and well-understood. "Well understood" means that the term is in common everyday language, general usage (in general settings and not just in a unique industry) and therefore does not have to be defined. However, be careful! Choose these "well-understood" terms carefully and make sure they really are well-understood. An example of a well-understood term might be "Person." It refers to a member of *Homo sapiens*. However, an example of a poorly understood term is "Customer." You think you know what it means, but do you really? "Customer" should always be explicitly defined for every business.

### 4.3.3 Miscellaneous Guidelines

1. A definition should **never** be a tautology, that is, defined by itself. This is also called a circular definition. Common examples of tautological definitions are:

   ✦ Customer ID is defined as "The identifier of the Customer."
   ✦ "Metal is something made of metal."

2. Parts of speech should agree. For example, a noun should be defined with a noun, a verb with a verb, and so on. Do not use an adverb phrase like "is when" or "is where" in the definition text.

3. All terms used in the definition should be either defined in the glossary or lexicon or be considered atomic/basic terms.

4. Distinguishing characteristics should be stated precisely.

5. Avoid classes that are too broad. A broad term or class should be large enough to include all members but not too large that it doesn't add any value.

# 4.4 Communications and Search

In the last section we discussed the importance of communicating ideas clearly and precisely to other people. There is, however, another view of communication: How well are ideas in the "knowledge base" represented so that they can be found? And how easy is it to express a search in a way that a computer can locate exactly the type of information you are looking for? This is also a form of communication, though one that is often overlooked.

Let's first discuss the Search Problem and its ramifications to the corporation.

## 4.4.1 The High Cost of Not Finding Information

Susan Feldman wrote several articles by this name (Feldman, 2001, 2004), and we also found a blog entry with the title, "The High Cost of Not Finding Information" (French, 2004). What exactly is involved when businesspeople can't find the information they need?

We all know about what happens when we lose our car keys. At first, it is a minor irritation. The problem begins to escalate, we panic, we waste a lot of time, we become more and more frustrated, and we begin to realize what being late means to the rest of our day. This escalates the problem to a higher level. Finally, we get desperate, and the problem of finding the keys becomes a Major Emergency as we feel our blood pressure rising. If there are any other people about, they are immediately enlisted in the Great Cause. Relief hits when we finally find them (incredibly, always in the last place you look!). However, the frantic problem of being late still looms, and we dash out the door, desperately trying to redeem the time by driving fast so we can make up some time, minimizing our lateness without getting into an accident.

Sound familiar? We have all had experiences like this. Is this the same type of experience that people would have if they were unable to find information to do their jobs?

### 4.4.1.1 Information and "Knowledge Workers"

Peter Drucker first created the term "knowledge worker" in the late 1950s and early 1960s. The economy of the twenty-first century is an information economy, and most workers today are knowledge workers who produce abstract work products consisting mainly of information, not tangible items like cars or pencils. Therefore, the know-how of the knowledge worker is not necessarily knowledge of everything, but knowing where to find it. Samuel Johnson, who compiled the first English dictionary in the 1700s, said:

**Figure 4.4**  Searching for a Needle in a Haystack.

> Knowledge is of two kinds. We know a subject ourselves, or we know where we can find information upon it. (Quoted in Chisholm, 2001)

The car keys example has its parallel in information searching, for sure. It is very frustrating when we do a search on Google, and we can't find what we need. To make matters worse, many times too much information comes back from a search and plowing through it all takes forever. We seem to be drowning in too much inform ation. We have all had the experience of doing a search on Google and noticing that our search had over one million hits.

How do you sift through this thicket of information and find the one fact that you need? As Susan Feldman says,

> Everyone seems to be working longer hours and getting less and less done…. We spend hours trying to track down something that we found only yesterday, but it seems to have disappeared…. In short, we spend a lot of time spinning our wheels looking for things and not finding them. (Feldman, 2004)

Figure 4.4 illustrates the proverb "needle in a haystack," which seems to describe much of our searching for information.

We had this experience when writing this chapter. Two nights ago the Susan Feldman article was located on the Internet, and when we wanted to insert the reference in the chapter, we could not find it! It took over an hour to finally find it, and when we did, the Web page did not come up, presumably owing to problems on the host's server.

### 4.4.1.2  *Trying to Track Down Information*

Let's extend the Lost Car Keys analogy into the information space. Consider the sequence of events that occur when you receive a request from the IRS

Finding data in the
massive amount of
files and data bases

**Figure 4.5** Drowning in Data.

to document a claim you have made on a past income tax return. How long does it take you to find the data to do the verification? The real problem is not verifying the amount or the date of the transaction in question, the real problem is in finding the check or the checkbook where the date and the amount is written down. Figuring out where to look is the biggest problem in understanding far-flung and disparate pieces of data. Metadata serves as an index to point you to the information you need quickly. Without metadata, what you are looking for could be anywhere. It is metadata that saves you enormous amounts of time when trying to find a particular piece of information.

Figure 4.5 shows that information technology is buried in data and numbers and that it is metadata that allows these massive volumes of information to be examined efficiently. It is a graphic all of us can relate to!

### 4.4.2  Quantifying Search Problems

Susan Feldman headed a research endeavor by IDC (International Data Corporation) published in a 2001 article entitled "The High Cost of Not Finding Information" aimed at quantifying the costs associated with search problems. How costly is it to the typical enterprise consisting of knowledge workers when these employees can't find the information they need?

Here are some quick facts that the IDC research found:

✦ The typical knowledge worker spends from 15 to 35% of his or her time searching.

✦ Only 50% or less of all searches are successful.

- ✦ Only 40% of survey respondents reported that they were able to find what they needed on their corporate Internet (Feldman, 2001).

- ✦ It should be noted that the IDC study was conducted in 2001 and again in 2003. Most intranets, and use of the Internet as a whole, have matured since then, so it could be that users are getting more search-savvy. But this is speculation. It would be enlightening if IDC would repeat its survey today.

Feldman backs up her statistics by noting that others have found similar results, notably:

- ✦ Ford Motor Company

- ✦ Working council of Chief Information Officers (CIOs)

- ✦ Association for Information and Image Management (AIIM)

- ✦ Reuters

- ✦ Kit Sims Taylor

Here are some attempts to quantify the cost impact of failed search in the enterprise.

### 4.4.2.1 Attempts to Quantify Search Impact

Feldman identifies three types of costs that can be quantified:

- ✦ Employee time wasted

- ✦ Duplicating/reworking information

- ✦ Opportunity cost

On the positive side, Feldman and Seybold identify two areas in which increased search capacity has a positive impact:

- ✦ Decrease in call center volume

- ✦ Increase in sales (conversion rates and shopping basket size—e-commerce)

Each of these areas is summarized below.

### 4.4.2.2   Baseline Assumptions

The IDC study begins with the following baseline assumptions:

- ✦ Each employee costs the enterprise $80,000, which includes salary plus benefits.

- ✦ The average knowledge worker spends 2.5 hours/day (30%) searching for information.

- ✦ The enterprise employs 1000 knowledge workers.

- ✦ 50% of information is not centrally indexed (housed in silos as on someone's notebook computer or a database).

- ✦ 50% of Web searches fail/are abandoned.

### 4.4.2.3   Employee Time Wasted

Based on these assumptions, Feldman calculated that the enterprise wastes $48,000 per week, or almost $2.5 million a year in searches. This number is an estimate only; she did not factor in employee vacations.

### 4.4.2.4   Duplicating/Reworking Information

Knowledge workers inadvertently re-create information because they can't access the original work products. IDC calls this a "knowledge deficit." Feldman references a study by Kit Sims Taylor, which estimates that "one-third of productive time is spent in knowledge reworking . . . with only 10% of time spent in actual creation of new knowledge" (Taylor, as quoted by Feldman and Sherman, 2001).

IDC's study of European companies estimates this knowledge deficit at $5,000 per worker per year in 1999, growing to $5,850 in 2003 (IDC, 2000). Wonder what it would be in 2007?

The organization Feldman uses as an example would therefore spend $5M per year reworking information unnecessarily; information that already exists but that the knowledge worker was unable to find.

### 4.4.2.5   Opportunity Cost

Missed business opportunity is difficult to measure because revenue must be tied directly to an employee. One way to do this is through sales and revenue generated by a sales rep. If a sales rep cannot find information relevant to making the sale, then the sale may be lost. If the sales rep generates an average revenue, then this can be used to calculate the impact of failed searches.

Feldman uses a revenue number of $500K/year per employee, which translates to $240/hr. 1000 employees * 50% failed searches * 240/hr * 2.5 hours searching = $300K/week or greater than $15M/year.

### 4.4.2.6 Decrease in Call Center Volume

The impact of failed searches on call center volume can be measured. If both internal and external personnel can find the information they need on a Web portal, then this represents less HR or sales requests. Feldman reports that call center volume decreases by 30% when search is improved.

> Good online customer service can handle up to 90 percent of customer questions. Implementing premium search can immediately boost call deflection, cutting the number of calls in half. (Sue Aldrich, as quoted in Seybold, 2006)

### 4.4.2.7 Increase in Sales

Improved search can also add to the revenue, as is seen most prominently in e-commerce companies. Seybold states that the size of online shopping baskets sees an average increase of 300% when the search mechanism involved is improved. Feldman's numbers show that online retailers have experienced a revenue increase of over $125K/month and an average deal size increase of over 400%.

### 4.4.2.8 Conclusion: Findability Makes a Difference

It can therefore be concluded that the ability to find information is not just a "nice to have" but it drastically affects the bottom line. How, therefore, can findability be improved? Since this book is about business metadata and not about search tools, we are next going to focus on the impact of business metadata to the search experience.

## 4.5 Business Metadata and Search

Two different kinds of business metadata are involved in the search:

- ✦ Common metadata structure that all documents have, for example, Title, Author, Date of Creation, etc.
- ✦ Tags, categories, category key words, topics, etc.

This section assists both the searcher and the author of a document in improving the search capability in both directions. Authors and searchers need to be aware of both areas.

We can improve our two-way communication between the searcher and the computer in many ways, as we show in the following sections.

### 4.5.1.1  Business Metadata Techniques for Searchers

Searchers can learn a few techniques in how they express what they are look-ing for in the search engine. Here are two quick wins:

✦ Use precise words in the search. Earlier in the chapter we discussed the need for precise word usage and strong definitions. Use of the appropri-ate words in a search will improve our chances of success. If you are unsure, check either the Corporate Glossary (if it exists) or an online dictionary for the correct definition.

✦ Use fewer words to achieve a broad search and more words for a nar-row search as necessary. If you are looking for a specific article, you can type most or all of the entire title to find it. If the search is too narrow and no results are returned, then you can enter fewer words in the title or a general topic. Often, you may think you know the exact title, but if you have just one word wrong, the search will fail to find it. Try entering the main words in the title instead of all the words.

### 4.5.1.2  Business Metadata Techniques for Information Providers

One of the most basic ways of improving the ability to find information on the Internet is to improve the names of documents. A wonderful short article by Kevin Hannon of InfoCurators (Hannon, 2004) illustrates how searches won't be able to hit their target due to the nonsensical names that the files have. Such ridiculous, meaningless names make the files virtually invisible over the corporate intranet. Here are a few examples that he cites, but we all surely have a few of our own that are just as crazy:

✦ Acme covermth                     Acme's Annual Report

✦ Microsoft Word-006702_1.doc       Technical field document that is really a pdf

✦ Microsoft Word-06682_0.doc        Safety requirements for a laser product

Hannon provides an example of naming Web pages and illustrates how pages will not be returned, based on who is doing the searching. He shows how using the company name as a prefix in a Web page name will not cause the page to come up on most search engines because the beginning of the name is primary. The example he uses is a cancer information site. Only doctors would append the term "disease" after the name of the ailment, so including this term in the page name will increase hits for doctors doing searches but decrease searches by nonmedical practitioners. If the aim of the Web site is to provide information to the medical community, then this naming technique will probably work just fine. However, if the goal is to provide information to the public at large and to disease sufferers and their families, perhaps this term should be left off the page name.

### 4.5.2  *Classification*

As we have seen, the title is a very valuable piece of business metadata. Even the individual words that are the components of the title are business metadata. It could be said that the file name or article/Web page title may be the most important piece of business metadata because it represents the primary way that things are found. However, second to this is how documents or files can be classified: what is the topic of the file or article? What topics are related to it? Can you find not just the specific article you're looking for, but related ones? The next section illustrates how searches can be assisted by using classification schemes.

#### 4.5.2.1  *Taxonomy*

To most people, the word "taxonomy" (if not confused with stuffed animals—"taxidermy") means the classification of the animal kingdom. This is perhaps the most famous example of a taxonomy, but it fails to illustrate how in this modern, Internet world taxonomies can be useful to searching for information. A taxonomy is a hierarchical classification system. It can guide how Web pages are organized on a Web site, and it can help customers quickly navigate the site and pinpoint items they would like to purchase quickly and easily.

For example, say you'd like to purchase a purple skirt. You go to a department store's Web site and you first distinguish that you'd like to look at the section called Women; see Figure 4.6. Next, you pick Skirts. Notice that "Skirts" are not a featured item like Dresses, Coats, Suits, or Jeans are. Oh well. You then click on Skirts on the left hand side; see Figure 4.7. Next the Skirts part of the online catalog is displayed; see Figure 4.8. There are some user-controlled options, but color is not one of them. A really good Web site would allow you to type "purple skirt" in the search window, and it would bring up all the skirts that have purple in them. When you do this in the Macy's site, it brings back two choices that surely look like pink, and not purple!

As we have seen in the Macy's example, the taxonomy organizes the items by their classification and enables navigation by beginning with a broad term and allowing the user to get more and more specific navigating through the categories until the precise item is located.

**Figure 4.6**   Highest Level Hierarchy: Women.

### 4.5.2.2   Basic Rules about Taxonomies

A really precise taxonomy is a parent-child-type hierarchy and is commonly called "IS-A," meaning the child is a type of the parent, and expresses a succession of broad to narrow relationships (just like the controlled vocabulary concept we learned earlier). For example, a fork is a type of cutlery or eating utensil. Strict, technical hierarchies use IS-A classification as a rule that should never be violated.

However, the data doesn't always fit nicely into parent-child classifications, and it is important to also be reminded of the function of a Web navigation taxonomy, which is to guide the user to the material he or she wants with a minimum of clicks, and to keep time spent in the Web site at a minimum. A physical store's goal is to keep you in the store for as long as possible so that you will impulse buy. If a Web site tried to do that, no users would buy anything from them! Therefore, it might be convenient for search purposes to put a document in more than one category.

Zach Wahl, internationally known taxonomy guru, makes the distinction clear between a strict, formal taxonomy (such as classification of the animal kingdom or pharmaceuticals) and a business taxonomy. The purpose of a business taxonomy is to navigate a Web site and facilitate "findability." Wahl says:

> [A] successful business taxonomy must be designed for intuitive browsing by end users. Design at every stage of the business taxonomy must, therefore, consider whether the average user will be able to understand both the terms and the hierarchy of the taxonomy and react to it in a meaningful and consistent manner. If

**Figure 4.7** Selecting "Skirts" on Left Side of Screen.

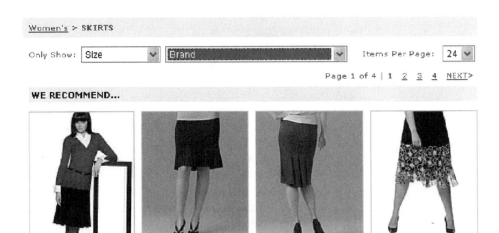

**Figure 4.8** Browsing Skirts at Macy's.

this is done effectively, the end user will receive a powerful "findability" tool, enabling them to discover information through browsing the taxonomy and view information in an intuitive and consistent manner. (Wahl, 2006)

Earlier we stated that you should know who your searchers are; this is key in designing any taxonomy. However, since the Web invites an endless variety of users from all walks of life, the taxonomy must be understandable to all.

### 4.5.2.3   Lowest Common Denominator Factor

The example from the preceding section about names from the medical community with both doctors and patients/family members searching for information about diseases highlights an important factor to keep in mind when designing taxonomies: the lowest common denominator. Instead of having separate taxonomies for distinct communities that take into account specific technical vocabulary differences, try using the simplest terms that everyone will understand. More from Zach Wahl:

> [T]he business taxonomy must be explained with simple terminology that avoids jargon or technical complexity that could confuse potential users. When considering the terms for a business taxonomy, the designers should identify the "lowest common denominator" of user types and build using terms and topics that will immediately resonate with them. (Wahl, 2006)

### 4.5.2.4   Language and Vocabulary

Different industries have their own jargon; so do different companies and even different divisions within a company. Should a taxonomy be customized for these differences?

There are two different philosophies about taxonomies:

◆ Single, master taxonomy

◆ Multiple, "facet-based" taxonomies for different subgroups

Kevin Hannon points out in an article called "Enterprise Taxonomies: One Large or Many Small?" the differences between having a single, master taxonomy that spans the enterprise as opposed to individual taxonomies in each functional area (Hannon, 2005). A master taxonomy collapses all vocabulary differences into one standard vocabulary. Normalization of vocabularies across departments may not always be desirable because searchers each want to construct their navigation based on their own nomenclature. Smaller, individual taxonomies can take into account these different "dialects" across the company and may help in allowing the users to use their own jargon that they understand. The users may get confused by the requirement to use universal terms because they don't think in these terms.

This approach only works, however, if you can guarantee that only the users familiar with the specialized vocabulary will be using that specific section of the taxonomy. The point we made earlier is that it is usually possible that anyone can access any part of the taxonomy. If access was restricted to a specific community, it might be possible to use a specialized vocabulary without confusing noncommunity members. The moral again seems to always be: "Know your searchers."

### 4.5.2.5   Simple Is Best

Business taxonomies used for searching should therefore be simple. The top list of categories should be very broad and phrased in language easily understood by all users. Whereas a technical hierarchy might go as many as 12 levels deep, Wahl points out that business taxonomies usually consist of about 8 top-level categories and each category has no more than 3 subcategories. Remember, too many clicks chases the users away! Wahl sums this thought up as follows:

> In other words, the business taxonomy sacrifices detail for usability and consistency. (Wahl, 2006 )

There is no universal, "right" way to build a taxonomy. There are, however, principles or guidelines that can help, and the most universal guideline is know your search community. A taxonomy should also always be considered "under construction," and the search experience should continually be monitored and improved over time. If people are frustrated by the search experience on a company's intranet, it will not be used, and valuable time will be wasted as employees run around asking each other for documents when they could have found them quicker online.

### 4.5.2.6   Correctly Categorizing Documents for Search

Where does a document belong in the search hierarchy? Who decides? A document may be authored or owned by one division of the company but perceived as being part of another functional area, for search purposes. For example, Hannon (2005) points out that tuition reimbursement policies may be set by Finance but are considered related to HR, so the average searcher would expect to find tuition reimbursement guidelines under the HR category; the same applies to something like Affirmative Action policies, which may be written by the legal department but should be searchable under HR. Therefore, the originator of the document may not always be the appropriate place for it to reside for search.

The decision of where documents belong is a decision for governance.

### 4.5.2.7  Governance and Taxonomy

Zach Wahl points out that it is critical to have a cross-disciplinary team assisting in taxonomy creation (Wahl, 2006). Every class of user type should be represented, so that all types of users' needs will be considered in the construction of the taxonomy. This team can form the governance body for the taxonomy. The main point is to get user involvement and buy-in from the business so that they have some ownership and don't write off enterprise search failure as an "IT thing." Governance was the sole subject in Chapter 3.

Governance also helps decide where documents belong and what classifications are appropriate. The author usually thinks he or she has a good idea of where the document belongs, but he or she may not understand how a user might go about looking for the document. Tools can be very helpful to decipher what documents are about; see Chapter 12, Unstructured Business Metadata.

Documents that are consistently miscategorized are signs of a faulty, confusing taxonomy. For this reason, the Web site's search metrics should be monitored periodically. The existence of many abandoned searches could be an indicator that the taxonomy is hindering, not helping, the search process.

### 4.5.2.8  Self-Organizing Tags

What if you let everyone create their own tags for documents (both their own and everyone else's) and share them? Would this make searches easier for everyone?

This self-organizing tagging structure is called a *folksonomy*, made popular by a Web site called del.icio.us. It follows the "Wisdom of Crowds" philosophy (made popular by the book of the same name) that a crowd is smarter than one person alone. This subject is discussed in more detail in Chapter 6, Business Metadata Capture.

## 4.6  Summary

Bad communications have dire consequences, ranging from major disasters that cause loss of life or billions of dollars to bad business decisions. This chapter has shown how business metadata can potentially prevent such disasters and foster good communication both between people and between the human and the computer. In addition, we have seen how much failed searches really can cost organizations, and it is a great deal of money—in the millions of dollars. Business metadata can help improve search and increase the "findability" of information. It involves Best Practices, in both defining the terms that we use and showing how we classify our information.

# 4.7 References

✦ Carliner, Saul. "Information Developer's Toolkit, Preparing Definitions." 2002. http://saulcarliner.home.att.net/id/definitions.htm

✦ Chisholm, Malcolm. "Is the Metadata Repository Dead?" *DM Review*, May 2001. http://www.dmreview.com/article_sub.cfm?articleID = 3335

✦ Feldman, Susan. "The High Cost of Not Finding Information." *KM World*, March 1, 2004. http://www.kmworld.com/Articles/PrintArticle. aspx?ArticleID = 9534

✦ Feldman, Susan, and Sherman, Chris. "The High Cost of Not Finding Information." *Viapoint*, 2001. http://www.viapoint.com/doc/IDC%20on% 20The%20High%20Cost%20Of%20Not%20Finding%20Information.pdf

✦ Hannon, Kevin. "Enterprise Taxonomies: One Large or Many Small?" Information Curators, 2005. http://colab.cim3.net/file/work/SICoP/ontac/ meeting/2005-10-05/single_vs_multiple_taxonomies_hannon.pdf

✦ Hannon, Kevin. "Metadata Is Money." InfoCurators, 2004. Available on request from www.infocurators.com.

✦ IDC. *European Knowledge Management Fact Book*. IDC #21511, January 2000.

✦ Isbell, Hardin, and Underwood. "Mars Climate Orbiter Team Finds Likely Cause of Loss." Mars Polar Lander (JPL), http://mpfwww.jpl.nasa.gov/ msp98/news/mco990930.html

✦ Lloyd, Robin. "Metric Mishap Caused Loss of NASA Orbiter." CNN, September 30, 1999. http://www.cnn.com/TECH/space/9909/30/mars. metric.02/

✦ Seybold, Patty. "Where Do Search and Findability Fit in Your Business Strategy?" Outside Innovation, 2006. http://outsideinnovation.blogs.com/ pseybold/2006/06/where_do_search.html

✦ Wahl, Zach. "Masterclass: Business Taxonomy, Part I." Inside Knowledge, October 31, 2006. http://www.ikmagazine.com/

✦ Wikipedia. "NATO Bombing of the Chinese Embassy in Belgrade."Referenced on October 26, 2006. http://en.wikipedia. org/wiki/NATO_Bombing_of_the_Chinese_embassy_in_Belgrade

# Initiating a Business Metadata Project

## 5.1  Introduction

As organizations moved to an understanding of the need for enterprise information, rather than just application information, corporations recognized that they needed to do something about their metadata. It is with that understanding and the thirst for enterprise information with integrity that organizations attempted to consolidate their information. First, information was collected and consolidated into a data warehouse. But quickly organizations saw the need to consolidate enterprise business and technical metadata as well.

The first attempts at a corporate repository for metadata were clumsy and closely focused on IT. Data dictionaries were created, followed by mainframe repositories. These initial attempts at enterprise metadata repositories were less than sterling. Most were not sustainable and lacked business metadata capabilities. Today the enterprise metadata repository technology is still quite limited in a number of products, but functionality and support for business metadata have improved. We not only now have the IT metadata repository products but also portal and collaboration products that can be implemented by business teams. A number of implementation options are available that do not require a million dollar capital investment just to start the metadata project. Today the issues are more about defining the plan, delineating the scope of the project, and getting the project initiated.

Essentially one must begin the metadata project with the end result or outcome in mind. This may mean that the metadata project is a business unit internal project, or a local metadata tool effort, or it could be an enterprise-wide project requiring significant capital and resources from many business units. Metadata projects may be very diverse; scope and objectives, source technologies, or implementation and usage technologies may all differ. Hence, we emphasize the need to clearly define the desired outcome or objectives of your metadata first. Plan and scope the effort to maximize its business value. Often the metadata objectives will require a significant level of metadata integration and consolidation. Thus, we need to discuss why we want to initiate metadata projects.

# 5.2 Why Consolidate or Integrate Metadata?

So why would an organization want to consolidate business and technical metadata to create an enterprise metadata repository? Among the many reasons that we could list here are the following:

◆ To capture the metadata from the corporation's staff. The people who have extensive knowledge of the enterprise processes, data, and metadata are leaving the enterprise through retirement or other reasons. These individuals carry a vast amount of the corporation's metadata in their heads. One can consider these individuals to have metadata repositories in their "gray matter." Thus, we often allude to the corporation's metadata repositories as being in carbon-based life forms that have legs (and each is an isolated local repository). The enterprise can lose significant business metadata as individuals leave the enterprise unless they establish a metadata repository.

◆ To aid staff members in understanding an enterprise business process and the IT implementation of the process (for communications and productivity).

◆ To look at metadata and information uniformly across the enterprise (for consistency and quality).

◆ To understand the cross-functional business and technical implications for change to an enterprise process or system (for reuse, the impact of change and organization management).

◆ To come up with a rational plan for consolidating entire systems in the enterprise (reuses and cost reduction).

For simplicity's sake, we could then say that organizations often desire to consolidate and integrate metadata in order to reduce the cost of operations, better communications, improve productivity, maximize reuse of resources, and enhance the quality of the organization's knowledge and service delivery.

Another reason to consolidate metadata involves the economies of scale that can be enjoyed through consolidation. Having a single system do the work of five or six smaller, unintegrated systems mitigates the cost of processing. When data and metadata are scattered across the corporation in an unorganized manner, there is no confidence in the data. In such a situation, the same data exists in five different forms throughout the corporation with five different values and most often with no metadata to help people understand the context and/or account for the differences. People are making decisions on the basis of incorrect, incomplete, or out-of-date data. The lack of metadata for nonintegrated corporate information is a major pitfall for large organizations.

The general response has been to consolidate data, thus improving the integrity of the data as well as the metadata available. Data is consolidated either (1) into a data warehouse or (2) into an enterprise metadata repository. Books, articles, seminars, and case studies all exist with regard to the building of data warehouses and will not be discussed in this book.

An enterprise metadata repository should contain metadata from all over the corporation. The ability to view metadata is a critical function that many metadata projects often ignore. The consolidation of metadata can be quite challenging in itself. If the metadata cannot be viewed, then many will question why the metadata project was attempted at all. Business metadata is all about bringing utility to the business and enhancing the understanding of data, as a means of facilitating businesspeople's job performance.

For an example, let's look at an implementation of the Corporate Information Factory (CIF). From the CIF's perspective, there is a need to gather and consolidate enterprise metadata. Figure 5.1 shows a CIF diagram.

The figure shows that there are many different architectural structures in the CIF. These structures have been built over time and support different forms of information processing. Some architectural components support historical

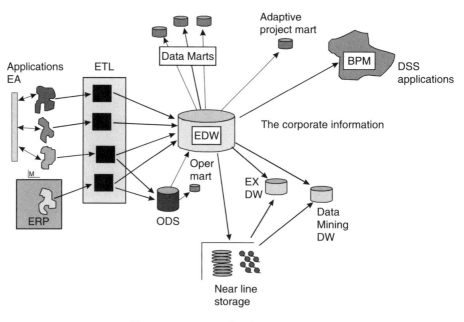

**Figure 5.1** Example of a CIF Diagram.

data, whereas others support current valued data. Some support the clerical community; some support the managerial community. In a word, many forms of data and many different technologies can be found in the Corporate Information Factory.

Metadata exists wherever there is a different architectural component in the CIF. Figure 5.2 shows that metadata for each architectural component is scattered throughout the CIF.

## 5.3 Metadata Project Planning and Scoping Considerations

As discussed in previous chapters, metadata projects can be categorized as:

- ✦ Centralized or enterprise implementations
- ✦ Local implementations
- ✦ Hybrid, incorporating aspects of centralized and local implementations

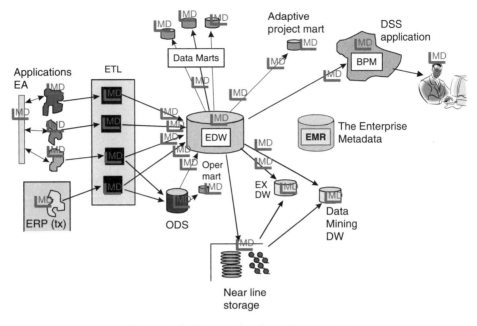

**Figure 5.2**    Where Metadata Exists in a CIF.

The objectives of the metadata project and funding approach will generally be tightly coupled. However, the scope of effort can be flexible within each of the available approaches. The following discusses some potential scoping issues you may need to address when you are planning your metadata data project.

### 5.3.1  *Business Metadata Versus Technical Metadata*

Another strategic consideration in building an enterprise metadata repository involves deciding what kind of metadata to include. One way metadata is classified is by technical metadata versus business metadata. Both kinds of metadata regularly exist in the information environment. As discussed previously, technical metadata provides a technical description of data and includes table names and descriptions, attribute names and descriptions, keys, indexes, and row counts. Business metadata describes other data but is couched in terms useful to the businessperson. Very few, if any, technology terms are found in business metadata. Contracts, agreements, billings, and warranties are full of business metadata, as are many other documents. If the enterprise metadata repository is to be used for general purpose processing, it may make sense for it to contain both kinds of metadata. Making the decision as to what kinds of metadata belong in the enterprise metadata repository is one that must be done strategically, in advance.

Building the enterprise metadata repository for both technical and business metadata can be a complex and lengthy task. It is strongly advised that it be built iteratively. Just like a data warehousing environment, one should not attempt to build an enterprise metadata repository as one large long-term project. There are many ways of organizing these iterations.

### 5.3.2    Different Iterations of Development

Many different approaches can be used to define how the iterations of the enterprise metadata repository can be divided. Some of the ways could include the following:

✦ *By geography*. First one country has its metadata gathered, then another country.

✦ *By time relevance*. The newest metadata is collected first.

✦ *By source technology*. All IBM metadata is collected before HP metadata is collected.

✦ *By business or technology application*. The inventory control application is serviced first, the stores management application is serviced next, and so forth.

✦ *By business versus technical*. All technical metadata is gathered before business metadata.

✦ *By business function or business unit*. Both the technical and business metadata is gathered for a given business function or business unit. This is often done for business metadata. For example, the Business Terms from Sales may be the first metadata loaded into the Business Terms Dictionary.

✦ *By business application*. The metadata from the Order Entry application and business processes will be acquired first.

Obviously, we would suggest that the metadata loaded first should produce the greatest benefit to the business. This implies that a priority is defined and that a relative value for metadata has been determined. However, if expediency is important, such as for the implementation of a metadata pilot project to demonstrate immediate value, the most convenient and easily accessible metadata could be loaded first.

### 5.3.3   Technology Tool: Local Metadata

Each different technology architectural component or tool has its own metadata, called "local" metadata. Local metadata is most often technical metadata and is closely tied to the technology that it supports. Business Objects has its own online analytical processing (OLAP) metadata; extract-transform-load (ETL) software has its own metadata; spreadsheets have their own internal metadata; data warehouses have their own metadata; the enterprise resource planning (ERP) application has its own metadata; and so forth. Each local metadata store is used to describe and control the metadata found within the confines of the architectural component. Each of the local architectural components is self-contained as regards technical metadata. Of course, business metadata is embedded in most of these technology tools as well.

What is missing is an enterprise description of the metadata embedded in these local tool repositories. Although there are lots of local metadata, there is no global description—an enterprise consolidated description—of the metadata found in the corporation. The purpose of the enterprise metadata repository then is to collect the local metadata and render it into a global form that is useful to the entire enterprise.

Building an enterprise metadata repository is a large undertaking for a small organization; for a large multinational organization it can be a colossal undertaking. Enormous amounts of data need to be considered, and the underlying metadata is constantly changing. For these reasons, building an enterprise metadata repository is not a short-term project. And even after it has been built, it requires an ongoing commitment to keep it current and accurate.

To attempt to build an enterprise metadata repository in a single push is to risk failure. The most successful enterprise metadata repository development efforts occur in different phases over time.

## 5.4   Defining the Scope of the Metadata Repository

At the start of an enterprise metadata repository effort, it is wise to develop a plan. The first consideration in the plan is to define the general scope of what is to be included in the enterprise metadata repository. Figure 5.3 presents an example of a CIF that has been mapped out to determine what the enterprise metadata repository should include. Again, this is just an example, for a data warehousing environment or CIF is just one potential scope for an enterprise metadata repository.

Figure 5.3 shows that the enterprise metadata repository has been designed to include the data marts (multidimensional technology), the data warehouse, the operational data store (ODS) oper marts (specialized data marts populated

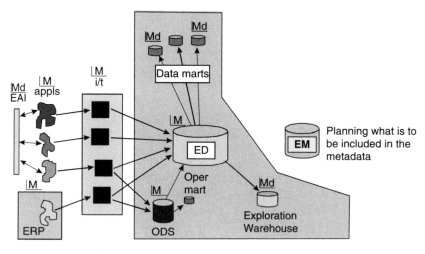

**Figure 5.3** Determine the Scope of Metadata.

directly from the ODS), and the exploration facility (for data mining). Determining the boundaries of what is to be found in the enterprise metadata repository before construction begins is a good way to avoid confusion at a later point in time.

In some circles, the definition of what will be included in the enterprise metadata repository project is called a definition of the scope of integration. Scoping the iterations of the metadata repository is quite similar to scoping a data warehouse or any iterative software implementation. We recommend that you follow the same guidelines that are already published. However, certain metadata sourcing considerations must be considered when defining the scope of the metadata iteration.

### 5.4.1 The Sources of Business and Technical Metadata

Many different potential sources of metadata may need to be consolidated in the scope of building the enterprise metadata repository, either local or enterprisewide. Each source of metadata has its own unique considerations. For each of these sources, at a minimum you will have to consider the following issues when you scope the effort:

✦ Stability of the source metadata

✦ Frequency and timing of the source metadata acquisition

+ Quality, controls, and audit checks for the metadata as well as the acquisition processes

+ Requirements for maintaining history, versioning, and archiving of the metadata

+ Metadata integration requirements

+ Business usage and presentation of the metadata

+ Timing and business cycle for presenting metadata

+ Security for access of the metadata

+ Security of the reporting and printed versions of the metadata

Planning and scoping the metadata project is not always a simple issue. Actually, it can often be more difficult than planning for a standard data integration effort. Organizations frequently fail to consider the issues of metadata history management, metadata usage and prostration, or metadata security.

## 5.5 Summary

There are many reasons we want to capture and consolidate metadata. Historically, we have not completed business or technical metadata projects based on achieving a given financial business return or ROI. However, metadata projects can yield significant, measurable productivity improvements. What is the value of having business metadata and process definitions available to escalate the training of new employees? What is the economic value of having the technical data lineage to reduce the cycle time and to improve the quality for application systems changes? These productivity improvements can be measured and monitored for purposes of reporting the value of metadata projects.

A consolidated metadata data store can be very useful. The metadata for the consolidation is sourced from many places in the enterprise. The metadata that resides in the different components of the technical applications and business units is called the "local" metadata. The local metadata can be accessed and sent to an enterprise metadata repository.

As the local data is sent to the enterprise metadata repository, it is subject to many different kinds of issues including editing. Among the forms of editing are removal of extraneous words and symbols; resolution of synonyms and alternate spellings; and the joining of expanded definitions and descriptions.

The enterprise metadata repository must be built iteratively. The work that is to be done can be segmented or scoped in many ways—by geography, technology, application, business unit, and so on. In planning the metadata project, one should always consider the desired end result in terms of what will be delivered to support business processes. There is little value to just building a database of metadata. Planning and scoping must define the objectives in terms of the outcomes desired. Metadata quality, history, and security should be considered in project planning.

# Business Metadata Capture

**CHAPTER 6**

## 6.1 Introduction

This chapter discusses the challenges of capturing business metadata directly from businesspeople. Examples of types of business metadata that require special capture mechanisms from businesspeople are as follows:

✦ Business terms

✦ Definitions of business terms

✦ Linking of business terms to the data elements of one or more systems

✦ Business rules

✦ Optimal ways of performing the job ("knowledge artifacts"; knowledge encyclopedia entries)

✦ Categorization (of business terms, documents, Web pages, etc.)

This chapter first examines why knowledge capture is so important. Business metadata, after all, exists for businesspeople to use, and it should reflect their point of view. There has to be a way (and a place) to capture their perspective so that it can be accessed by other businesspeople. We will attempt to define what the corporate knowledge base really is and how it represents this business point of view.

Next, we discuss how to encourage businesspeople to share their valuable insights and information, and we present various technologies that can support knowledge capture. In addition, we will cover the subject of capturing knowledge from both individuals and groups or communities of users. The interesting aspect of metadata or knowledge capture from individuals is the ability of the individual himself to directly benefit from this exercise.

By sharing knowledge about a topic, people can actually increase the quality and value of the knowledge itself as well as make the group as a whole smarter. We term this kind of process *knowledge socialization*. The socialization of knowledge is critical to both the evolution of knowledge and its usefulness and has advanced greatly with the rise of the Internet. We will show how technology assists in knowledge socialization and describe the critical role that socialization plays in knowledge capture.

This chapter also explores a special kind of stewardship called "Governance Lite" which presents one way to balance the need for some governance with knowledge capture requirements. In the process, we will explore some of the unique features of the knowledge capture culture as it pertains to governance. We will also discuss the role of publicity in encouraging people to share their valuable knowledge. Lastly, individual knowledge capture is revisited, and practical ideas are presented to help us all be more productive in capturing our moments of brilliance and insight so we can remember them later.

## 6.2   Why Bother to Capture Business Metadata?

As we have seen, business metadata can add context to existing data and be extremely useful. Where does business metadata originate? The obvious answer is from the businesspeople themselves. Some business metadata can be "mined" from unstructured data that already exists; this type will be covered in Chapter 11. Other business metadata can be transformed from technical metadata: metadata that is translated from technical statistics or other representation into "business-speak" so that businesspeople can understand it. Chapter 7 will discuss the transformation of technical data into business metadata. But the bulk of business metadata (the data that adds context to data) is floating around in people's heads. (See Figure 6.1.)

### 6.2.1  People Leaving

Average employee turnover is 12% per year. HR professionals know that the cost of this employee turnover is extremely high:

✦ Retraining is very costly.

✦ But what about all that hard-earned knowledge obtained by the School of Hard Knocks that's not written down anywhere?

✦ New persons will have to go through the same procedure to learn it themselves! Some may never even learn these lessons.

In addition to regular employee turnover, the "Baby Boomer" generation is now beginning to hit retirement age. Here are some statistics about recent and future changes in the workforce:

**Figure 6.1**   Business Metadata in Someone's Head.

✦ In 2006, Baby Boomers—approximately 75 million people born between 1946 and 1964—began to turn 60 (Segal, 2006).

✦ In 2000, 12.9% of the workforce was over 55 years of age.

✦ Somewhere between 2010 (Bureau of Labor Statistics) and 2015 (U.S. Department of Labor), 20% of the workforce will be over 55.

### 6.2.2 Other Business Motivations for Knowledge Capture

In addition to employee turnover, here are two more business motivations for knowledge capture, and there are probably lots more out there!

#### 6.2.2.1 Cross Selling in Other Geographic Regions

Imagine a support arm of a corporation called ABC Corp. whose mission it is to become more competitive in National Accounts. The ABC's sales staff typically focuses on "low hanging fruit"—local companies. Large companies with a presence in multiple states have support challenges: You, as an ABC sales rep, have to prove that you can support them in locales other than just one. ABC needs to reach out to all the state offices and get information from them: What are your successes? What has worked for you? ABC Corp. needs to encourage the local sales people to share what has made them successful in their local area and what makes the company uniquely competitive in their region. This issue is very important when the sales people are working on accounts that have a presence in multiple states: a sales rep from one region selling to a corporate headquarters needs to convey how his or her firm can support the other remote locations, not just the headquarters. This company needs to foster the "knowledge capture culture" across geographic regions.

#### 6.2.2.2 Unification of Business Terms and System Speak

One firm went through a long and painful migration to a combination customer relationship management (CRM) and financial management package, consolidating hundreds of small and large legacy systems. Each system had its own vocabulary and semantics, as did the new CRM package. How could everyone be trained to speak the same language? The obvious answer was to create a business glossary.

One major objective of this particular glossary was to capture the language of the business directly from the business users themselves. In addition, the company wanted to have "authorized" business terms. So this glossary project involved both outreach into the business community and governance over what was submitted. (The real-world knowledge capture example used later in this chapter is from this glossary project.)

# 6.3 The Corporate Knowledge Base

### 6.3.1 *The Corporate Glossary: Beginning of a Knowledge Base*

In Chapter 4, we discussed the importance of well-defined terminology and standard vocabulary in an enterprise. The glossary is also a great place to begin a knowledge capture initiative and to start encouraging businesspeople to contribute their expertise.

### 6.3.2 *What Is the Corporate Knowledge Base?*

The Carbon-Based Life Form (i.e., human being) is the main repository of the Corporate Knowledge Base, including business metadata. When each person leaves the corporation, a piece of the metadata repository is leaving, and potentially critical corporate knowledge goes out the door with him or her.

What is the Corporate Knowledge Base? It is essentially everything the organization collectively knows that pertains to its business. Some of this knowledge is contained in databases; most of it is not. Much of it is in unstructured data like e-mail, PowerPoint presentations, word processing documents, Acrobat files (.pdf), and the like, but the vast majority is floating in people's heads. Here are a few things that are included in the Corporate Knowledge Base:

✦ Its mission

✦ Its customers

✦ Its competitors

✦ Its products

✦ All the job components necessary to accomplish its mission

✦ How all the jobs integrate and work together to accomplish the mission

Not only is the stuff that is floating in people's heads not written down or articulated in any way (such that some people may not even be cognizant that they know it), but there's no validation standard for this knowledge, so some of it may be wrong. If this amorphous knowledge could be exposed, then these errors could be discovered and corrected. But since it exists only in the world of each individual, it can be the basis for many poor decisions, which can cost the business dearly.

### 6.3.2.1 What Does the Individual Worker Know?

The term *knowledge worker* was the creation of Peter Drucker in 1959. As he defined the term, a knowledge worker is a person whose primary role is to gather and package information so that others can use it.

People have individual knowledge locked in their heads, which they do not articulate to anyone else; some may not even know that they know it or may not have even articulated it to themselves! Much of this knowledge is completely instinctive or intuitive, and the person takes it for granted: "Of course I know to look that up in the Policy and Procedure Manual, Chapter 8 … Doesn't everybody?!"

Most workers know what their individual job entails, and some even know how to optimize their jobs. This individual knowledge is often not available to others. The strange thing is that the individual may often not have it available for recall when needed!

As mentioned earlier, people often have insights into how to do their job better, but often, these insights are lost because there is no easy way for a person to capture them. Traditional knowledge management has typically ignored this aspect of corporate knowledge—knowledge capture at its most fundamental level: individual knowledge capture.

The fact is people are generally poor documenters. For example, how many good ideas and insights have you lost because you couldn't write them down when the thought occurred to you? And then, even if you did write it down (usually on a sticky note), it still got lost because you lost the piece of paper!

Then there's the aspect of "tacit knowledge," which is the same thing as "know-how"—the stuff we intuitively know but can't readily explain. Michael Polanyi coined the term *tacit knowledge* to mean "a form of knowledge that is apparently wholly or partly inexplicable" (Wikipedia, July 13, 2006).

Knowledge acquisition is hard work. It includes both socialization and individual thinking, and it must be consciously planned for and cultivated.

In this chapter, we will focus specifically on use of technology to assist business in knowledge capture and dissemination. For further reading, the interested student should consult von Krogh, Ichijo, and Nonaka, *Enabling Knowledge Creation* and Nancy M. Dixon, *Common Knowledge*.

Most business metadata must be captured from businesspeople directly. After all, it is data in "business speak" that constitutes business metadata, so it is natural that the source of this metadata are the businesspeople themselves.

# 6.4 Principles of Knowledge Capture

How do you encourage people to share what they know? If people would share their knowledge freely, the business would have much to gain. People would learn from others faster and easier, and the business itself would advance and improve greatly. In this way, we might achieve the dream of the "Learning Culture." As we saw earlier in the chapter, employee turnover erodes the knowledge base. Encouraging people leaving their position to share their business know-how would result in less of a liability to businesses.

Sharing knowledge has two facets. For one, people don't want to share their knowledge (that's the sinister side), and even among those who do want to share, it isn't easy to do so. Some corporate cultures perceive knowledge as power. In these cultures, the result is knowledge hoarding and much resistance to information sharing. Even when sharing is perceived to be beneficial, how does one share information? Do you write it down? This is clumsy. Nobody takes dictation anymore, and voice recognition software is getting better but it's not perfect by any means.

To achieve knowledge capture, then, it must be easy. It must be able to fit into the daily routine of the businessperson. People shouldn't have to do anything special, or if they do, whatever the additional step is, it should be part of the normal workflow. People should not have to "go out of their way" to share knowledge.

The culture piece is always a challenge at least as long as people perceive that individual knowledge provides them with special leverage over others within the corporation.

## 6.4.1 What Is the Knowledge Capture Culture?

The knowledge capture culture has two main aspects, technical and cultural, and they should be in mutual harmony:

- ✦ Corporate culture (which is a human thing) encourages and rewards knowledge capture.

- ✦ Systems (both manual and automated) are organized in such a way that will make both the capture and dissemination of information easy.

In the knowledge capture culture, everyone has bought into the vision of knowledge management and understands the advantages of knowledge sharing (we all become smarter!). Consequently, sharing is valued. It is most potent if each individual perceives how they will benefit personally by knowledge sharing.

Which aspect is more difficult, the people or the systems? Perhaps the answer is the first, the people factor. Human issues are always a challenge. Everyone, for example, has likely felt the sting of company politics at some point in their career.

James McQuade presented an excellent paper at the DAMA (Data Administration Management Association) International Conference in 2005 called "Combining Business Metadata Delivery with Knowledge Management." His company, Giant Eagle, is a supermarket chain that is trying to encourage store managers to publish knowledge artifacts, thereby creating insights into the business that can contribute wisdom to others in geographically distributed areas. McQuade stressed that the people issues were the most important and support for knowledge capture must be available in every level of the knowledge creation chain.

The knowledge capture culture makes it easy to share information with systems that facilitate both capture and sharing.

Von Krogh et al.'s book, *Enabling Knowledge Creation,* begins by stating that knowledge is a competitive advantage, and its creation must be nurtured. This process is enabled by five main emphases:

+ Instilling a knowledge vision

+ Managing conversations

+ Mobilizing knowledge activists

+ Creating the right context

+ Globalizing local knowledge

The book points out that knowledge is created most often in "microcommunities" where a small group of individuals work together and establish a community of trust. We might refer to this entity as an unofficial "mini-collective." Much of the book talks about how trust can be nurtured; one way is to provide bonuses when the team succeeds.

# 6.5    Socialization of Knowledge

Some tacit knowledge can be captured by socialization, in the mini-collectives where camaraderie incubates and nurtures knowledge creation. It is on the mini-collectives that the traditional knowledge management discipline has focused its efforts. It seems, however, that the socialization of knowledge is much broader than mini-collectives.

### 6.5.1.1  Knowledge Socialization and the Wisdom of Crowds

Don Tapscott, in *Wikinomics*, uses the term *collective intelligence*, which he defines as "the aggregate knowledge that emerges from the decentralized choices and judgments of groups of independent participants" (Tapscott, 2006, p. 41).

Tapscott also discusses James Surowiecki's provocative book, *The Wisdom of Crowds*, in which Surowiecki proposes that a crowd or a group is usually more accurate than an expert alone. The subtitle of his book is *Why the Many Are Smarter than the Few and How Collective Wisdom Shapes Business, Economies, Societies and Nations*. Four conditions must be met for a crowd's collective intelligence to produce more accurate outcomes than a small group of experts:

- ✦  Diversity of opinion

- ✦  Independence of members from one another

- ✦  Decentralization

- ✦  A good method for aggregating opinions

Tapscott believes that mass collaboration to create collective intelligence in nearly every endeavor of life, ranging from science to business, will be the "next big thing," revolutionizing life and business as we know it.

### 6.5.1.2  Why Do We Need Experts?

It is obviously easier to refer to one source than have to check multiple sources for every question that might arise. For example, if you need the weather for the day, do you check one source or multiple ones? Your answer will probably be based on how important the information is to you. For example, if you are in charge of the next space shuttle launch at Cape Canaveral, you will probably check multiple sources for the weather, and certainly the ones known to be the most accurate. But if you just need to know if you should wear a coat to work that day, probably the local weather station will do, and one source will suffice.

Surowiecki brings up various problems associated with "expert status":

- ✦  It may be difficult to distinguish between expert knowledge and just pure luck; this is how superstitions start.

- ✦  The expert may not even know that he or she is an expert; knowing something and knowing what you know may be two different skills.

It seems that we need the security of consulting an expert, even when he or she may have dubious credentials. Surowiecki uses the term *seer sucker* to capture our inherent need for an expert: Even though no expert seems to exist, a sucker will still be found to serve as one.

The credibility of experts is a topic worth consideration. Deborah McGuinness, in her talk entitled "Making Web Applications More Trustable" at SemTech in 2006, presented some ideas about how some sources of knowledge are more credible than others. One way you can measure credibility is to assign weights to people's opinions. Some Web sites already do a version of expert weighting, based on users voting on whether a book review was helpful, or whether a person's list is useful. Amazon and eBay have weighting systems for reviewers and merchants based on the feedback users provide. Surowiecki says that individual weighting is unnecessary, that the crowd already factors this in naturally by balancing out dummies with experts. The diversity factor counts for a great deal. Surowiecki also states that experts can be biased and that other opinions can balance out the bias. It is the diverse nature of a crowd, he says, that enables it to be smarter than any individual expert. A group that is very homogeneous is not as smart as one with diverse points of view.

One reason for the power of the group is the "permission" to dissent from the group's consensus. The more dissension that is voiced, the more people will not fear expressing differing opinions, thereby adding to the group's ability to consider several alternatives and to arrive at a sound conclusion. Therefore, an important characteristic of a "smart" group is one in which dissension is permitted. This matter touches on the trust issue mentioned earlier concerning the knowledge capture culture.

No matter how smart a group is, however, nothing can take the place of an expert when you have to have brain surgery or are in any other life-threatening situation in which only the opinion of an expert can save you. Obviously, experts have a vital, primary role in certain situations. But even in such dire situations, there is a time for a "second opinion," and you should consult with several experts. It might be argued that this presents the best of both worlds: diversity of opinion of experts!

## 6.6    Technology That Fosters Knowledge Socialization

Even though we have a propensity to rely on experts, this does not diminish the power of socialization in the creation and evolution of knowledge, and the importance of collaboration in the workplace. Today, many advances in technology have provided new ways to socialize knowledge.

The Internet has perhaps had the greatest influence on socialization, permitting virtual socialization, which has created a new reality of social interaction. Is it more personal or less so? Some might argue that this new interaction is less personal because it is not face-to-face. However, because of the mere fact that it fosters some anonymity and that it creates a vehicle for people to be open in a new way, people feel that it is safe to share things that they might not feel comfortable doing in a face-to-face venue.

### 6.6.1   *Social Networking*

Social networking allows each participant a means to connect to other people with like interests or something in common. For example, Classmates.com was the first such site, which enabled people to find others from their same alma mater (high school or college that they graduated from). Perhaps the most famous is MySpace, a social networking Web site based in Santa Monica, California, that offers an interactive network of blogs, user profiles, groups, photos, and an internal e-mail system. According to Alexa Internet, as of July 2006, it was the world's fourth most popular English-language Web site and the sixth most popular in any language. It is the most popular site in the United States, accounting for 4.5% of all Web site visits.

The page shown in Figure 6.2 came from Wikipedia and belongs to MySpace's founder. Tom's blogs are listed on the right.

**Figure 6.2**   MySpace Example.

### 6.6.2 *Portals and Collaboration Servers*

Collaboration software, otherwise known as **groupware**, has been around for a while, manifested in Portal software and before that, in environments like Lotus Notes. Among its features are shared areas, usually project or team focused, where team members can post documents, calendars, have threaded discussions, and so on. Some collaboration environments feature e-mail archives that are browsable by all team members. In this way, it enables the team to have ready access to the history of e-mails between the group.

Using a collaborative environment can be an effective way to capture knowledge and can allow team members to socialize the knowledge, especially by using the threaded discussions. Figure 6.3 shows an early implementation using Lotus Notes and a subcomponent called "Team Room."

Team Room's most important feature was its tight integration with the e-mail system. It provided the following benefits:

✦ The user could easily switch environments with one mouse click, from e-mail to Team Room and vice versa.

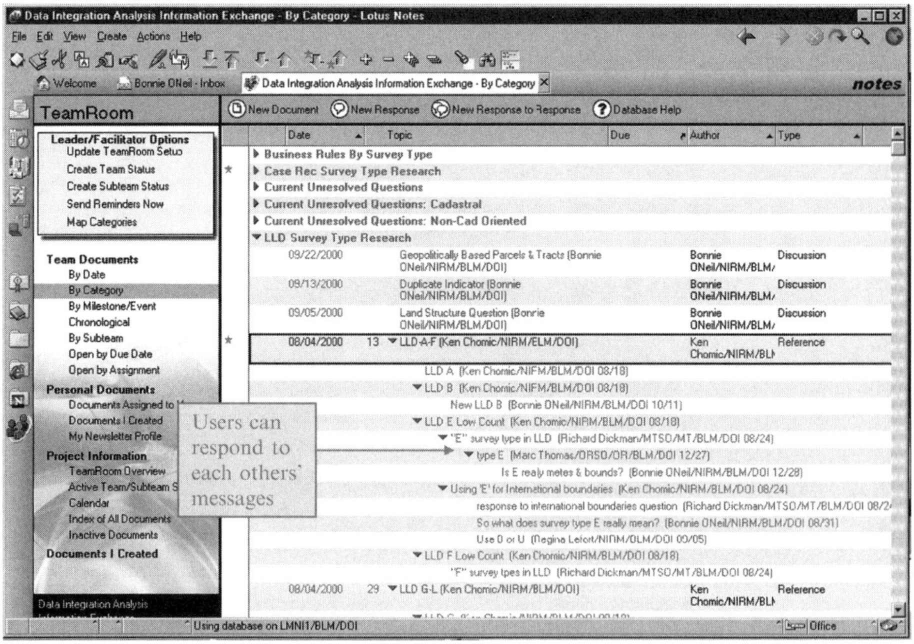

**Figure 6.3**    Example of a Collaboration Environment in Lotus Notes' Team Room.

◆ The user could easily add checking Team Room for new postings daily as part of his or her normal workflow, because it didn't require accessing a new tool; it just became part of the process of getting e-mail. In other words, no new process was required; adapting the old process was sufficient.

◆ E-mails could be sent automatically when documents or discussions were posted or updated.

We used Team Room very successfully on a project and got everyone contributing actively. It also helped that the project that the Team Room was used with was a highly visible one and that there was some rivalry between different departments and functional categories. Each of the groups didn't want other groups to get the upper hand, so they were constantly competing to have their voice heard and to have their own opinions considered on the project. In this case, the rivalry between functional areas fueled sharing rather than stifled it. Team Room provided the groups with a vehicle to be heard, and consequently, they were active users.

Notice that each individual's contribution is stored separately. There is no implementation of the notion that knowledge is being incrementally built. The threaded discussion tells you who said what when, but there is no sense of creating a piece of knowledge jointly. The only way to accomplish this is by serially working on a document: each team member downloads the document, checks it out, works on it a bit, and checks it back in. Then, each team member updates and adds its contribution to the main knowledge artifact.

Most of us today recognize the "twisty" indicator that is commonly used in Web sites and other hierarchical structures to indicate the presence of entries below the current entry. If you click on the twisty, it reveals the lower level discussion threads. Notice, too, that the collaborative environment supports commenting on a document (which is what "reference" means on the right side), as well as a discussion thread that is not related to a document (labeled "Discussion").

Team Room also had a chronological view indicating which days had entries that the user had not viewed. This enabled users to look at only what was new. (See Figure 6.4).

Some collaborative environments require some monitoring to be effective. The Lotus Notes environment seemed to require a little monitoring, since it was so new. Nowadays, portals are common, so it is probably less important.

On our project, we provided individualized training to new users by phone. Because users were geographically distributed, phone training was cost effective and still seemed to get the job done. The phone training included simple ways that checking Team Room could be integrated into the person's usual workflow. The technical project lead posted e-mails weekly or bi-weekly with project status items and what had been newly posted on the Team Room.

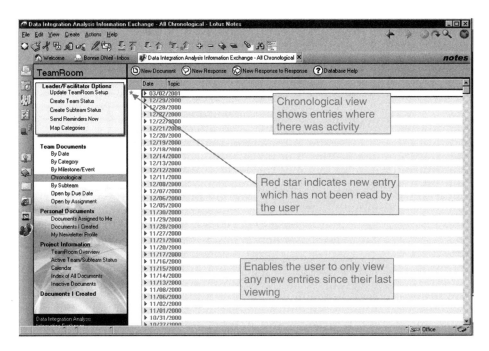

**Figure 6.4**   Team Room's Chronological View.

The e-mails also highlighted special items that needed feedback from users. E-mails occasionally posted controversial issues to make sure everyone was awake and using Team Room. E-mails could also be automatically generated and could include a link directly to the relevant Team Room entry. This made it even easier to access the Team Room.

Team Room included what I call the "Big Brother feature," which enabled the technical lead to monitor usage, showing who, what, when, and whether anything was posted. Most users were passive, and as is true of other typical groups and communities, you always have a few vocal ones in every bunch. But we found that even the shy members would post a response every now and then. We found that usage increased when an e-mail blast with a controversial issue had been sent, which is what we expected (and, indeed, this was the purpose of the blast in the first place!).

This particular project's success was owed in no small part to the Team Room environment. Collaboration environments can make a huge difference with geographically distributed teams. The secret to our project's success with collaboration was the periodic checking for new items. It was less onerous for users to read a few postings every day than a massive amount in one session. Think of how you read e-mails; isn't it easier to read a few in the morning and some in the afternoon rather than a whole day's worth at one sitting? Remember what it's like when you come back from vacation?

The project's main focus during the phase when we used Team Room was on business rule gathering and validation. We followed up the discussions with an on-site meeting. The meeting was extremely productive because everyone, having periodically checked Team Room, was up to speed on all the topics. We were able to go through each business rule and get validation right away, and the discussions were informed and very meaningful. People were prepared!

The collaboration software caused a huge leap in productivity for this on-site meeting. We actually finished half a day early, which never happens! Everyone was amazed; people from out of town actually had a little sight-seeing time!

Since this project's conclusion, the collaboration features of Team Room have been absorbed by the Lotus Notes Domino Server, and other vendors have impressive product offerings, like Microsoft's SharePoint. There are many collaboration/groupware products to choose from.

### 6.6.3   Wikis and Knowledge Socialization

#### 6.6.3.1   Introduction to Wikipedia and Wiki Technology

**Wikipedia** is an open-source encyclopedia on the Internet. It is the "People's encyclopedia"—anyone can contribute content or update an existing entry. In this way, everyone can participate in it and own it. Wikipedia is democracy in action: "Of the people, by the people, for the people."

Wikipedia traditionally has very little governance, its purpose is mainly to filter out foul language. Furthermore, it has no verification of facts; it is supposed to govern itself. If someone contributes something that is incorrect, someone else comes along and edits it. The self-governance seems to work, and it is widely quoted. It is a great source for general information about almost any subject. (See Figure 6.5 for the entry on "Data Warehouse.")

No one is acknowledged as the author of a Wikipedia entry. If you want to know about an article's origin and history, you can click on the "history" tab to see who edited it—that is, if the person did not edit anonymously. You can create a username in Wikipedia or you can choose not to do so. Either way, you are allowed to edit anyone's article. If you edit without logging in, your IP address will be shown in the history of the page.

Wikipedia is built on top of software called a wiki, which enables the free-flow collaboration discussed here. It is self-organizing; a topic of discussion can be created at any time by anyone. It does not require fitting a topic into a rigid hierarchy. It builds trust between contributors and a sense of collaboration. It is bottom-up collaboration.

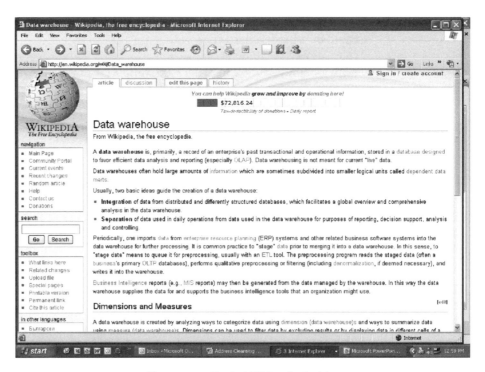

**Figure 6.5** Typical Wikipedia Article.

Wikis are an extremely powerful tool for collecting business metadata of all kinds. They allow information exchange on a topic of your own choosing, and they become more useful to everyone the more people contribute. They are used for all facets of life; some people even use wikis for keeping in touch with family.

The wiki seems to have become the symbol of the new collaboration that Web 2.0 has fostered. This is why Don Tapscott chose to create a name for this new collaboration phenomenon derived from the word wiki; he calls it **Wikinomics** [Tapscott, 2007].

### 6.6.3.2   The Role of Wiki in Knowledge Capture

As we have seen, the "crowd factor" can be a positive influence on the accumulation of knowledge. Wiki technology is perhaps the crowd at its best. Wikis enable one article or encyclopedia entry to benefit from a crowd or a multiplicity of authors, each person modifying the same entry.

This has a great psychological payoff: Everyone who edits the entry feels that they are contributing to the universal source of knowledge. They, like everyone else, have the power to either create new knowledge or edit and contribute to existing knowledge.

### 6.6.3.3   Difference Between Wikis and Portal Collaboration

You might say, "We are using a portal collaboration area with groupware to encourage people to share insights and questions. What advantage does using a wiki bring?"

Wiki technology offers these advantages:

✦ A wiki allows entries to stand alone, classified according to their title. Collaborations consist of threads, and an entry is always stuck in the hierarchy of the thread and the message to which it was responding.

✦ A wiki is self-organizing, meaning that entries do not have to fit into a preexisting taxonomy or classification scheme. People are free to create a page on whatever topic they would like.

✦ A wiki has a page for threads if they are desired. But the thread is attached to the entry and not the other way around.

✦ With a wiki, anyone can update another's entry. This is not so in collaboration software. A message on a thread always stays the same, even if someone wants to edit it later. Some collaborations allow you to edit your own post, but certainly not someone else's.

An important motivation for encouraging people to contribute knowledge is the satisfaction that they are contributing to an overall knowledge base—something bigger than themselves. Being able to edit existing entries provides some of this satisfaction.

### 6.6.3.4   Limitations of Wikis

Lately I have come face to face with a limitation of wikis as a knowledge dissemination mechanism: They are a "roach motel." It means that you can get data in, but you can't easily get data out, in a different form. On one project, we wanted to use a wiki for a project dictionary and then give it to the client when we were finished. The only problem was that it existed as a wiki only and there was no way to export it to a text file, Excel file, database, and so on. This ability to export the data is very useful because you can repurpose the dictionary and have it referenced from different applications by importing it into different tools.

Now of course this may not be true of all wikis; as you probably know there are many flavors. You can get a taste of them by visiting www.wikimatrix.org and comparing them to each other. Unfortunately, however, it is true of the vast majority at the time of this writing, including MediaWiki, the most famous of them all. (Wikipedia is built on this one.)

This inability to repurpose wiki data can be a major stumbling block for using a wiki to collect business rules, which is not a very useful exercise if you can't easily repurpose them into your applications or rule engines.

### 6.6.4   *Wikis and Governance*

On the downside, wikis can be very chaotic because they lack governance. Entries change day to day; when you quote an entry as an authoritative source, you should also supply the date that you accessed it, since it is so subject to change. Some CIOs are afraid to launch wikis in their organizations for fear that they will become a forum for corporate gripes.

#### 6.6.4.1   *Why Some Governance Is Usually Necessary*

Even Wikipedia has had to face the governance issue. In several high-profile cases, damaging information was published on its site, resulting in legal ramifications. For example, an article that was allowed to remain up for 132 days said the following:

> John Seigenthaler Sr. was the assistant to Attorney General Robert Kennedy in the early 1960s. For a brief time, he was thought to have been directly involved in the Kennedy assassinations of both John, and his brother, Bobby. Nothing was ever proven.

This information was patently false, posted with malicious intent.

Does this mean that Wikipedia is inherently unreliable? In academia, professors often do not allow it to be used as an authoritative source. Obviously, millions of people rely on Wikipedia for knowledge all the time (including me). How do you balance out your need for truth with the fact that Wikipedia might contain errors?

As a matter of fact, everything could contain errors. Very high-profile mistakes, for example, have been made in the news media in recent years. So what's a poor person in search of the Truth to do?

It seems it is OK to use Wikipedia, but in order to be wise and judicious, one should, balance it with other sources as well. After reading the *DaVinci Code*, I, like many other readers, went in search of what was fact and what was fiction. The first place I looked was Wikipedia, but I also visited Web sites like Opus Dei to let them speak for themselves. In addition, I consulted other sources, followed links, and so forth. At the end of my journey I was convinced that Wikipedia did a very good job of reporting the facts (and that the *DaVinci Code* was excellent fiction!).

# 6.7 Balancing Out the Need for Governance with the Need for Contributions: "Governance Lite™"

If anyone is allowed to create or update a dictionary entry, then some control is needed to reconcile terms cross-functionally with other groups in the organization who may have different usages for the same term. This creates the need for some level of governance. One such project involved a dictionary, and the question came up about an "authorized" vocabulary. The organization involved decided that it wanted to have an individual or group to authorize vocabulary, which then brought up questions about who was in charge of the authorization? However, the requirement for governance had to be balanced against the other side of knowledge capture, which involved encouraging business-people—the people who know the vocabulary the best—to supply the terms and definitions themselves. They know best, because they are on the ground floor. Too much authorization red tape will discourage them from supplying the terms in the first place, and then authorization will be a moot point.

We have all experienced corporate initiatives that have been burdened with too much governance. The governance gets in the way of flexibility: The business needs to be able to change the definition of a term when the business itself changes. The resulting situation involves definitions that may have been correct at one point in time, but as things change, they never are in synch with the business as time goes on because it takes an act of Congress to change the dictionary. "Governance Lite™" is a concept that was created (by Bonnie O'Neil) in the context of a dictionary project in order to create a flexible structure to accommodate both the need for governance and the need to keep it constantly in synch with the business.

## 6.7.1 How Governance Lite™ Works

Governance Lite™ in a glossary scenario works as follows: Anyone in the organization can create a Business Term entry in the glossary. If a user looks up a term in the corporate glossary and it does not exist, he or she has the option of creating a new glossary entry. When a new term is created, it has a state of "Candidate." Anyone can see all candidate terms, and the state will be shown to users of the Glossary.

The project had a "Terms Team" whose job was to rationalize and normalize terms. The Terms Team was electronically notified when a new term was entered into the glossary. The team then researched the term with other terms already in the glossary and made sure no conflicts existed.

The team also checked that the wording of the definition was accurate and that the definition followed the format mentioned in Chapter 4. Sometimes this work may have required researching reference documents and/or contacting line of business Subject Matter Experts (SMEs) directly. When the definition has been successfully researched, its state is changed to "Authorized."

When someone looked up a word in the dictionary, the state would be displayed along with the definition. In this way, the business was alerted to its use of a Candidate term. The business would therefore take steps to clarify the meaning of Candidate terms whenever they are used, since it is possible that a candidate can have more than one meaning.

The last two states are Replaced and Retired. Sometimes the business would determine that a term was not useful anymore and was no longer part of the common business language. In this case, its status would be Retired. Work was still ongoing regarding setting policies concerning retired terms when I left the project. The intention was that if the Terms Team uncovered a term that should be retired, the status would be set to Retired, and if no one commented on this or edited the definition, it would cease to be an active part of the glossary and would no longer be displayed to users.

Replaced means that the term was being phased out and was being replaced by a newer term. The new term essentially meant the same thing as the original term. This kind of situation was encountered as fallout of a system migration. The new system referred to a data element as a different name than what was in the old system. Management wanted everyone to assimilate the new system as fast as possible, and one of the ways to do so was to force everyone to use the new vocabulary. It was advisable in this case that the old terms remained (at least for a while, until people got used to the new vocabulary). These old terms would therefore have the status of Replaced, but they must also be linked to the terms that replaced them.

Figure 6.6 shows the four states of term governance.

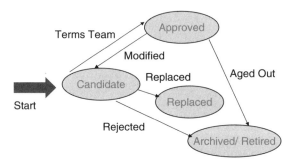

**Figure 6.6**   Term Life Cycle.

If an authorized vocabulary is desired, then there must be some governance to apply the "authorized" status. However, as we stated earlier, one of the objectives of knowledge capture is to encourage businesspeople to share; too much governance will accomplish the opposite and cause them to NOT share. In this case, it seems suitable for knowledge capture projects to apply reactive, not proactive, governance—governance after the fact. Essentially you are telling the users, "Give me what you've got, and I'll figure out what it means later." This is exactly opposite from how constraints work in the transaction world, where errors cannot be tolerated because they have an immediate impact on the bottom line. Transactions must have proactive governance: business rule verifications must be applied before data is entered into the system. Rules like "ship date must have to occur later in time than the order date" must be enforced and bad data must be caught before it is allowed to be entered into the system.

### 6.7.2   The Search for Technology

(**Technology Alert:** The following story is based on a client implementation conducted a few years ago. Later in the next section and at the end of the chapter, we will share some of the new tools available, including exciting Web 2.0 technologies that have greatly expanded the functionalities offered by this vendor—and others—so don't get discouraged!)

Let's continue with our case study about the corporate glossary: Since we were trying to capture terms and definitions from the businesspeople, we looked at wiki technology for an answer. We looked at MediaWiki's technology, which is the same software that is used for Wikipedia. We also looked at using our portal software—we used Plumtree (now part of the BEA Aqua Logic suite of products).

Plumtree had two types of development: custom and straight out of the box. When you use the latter, with a tool called Studio, you can implement very quickly. The tradeoff is that you cannot do any custom development. Since we wanted to launch our glossary quickly, we wanted to use the straight out-of-the-box software, if we could. We had to then get creative in how we implemented it. One other constraint: we had no budget, so we had to figure out how to get around product limitations without programmer support. Studio doesn't require a programmer, so this was a vote in its favor.

Neither Studio nor MediaWiki provided an easy solution to our governance requirement. We wanted to be able to display a field that was updatable only by the Terms Team. It was not possible to do this in Studio because it was "all or nothing"; if the field is shown it must be editable. MediaWiki would allow customization, but it required a programmer, so we were out of luck there.

We finally chose Plumtree, and we managed to get around this requirement by not displaying the Status field in the insert/update portlets, but it would be shown in the read only portlet.

We had one more technology problem; however, we needed to be able to allow someone to update an existing entry and have the term's status switch to Candidate again when someone edited it. Since Studio does not keep a history and seemed to have an internal mechanism that disabled database triggers, we did not have a way that someone could edit an existing term and the status would change behind the scenes. As was the case with the status field in general, we realized there was no way to implement this without a programmer. So we created a workaround: every time someone wanted to edit an existing term, they would actually have to create a new term, use the same term name, and copy the definition using copy/paste, and then edit the definition.

We knew this was a shabby workaround, especially because it violated two fundamental principles that we mentioned early on in this chapter:

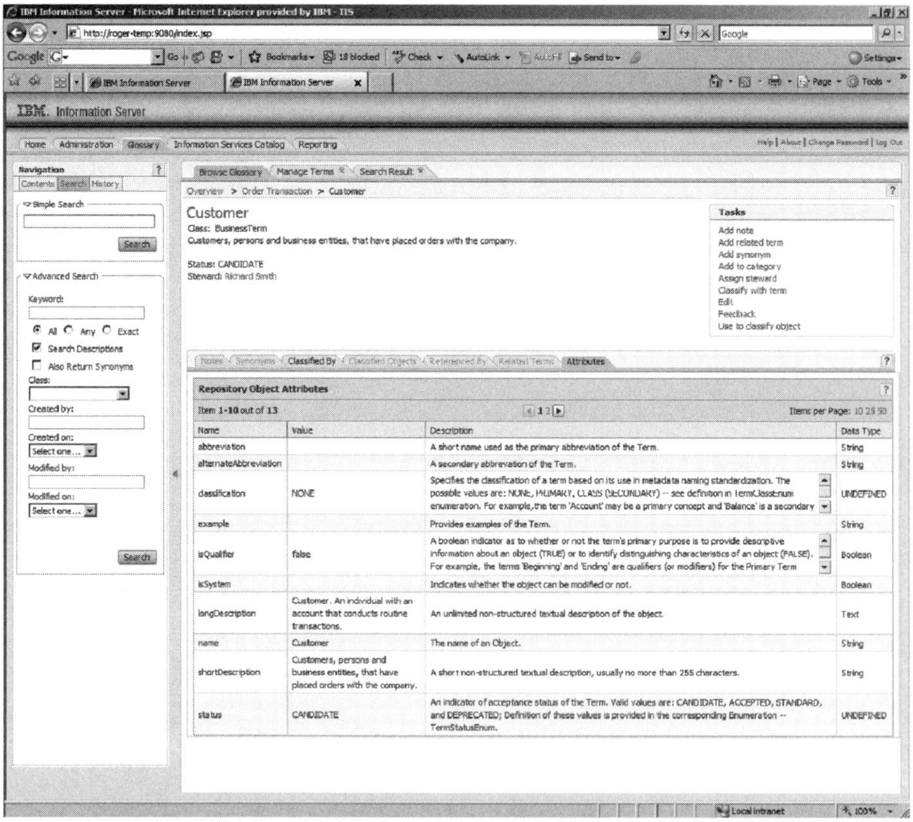

**Figure 6.7** Term Information.

✦ Knowledge capture must be easy; this was extremely clumsy and required too many mouse clicks.

✦ It did not deliver the psychological satisfaction of the user updating the corporate knowledge base by "feeling the power" of editing someone else's definition.

However, you get what you pay for, and since we had no budget, this was at least a way that we could deploy a dictionary in the least amount of time, even if it wasn't perfect.

### 6.7.3   Business Glossary Technology

IBM has recently released a commercially available glossary product that even supports Governance Lite™. It comes with the Information Server, IBM's

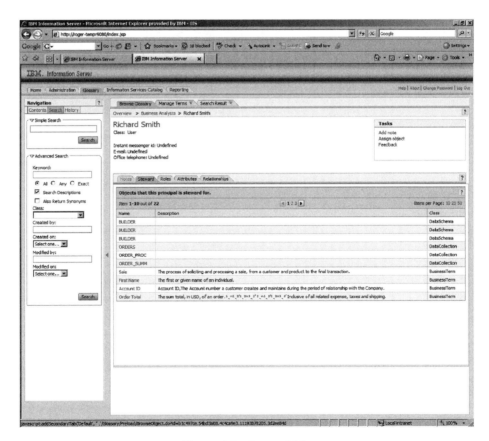

**Figure 6.8**   Stewardship.

integrated metadata repository (we discuss the repository in more detail in Chapter 9).

Figure 6.7 shows a glossary entry. The Business Glossary has many attributes for a business term. Of special note is the "Status" Field, where "Candidate" is shown. Note the business metadata it provides, which is a nice description of what each field means. They use slightly different terms for the states of Governance Lite™ shown in Figure 6.6.

Stewards can be named, and the terms they manage can be displayed. Figure 6.8 shows a steward and the objects that he manages. Notice that other types of objects are also shown. This is a feature of their integrated metadata repository.

# 6.8 Publicity

One of the immediate goals of the dictionary project was to get the business to familiarize itself with the glossary and to use it. The project therefore launched a publicity campaign, which included a contest, to generate excitement and awareness of the glossary. Every time someone entered a term, his or her name was entered into the drawing to win a gift certificate for company merchandise like polo shirts, tote bags, and so on. There was an article on the corporate portal, as well as in the e-magazine, advertising the dictionary and contest. Posters were displayed in each regional office announcing the contest. Figure 6.9 shows the poster.

The purpose of the contest was twofold:

✦ To get a jumpstart on collecting as many terms from actual business-people as possible

✦ To get people familiar with the glossary so that they could start using it in their daily work

The publicity worked; we received a fair amount of entries. Of course, we received a few bogus entries from people just trying to get credit for the contest; when the terms team called up the submitters asking for clarification, the truth came out. But we received only several of these invalid entries. One of the lessons we learned definitely involved the publicity; any time you are trying to coax information out of businesspeople, you have to promote it and, at least in the beginning, add a little extra incentive and make it worth their while to share information.

**Figure 6.9**   Publicity Poster for the Dictionary Project.

### 6.8.1   Visibility versus Usefulness

Our manager was looking for a small project with high visibility that would help all businesspeople in the company see the value of data management. Many people recognized the value of a dictionary, but, alternatively, many saw it as trivial. It is obviously not a high-visibility project.

Once established, however, it is **there**. When a new employee needs to understand business jargon, he or she has a place to go to find out what the word means. The dictionary's value may not be measured in a number of hits. It is valuable because it is there when you need it.

Here is a quote from one of the employees:

> I've been begging for someone to give me a Dex Dictionary since the day I got here. This will be especially useful for trainees and new folks like me. Being new, it's embarrassing to keep asking questions like what is CCU? What's CMO? What's a bag? This will be a great resource.

## 6.9 Knowledge Capture from Individuals: The Individual Documentation Problem

The bulk of this chapter has discussed knowledge capture from groups, and indeed this has been the focus of traditional knowledge management approaches since their inception. However, as noted earlier, there is another area of knowledge capture that has been mostly ignored by knowledge management authors: capturing elusive tacit knowledge from the individual.

As we have stated, people are poor documenters. We don't like to record ideas or make lists, and when we do, we usually record it in a place that can't be retrieved easily, or even made sense of. Think of the sticky note phenomenon; you don't have a proper note pad handy, and so you use a sticky note. Then, sure enough, later you may say "where's that sticky note that I wrote down John's phone number on?" So the sticky note doesn't really benefit you at all, because it is not the best method for search and knowledge recall.

Here are a few ideas, some of which come from a wonderful book by David Allen called *Getting Things Done*.

◆ Keep a Next Steps list, and keep it open on your desktop. Then when an idea hits you like "I have to go to the pharmacy and pick up my prescription" it is on the list. Check the Next Steps list frequently throughout the day.

◆ Keep an Idea Incubator where you can jot down ideas that come to you as fleeting thoughts throughout the day.

◆ Use the notes feature in your e-mail application to record thoughts.

◆ Use notes on your phone if you have such a feature on your phone.

David Allen suggests that every task that has more than one step is really a "project" and you should record the Next Step in your Next Steps list. Don't try to do all the steps at once because this is one way you will stall yourself.

I have a Tablet PC, and I find that it is a great place to record ideas. I use One Note, which is a virtual spiral notebook, perfect to take notes on during meetings. The key is that it is searchable. This means you can easily retrieve the answer to questions such as, "What was that item said in the meeting by John about last month's profitability?" You can either go quickly to the notes you took on that day in that specific meeting (based on how you have organized your notebook) or use the search facility that searches the entire notebook.

Tablets also come with voice recognition software, so you can actually dictate to it and it will transcribe your words into text. It can still be a bit temperamental, so this feature isn't quite all here yet. But soon you should be able to dictate a knowledge artifact and have it record and store for you.

You can use a personal wiki for recording spontaneous ideas. Wikis are well suited for storing "nuggets" of knowledge. These ideas can then be accessed at a later time, when they can help the knowledge worker do his or her job better.

# 6.10   Web 2.0 and Knowledge Capture

*Web 2.0* is the term coined by Scott O'Reilly to group all of the new power of the Web in recent years. It includes (to name a few):

✦ Wikis

✦ Blogs (short for weblogs; dated postings by an individual on any subject imaginable)

✦ Folksonomy and dynamic, collaborative tagging (example, del.icio.us)

✦ Social networking (example, MySpace)

✦ Customization/personalization of newsfeed (example RSS feeds)

✦ Mashups (dynamic integration of disparate types of information into one presentation format)

As we discussed earlier, wikis have ushered in a whole new way of collaborating: bottom-up, self-organizing, and open, they present a new forum for people to freely contribute to a body of knowledge. They are also informal. If two people get together in the break room to troubleshoot a problem, when they arrive at a solution, there is no corporate memory recorded. Thus, if the same problem were to reoccur, they would have no knowledge base to refer to. A wiki, however, can be used to socialize the problem and to record that process of socialization, which will allow subsequent troubleshooters to not only trace the steps that were taken, but also to see the rationale behind each step. This is business metadata at its best.

But Web 2.0 has gone beyond wikis. We will close the chapter with a brief sampling of two exciting examples of Web 2.0 that provide business metadata capture using mashups and folksonomy/dynamic, user-defined tags.

## 6.10.1   Mashups

BEA's Aqua Logic product Pages provides the business user with a means to create his or her own customized mashies, with no programming. Figure 6.10 shows a wiki editing area, appearing as a to-do list, adjacent to a pipeline report.

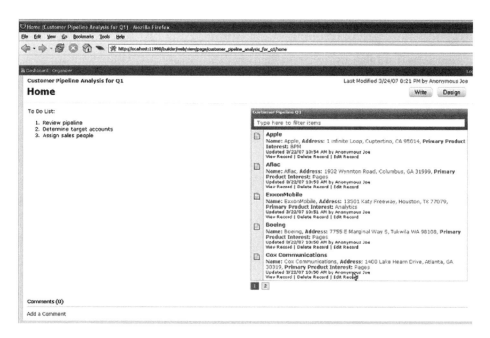

**Figure 6.10** Wiki To-Do List Next to a Pipeline Report: Simple Mashup in BEA Aqua-Logic Pages.

The to-do list and the pipeline report are not intrinsically integrated in any way. Imagine if I displayed two business intelligence (BI) reports from the data warehouse and annotations about each. Businesspersons can create combinations of reports like this themselves, adding the annotation, and can then save it for use later. The businessperson has created valuable business metadata that meets his or her own needs. If the user can be convinced of the merits of sharing, then the business audience for this data and business metadata becomes larger and the reports more useful. This is an interesting instance of business metadata capture that starts out serving the individual, but has the potential for providing a much wider service to the business.

The mashup described in the preceding is very simple. A more interesting example, involving true integration, would show trend reports and a link to a weather site revealing that the dip in sales was attributable to several snowstorms in the area, corresponding to the dates that the sales started tapering off. Figure 6.11 shows a stylized representation of two BI reports and annotations explaining the dip in sales. But nothing illustrates this better than the weather data itself, and maybe even the inclusion of a Doppler radar picture would enhance it more.

Users can indeed create mashups with all sorts of different types of components. Figure 6.12 shows a user-defined mashup using BEA's new portal tool called AquaLogic Pages linking to Google Maps. It allows sales reps to be assigned based on their relative location to a new client in the pipeline report.

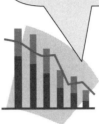

The blue line indicates sales projections. Notice how our actual revenue exceeded projections, but it still followed basically the curve we projected, with one exception; a low was projected in the middle that was not hit.

This sales decline was due to a series of snowstorms that hit the Denver area late 2006–2007. Red line is not sales projections here but is shown for emphasis.

**Figure 6.11**  BI Reports with Business Metadata Annotations.

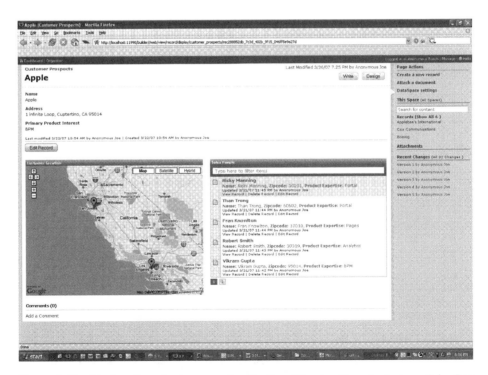

**Figure 6.12**  Mashup Functioning as an Application, Allowing Users to Assign a Sales Rep to a New Account Based on Geographic Data.

### 6.10.2 User-Defined Tags: Folksonomy

Just as wikis help to foster collective intelligence, tagging helps to harness it to find things easier. Chapter 4 discussed how taxonomies can help people find documents more efficiently. Usually, someone is tasked to write the taxonomy, and sometimes this person does not understand the content of the document. As we discussed in Chapter 4, many things don't fit into neatly organized hierarchies. Imagine putting together the Wisdom of Crowds with tagging and the bottom-up method of wikis. This is what del.icio.us does, and BEA's new Pathways product provides these things. Figure 6.13 shows a tag cloud on the left, reflecting the popularity of the tags created by the whole community. The tags are also associated with experts, so you can go to the appropriate person if you need more help in a particular area.

**Figure 6.13**  Tags and Experts.

These community-shared tags help everyone find documents more easily because the wisdom of the group in tag creation is superior to your functioning alone. The author of del.icio.us calls it "a way to remember in public" (Tapscott, 2006, p. 42). Also, tagging helps you find related information faster because people creating and using similar tags usually have similar interests. If you need to find more related documents, you can go to tags created by these other people with similar interests.

# 6.11 Summary

Capturing business metadata straight from the businesspeople themselves is very important and presents a problem that is both technical and cultural. In this chapter, we have tried to tackle both issues. We covered the socialization of knowledge and the role of technology in supporting this socialization in depth. The wiki phenomenon can play a large role in making knowledge capture easy, but it also presents some challenges. You must avoid the "roach motel"

The discipline of knowledge management seems to ignore the problem of knowledge capture from individuals. This chapter provides pointers on how you can more effectively capture your own knowledge and use it to make your life more efficient, as an individual. Others can also benefit from individuals' insights, too, but the one who benefits the most is the individual him- or herself!

Publicity to launch knowledge capture projects is an area in which IT as a whole is not very adept. Lastly, governance has a different role in knowledge capture projects as opposed to traditional online transaction systems. Reactive versus proactive governance is more effective, and we have coined the term "Governance Lite" to describe it.

Finally, the end of the chapter shared some new Web 2.0 enabling technologies and showed how these products help to capture business metadata directly from businesspeople, with no programmer involvement.

# 6.12 References

✦ Allen, David. *Getting Things Done*. New York: Penguin Group, 2001.

✦ Amazon.com. Review of *The Wisdom of Crowds*. http://www.amazon.com/Wisdom-Crowds-James-Surowiecki/dp/0385721706/sr = 1-1/qid = 1162589559/ref = pd_bbs_sr_1/103-0890407-7574238?ie = UTF8&s = books

✦ Dixon, Nancy M. *Common Knowledge*. Cambridge, MA: Harvard Business School Press, March 2000.

✦ McGuinness, Deborah. "Making Web Applications Trustable." *Semantic Technology Conference*, March 2006.

✦ McQuade, James. "Combining Business Metadata Delivery with Knowledge Management." *DAMA International*, 2005.

✦ Segal, Jonathan A. "Time Is on Their Side." *HR Magazine*, February 2006. http://findarticles.com/p/articles/mi_m3495/is_2_51/ai_n16101872

✦ Surowiecki, James. *The Wisdom of Crowds*. New York: Random House, 2004.

✦ Terdiman, Daniel. "Wikipedia under Fire." *Zdnet*, December 5, 2005. http://news.zdnet.co.uk/internet/0,1000000097,39240326,00.htm

✦ Tapscott, Don, and Williams, Anthony. *Wikinomics*: *How Mass Collaboration Changes Everything*. New York: Penguin Group, 2006.

✦ Von Krogh, Georg, Ichijo, Kazuo, and Nonaka, Ikujiro. *Enabling Knowledge Creation*. New York: Oxford University Press, 2000.

✦ Wikipedia. "Tacit Knowledge." Referenced July 13, 2006. http://en.wikipedia.org/wiki/Tacit knowledge

✦ Wikipedia. "Knowledge Worker." Referenced July 12, 2006. http://en.wikipedia.org/wiki/Knowledge_worker

✦ Wikipedia. "Internet." Referenced July 20, 2006. http://en.wikipedia.org/wiki/The_Internet

✦ Wikipedia. "Groupware." Referenced July 16, 2006. http://en.wikipedia.org/wiki/Groupware

# Capturing Business Metadata from Existing Data

CHAPTER 7

## 7.1 Introduction

This chapter explores all the general sources of metadata. Most metadata begins as technical metadata because it comes from a technical source. It is often collected as a by-product of the application, and it is usually not collected for its own intrinsic value. Throughout this discussion, we will be paying special attention to the business metadata that is embedded in these technical sources. Later in the chapter, we will discuss how this mostly technical metadata can be harvested and transformed into business metadata.

# 7.2 Technical Sources of (Both Business and Technical) Metadata

There are many different sources of metadata in existing systems and the digital environment. Each source has its own unique considerations. One of the typical sources of metadata is from Enterprise Resource Planning (ERP) applications.

### 7.2.1 Enterprise Resource Planning Applications

ERP applications are provided by vendors such as SAP and Oracle/PeopleSoft. ERP technology attempts to integrate all data and processes into one unified software application; in reality, most companies that implement them use various components of the system to run key parts of the organization, such as Finance. While ERP technology is operational and transaction-oriented, it is usually accompanied by analytical applications or modules. In the case of SAP, the analytical technology is known as BW (Business Warehouse).

ERP systems store lots of business metadata, including financial calculations, process logic, and business rules, which are often difficult to extract, because they are buried in the mechanics of the system.

The metadata found in ERP technology can be accessed in at least two ways. One way is to do a native read of the application internals, reading Oracle or DB2 files and interpreting the ERP metadata. The other way is to read the ERP metadata through a common interface supplied by the ERP vendor. It is always preferable to use the vendor-supplied interface, for several good reasons. The first reason is to isolate you, the customer, from vendor changes to the software over time. The move to new releases becomes easy to accomplish by using a vendor-supplied interface. The second reason is to minimize the possibility of misinterpreting the metadata, which is very easy to do. You can use it inappropriately if you are not careful. Even though the vendor guarantees the integrity of the interface, it is not guaranteed against misuse, so you must be very sure you understand the vendor's documentation and know what data is supposed to be sent and received.

### 7.2.2 Reports

Another good source of metadata is reports. The column headings of reports are full of business metadata, especially all columns containing summaries, averages, and aggregates of different types. Each aggregate is important to the business. It should be noted, however, that usually more metadata is hiding behind the scenes than is revealed by the headings alone, such as the formulas used to calculate the values in the column. Formulas are a very important type of business metadata, and formula definitions need to be tracked and available for businesspeople to access any time the aggregate appears. Often the report does not contain the explanation of the formulas, unless you have access to the program that generates the report. Then you must extract the formulas from this program.

One of the problems of using reports as a source for metadata is that typically a report includes lots of other data that is not business metadata, that is, the data itself. This means that useful metadata must be separated from the data; for example, column headings must be extracted and the data left behind.

### 7.2.3   Spreadsheets

Spreadsheets—especially the column headings—can be a good source of metadata, just as they are in reports; of course, it depends on how descriptive the column headings are. Since they can also be misleading, caution should be used in their interpretation into useful business metadata. Unlike reports, spreadsheets contain the formulas in the cells, so these will have to be extracted out. In addition to column headings, most spreadsheets have columns that provide descriptions. This is especially true if codes are used; the code itself will appear in one column, and in the adjacent column, usually to the right, the description of the code will be displayed. This is extremely useful business metadata. However, like reports, a spreadsheet usually contains many other data., the data values, and of course the data values are not metadata and will need to be eliminated from consideration as metadata.

### 7.2.4   Documents

Standard documents are full of metadata. The typical metadata found in a document includes title, author, and last modification date. Title and author are obviously important, but modification date may also be useful. In addition, the document itself may contain useful metadata. Unfortunately, the metadata inside the body of a document must be separated out from other data, and this separation is often less than trivial owing to the unstructured nature of the document. We will describe some techniques on how to perform this separation later in the chapter. In addition, Chapter 12 deals with the special challenges of unstructured data and further elaborates on techniques for capturing business metadata from these documents.

### 7.2.5   DBMS System Catalogs

A splendid source of technical metadata is the directories of information that come with a database management system (DBMS), usually known as the System Catalog or System Tables.

The DBMS system catalogs contain a wealth of metadata, usually all technical. Examples include the data type used to represent an attribute, the length of the field, and whether or not the field allows null values. As in the case of other sources, the challenge of reading a DBMS's system catalog entails separating out what technical metadata is useful and what is not. Like ERP systems, the DBMS vendor sometimes supplies a standard interface for the reading and extraction of the metadata. It is always good policy to use the standard interface of the DBMS vendor for the same reasons discussed above. Some DBMS vendors don't supply an interface but instead supply utilities and application programming interfaces (APIs) so that you can write your own tools to extract metadata. Cautions that were expressed earlier in the section concerning ERP vendors also apply here: notably, when the vendor changes the system catalog structure, you must modify your tools accordingly.

### 7.2.6   Business Intelligence Tools

Another good source for metadata is the Business Intelligence Tools (BI) environment—the user view of data served up by the data warehouse and data marts. The BI environment includes On-Line Analytical Processing (OLAP) tools. Such products produce cubes or pivot tables that enable drill-down and rollup analysis. Usually, OLAP multidimensional technology is found in the data mart environment.

OLAP multidimensional tools usually keep a generous supply of metadata about their content, for example, information about how data has been defined to drill down and roll up. Gathering and integrating metadata from the OLAP vendor is useful especially for technical metadata; however, drill-downs and rollups are important business metadata. Drill-downs and rollups define taxonomic structures, such as product hierarchies or organization hierarchies; these are very important to the business. Other examples of business metadata found in OLAP are "business names" of data elements and the mapping of these names to the underlying data from the database.

### 7.2.7   Extract-Transform-Load (ETL)

Obviously, the main source of mappings from source systems to data warehouse and data mart fields is the Extract-Transform-Load (ETL) environment, which is a great source of both technical and business metadata.

As a rule, the metadata found in the ETL environment is about data movement and transformations (naturally!). Most of the metadata found in the ETL environment is of the technical variety. However, ETL contains metadata that has all sorts of business ramifications, such as:

✦ Where the data came from

✦ What changes or transformations were made to the data, if any, in transit

✦ What summaries or other aggregations were created

✦ When the last load occurred and whether or not it was successful

This information is extremely important to many businesspeople, especially compliance and process analysts.

The raw content and format of mappings in ETL tools is not "business-friendly," however. Businesspeople are obviously not interested in pouring through load statistics for all intermediate jobs to determine whether the specific data they were interested in got loaded successfully. Nor are they interested in looking through hundreds of mapping diagrams to find the one they want. They simply want to answer the questions, "Where did this data come from? Which systems? Which fields? Which applications? What, if anything, was done to the data? What format changes or transformations were applied?" Business metadata can make this information accessible and understandable to businesspeople, but it takes both capture of the raw technical metadata and the conversion of the information into something that businesspeople can understand. This means the need for a translation of the technical metadata produced by the ETL tool to turn it into business metadata. This repurposing of technical metadata will be discussed later in the chapter.

### 7.2.8   Legacy Systems and On-Line Transaction Processing (OLTP) Applications

The original source of metadata that always needs to be considered is the metadata found in the OLTP environment in general, which includes both legacy and, more recently, built applications. This metadata includes:

✦ Application screen names

✦ Screen field names

✦ Help text for data entry in screens, including "hover text": explanatory text that appears when the mouse hovers over a specific area

✦ Pick lists for field data entry

✦ Data dictionary

✦ Application code (lots of hard coded stuff!)

Any discussion of legacy system metadata should also include user guides and general user documentation.

Many issues are associated with the metadata found in the legacy applications environment. Some of the issues are as follows:

✦ How up to date is the metadata? Has it been maintained over time?

✦ How complete is the metadata in the legacy application environment?

✦ How can the metadata be accessed? Usually, older technologies did not make metadata access especially easy.

✦ On the assumption that the metadata reasonably and accurately described that application, how relevant is it to our upcoming applications?

### 7.2.9   The Data Warehouse

Perhaps the most important source of metadata is that which describes the data warehouse.

The data warehouse stores and also creates a plethora of technical metadata, and occasionally some business metadata as well. In addition, in order to construct the data warehouse, a lot of research has to be done to understand how to integrate fields from diverse data sources. What is done with the results of this research is obviously the most critical consideration involved in capturing metadata from the data warehouse.

For example, did the developers document what they found in a metadata repository (best) or if not, did they document their findings in other documentation, like a Concept of Operations document or other explanatory document? Were they given documentation requirements? Were they given a specific format/template? If so, then there exists very valuable metadata, because for many organizations the warehouse is the lifeblood of data integration for the corporation. If not, it might be your fault! You will therefore have to consider using all the techniques of mining data from people's heads, as explained in Chapter 6, and go after the technicians who built the data warehouse to capture what they learned in the process of building it. This is because it is the process of building the data warehouse that is the most important source of metadata, and not the warehouse itself.

### 7.2.10    *Summary of Metadata Sources*

As we have seen, many diverse sources of metadata exist; this chapter has just explored a few obvious ones. Chart 7.1 summarizes some of the salient characteristics of the different sources for enterprise metadata, as presented in this chapter.

There is rich diversity in the plethora of sources of enterprise metadata, as seen in Figure 7.1. The sources feed into the Enterprise Metadata Repository (EMR).

| Source | Business/ technical | Vendor interface | One time/ ongoing | Editing special consideration |
|---|---|---|---|---|
| ERP | Technical | Yes | Ongoing | Important to use vendor interface |
| Reports | Business | No | Ongoing | Lots of junk to be edited out |
| Spreadsheets | Business | No | Ongoing | Lots of junk to be edited out |
| Documents | Business | No | One time | Must remove non metadata data |
| DBMS directory | Technical | Yes | Ongoing | Some extraneous data to be removed |
| OLAP directory | Both | Yes | Ongoing | Some extraneous data to be removed |
| ETL | Technical | Yes | Ongoing | Often contains meta process information |
| Legacy appl | Both | No | One time | Old technology hard to decipher |
| Data warehouse | Could be both | Yes | Ongoing | Might have to comb through documents |

Some considerations of different metadata sources

**Chart 7.1**    Characteristics of Metadata Sources.

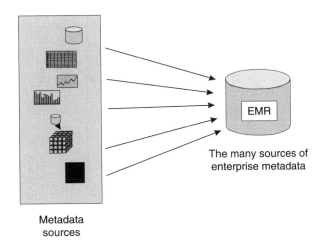

The many sources of enterprise metadata

Metadata sources

**Figure 7.1**    Diversity of Metadata Sources.

# 7.3    Editing the Metadata as It Passes into the Enterprise Metadata Repository

In almost every case, the sources of metadata must be edited before the data they contain is fit for the enterprise metadata repository. This is especially true when it comes to transforming technical metadata into business metadata.

In fact, extensive editing is often required in order to take the metadata from the source to the enterprise metadata repository. There are two basic styles of editing—automated and manual. Figure 7.2 shows all the different sources feeding an edit process that contains these two styles of editing.

### 7.3.1    *Automation of Editing*

It is axiomatic that as much editing as possible should be done in an automated manner. There is simply too much metadata with too much complexity coming from too many sources to try to edit it manually. Yet, there is such a lack of uniformity of metadata coming in from different sources that some amount of manual editing is inevitable. It is then natural that there is a mixture of manual editing and automated editing.

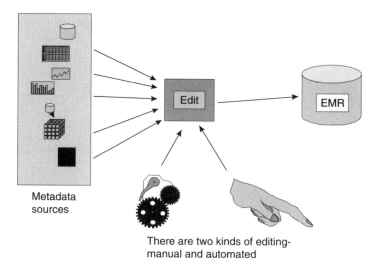

**Figure 7.2**    Manual and Automated Metadata Editing.

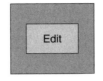

"...Forty dollars ..... . Judgment: this...... ..shall be paid ....... Interest bearing ..... notwithstanding ...day of July ....."

**Figure 7.3** Word Removal.

The simplest form of editing metadata in preparation for entrance into an enterprise repository is to remove data. Figure 7.3 shows an example of data that is removed as it passes out of the source.

One way to remove unwanted data from the metadata being prepared for the repository is to remove it manually with a text editor. But a more sophisticated way to accomplish this task is to use a "stop words" list. A stop word list is a list of all the words, phrases, and symbols that need to be removed. These lists are described in more detail in Chapter 12 on Unstructured Business Metadata.

The stop word list typically contains words such as "a", "an," "the," and "to," but it can be altered to contain anything. When the item in the stop word list is encountered, the item is removed from the text being prepared.

### 7.3.2 "Granularizing" Metadata

In many cases, the metadata enters the source analyzer in the form of a single document. Figure 7.4 shows that a DBMS System Catalog has been read and that different tables are found in the directory. Rather than keep the directory intact, the metadata manager wishes to break the system catalog into smaller component pieces, each piece containing table information separately.

The metadata manager uses a "granularization" piece of software to extract the different pieces of metadata, as seen in Figure 7.4. The figure shows that the enterprise metadata repository receives three separate tables, which have been extracted from a single directory.

### 7.3.3 Expanding Definitions and Descriptions

Another challenge for the metadata editor is the inclusion or joining of information. In many cases, the metadata comes from the source metadata in a raw state. It is therefore desirable to expand the definition and descriptive

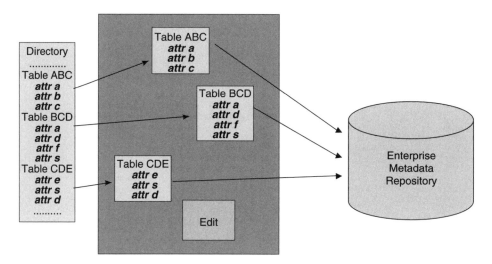

**Figure 7.4**   Breaking a Larger Source into Components.

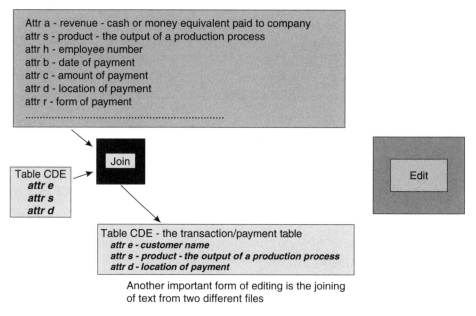

**Figure 7.5**   Joining Text from Two Different Files.

information found in the metadata coming from the source. A separate file is created with the definitions and descriptions that are desired. Then the source metadata and the expansions are "joined" together, as seen in Figure 7.5.

In Figure 7.5, two sources of data are joined on common information. The first source contains a simple list of technical metadata with table names and their associated attributes. This list is joined with a description of each column. The result is metadata going to the enterprise metadata repository in a much more complete, robust manner. In this case, the list now contains tables, their attributes, and a description of what each attribute represents.

Care must be taken with this approach. If at a later time, the same metadata source is reentered into the enterprise metadata repository, the join must be reexecuted. Otherwise the metadata that comes from the first source will be in a raw state and will lack the completeness required.

### 7.3.4   *Synonym Resolution*

Another form of editing is that used for the management of synonyms. Synonyms are different words or phrases that have the same meaning. The English language is full of synonyms: for example, "car" and "automobile"; "kiss" and "osculate." It is often important to locate and "resolve" synonyms. Suppose you want to consolidate metadata, and suppose you find that the same object is referred to by more than one name. One metadata source calls the object "rec_revenue," whereas another metadata source calls the same object "recognized_revenue." Yet another metadata source calls the object "rev-rec." You wish to ensure that the person using the enterprise metadata repository recognizes that these names are, in fact, referring to the same thing. You can use synonym resolution to tie them all together.

In Figure 7.6, there are three tables, all of which are really the same table. However, for some reason they have been named differently in different places. The metadata manager uses software that recognizes that the tables

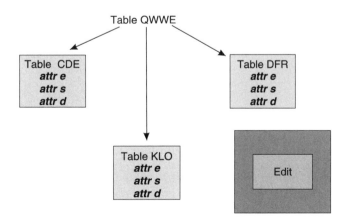

**Figure 7.6**   Synonym Resolution.

are really the same and performs resolution. There are several ways to do this. One way is to replace the table names Table CDE, Table DFR, and Table KLO with the name Table QWWE. This works fine as long as there is never any need to see what the original metadata information was. If, however, there is a need to retain the original information (often for traceability purposes, for compliance or legal reasons), you can append the common table name with the original name. In this case, Table QWWE is appended to the tables. The following results would appear: Table CDE_QWWE, Table DFR_QWWE, and Table KLO_QWWE. In addition, you can use a "Rosetta Stone" approach, named after the famous ancient stone showing the same text written in three different languages, which helped us decipher Egyptian hieroglyphics. This approach involves using a separate table to resolve the names, so you can see which tables are mapped to the central table, if you need to go back to the source data or need to be able to trace the data lineage. Figure 7.7 shows a Rosetta Stone mapping table.

Note that synonym resolution works for more than just table names. It works for any kind of metadata that exists. Also note that alternate spelling can be treated in exactly the same manner as synonyms.

### 7.3.4.1   Caution!

Care must be taken any time synonyms are resolved. The question must always be asked: Are they really synonyms? If two things are mistaken as synonyms, data can be mistaken as the wrong thing and merged incorrectly. The result will be many bad business decisions and the mixing of apples and oranges. This was discussed in greater detail in Chapter 4.

## 7.3.5   Homonym Resolution

The reverse of synonym is homograph or homophone, commonly known as homonym. In Chapter 4 we defined a homonym as two (or more) uses of the

| Source Table | Mapped Table |
| --- | --- |
| CDE | QWWE |
| DFR | QWWE |
| KLO | QWWE |

**Figure 7.7**    Rosetta Stone Mapping Table.

same word; you can also think of homonyms as two or more words that are spelled and pronounced the same but have different meanings. Some examples of homonyms are as follows:

✦ The **bill** of a bird and the restaurant **bill** for food

✦ You set the table with **glasses**; John wears **glasses** so he can see better

✦ A **mole** can be a small, furry animal, a skin anomaly, or an internal spy

Homonyms are known in semantics as "word sense" or the "sense" of the word. They can be managed when reading source metadata.

A very simple example can be seen using a very common word: "Name." Obviously, name can have many meanings. What kind of name is being referred to? For years, when referring to an attribute in a database query, you could reference the table name, next a period (.), and then the column name. For example: Person.Name and Product.Name helps to distinguish the type of name referred to. This kind of referencing can be used for homonyms. This type of approach can easily be applied to all sorts of other business metadata such as business terms. For example, to distinguish the term *revenue* as used in the Marketing Department from that used in the Finance Department, add a modifier: "Marketing Revenue" versus "Finance Revenue." Two very different calculations may be used for these two divisions, and so these are definitely homonyms and not the same underlying concept.

Figure 7.8 shows the resolution of homonyms. These three tables may be called the same name (CDE), but in reality they are not the same, and they need to be resolved.

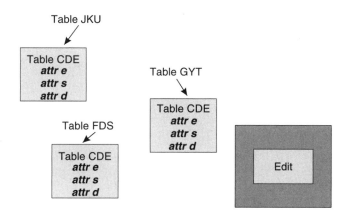

Recognizing and resolving homographs is another editing challenging

**Figure 7.8** Homonym Resolution.

Homonyms can be resolved by using the Rosetta Stone in reverse. In the example in Figure 7.8, the database name is required to distinguish each originating table name, since all the tables have the same name. Then the corresponding new name can be associated properly. In the case of business terms, a modifier is usually required, as in the example of revenue: *Sales* revenue versus *Marketing* revenue.

### 7.3.6 Using a Staging Area

As we have seen, a lot of editing is usually required when preparing data for entry into an enterprise metadata repository—so much editing in fact, and rather complex editing at that—that it often makes sense to use a staging area as a temporary storage facility. Then, after the editing is complete, the results can be transported into the metadata repository. Figure 7.9 illustrates such a process.

This process of metadata integration and transformation that occurs in a staging area is reminiscent of the data warehouse. Indeed, metadata repository management is often described as a mini-data warehouse process.

### 7.3.7 Manual Metadata Editing

If you have exhausted all possible means of automated editing, the only thing left is to edit the metadata manually. Obviously, it is not practical to use manual

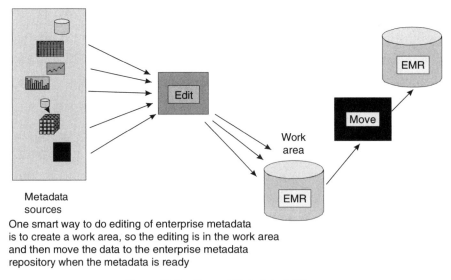

Metadata
sources

One smart way to do editing of enterprise metadata
is to create a work area, so the editing is in the work area
and then move the data to the enterprise metadata
repository when the metadata is ready

**Figure 7.9** Manual Metadata Editing.

editing as a repeatable process, so the challenge is to figure out how you can automate it. But sometimes manual editing is required for the initial load. Metadata can be manually edited and placed in the staging area we have just discussed, and then an automated process can be used to load it into the repository.

# 7.4 Turning Technical Metadata into Business Metadata

Most of the metadata mentioned in this chapter is technical metadata. Obviously, in its original format, technical metadata is not suitable for or comprehensible to business people. Therefore, it must be translated into the language of the business, in a format that businesspeople can understand.

The first step in any data delivery effort, and metadata is no exception, is to determine what metadata would be helpful for the business user. Determining the actual metadata needed may require analysis from the business point of view. Questions such as the following are asked of businesspeople:

✦ "What would be helpful background information to know about this report?"

✦ "What is your expectation about the data shown in the report, such as when it was last refreshed? Would you like to know if the data does not conform to your expectations, such as the last load failed to run?"

✦ "Are there any numbers on this report that you would like to know where they came from and if they were transformed in some way?"

The answers to questions like these will provide guidelines for business metadata; most of it will be technical metadata that is transformed into business metadata.

Once you have obtained the answers to these questions, you should next identify the technical metadata that contains these answers. For example, the businesspeople have identified the following:

✦ "I would like to know the exact formula that was used to calculate revenue on this report." **Technical Metadata:** Probably located in the ETL transformation, but may not be; it might have come from the source system, or it may even be in businesspeople's heads and calculated by businesspeople themselves (revenue is tricky! Always make sure it is well defined!).

✦ "I would like to know when this report's data was last refreshed." **Technical Metadata:** Load Success status, and the date.

✦ "I would like to know where (which applications) each of these numbers came from." **Technical Metadata:** Name of the source system or application that was referred to from the ETL mapping.

Each of these examples refers to metadata contained in the ETL processes, either in the load logs or in the mappings themselves. As you can see, it takes a certain amount of translation to determine what metadata is needed and where it needs to come from.

Here's a step-by-step guide to extraction of business-relevant metadata from technical metadata:

1. Determine what business metadata is required and embedded in the technical metadata that needs to be extracted.

2. Remove the relevant parts of the metadata from the original tool that captured it and store it elsewhere, often in a staging area. The prior sections of this chapter illustrate ways of doing this.

3. Next, determine what the captured metadata's reference point is from a business point of view. The reference point is where the businessperson starts from: He or she can be viewing a specific field or report and has questions about it. The reference point is the mechanism that enables the right metadata to be available at the right context for the business-person. The reference point for an ETL mapping is either the source field or the target field, or both. From a data delivery point of view, the target field is the reference point (where the businessperson starts from). The reference point for an ETL load job, from a business point of view, is the business intelligence report that contains the data that was loaded by the specific ETL job. The technical metadata then needs to be joined to this reference metadata that provides context for it.

4. Carry out the actual transformation from technical metadata into business metadata: How does the businessperson want to see this data? It could be very simple, such as a load date (is time also important?); however, there needs to be explanatory text around the metadata, such as: "The last date this data was loaded was Thursday, March 24, 2007, at 4:30 a.m." Business metadata usually contains textual explanations, in order to make it understandable to the business.

5. Implement and store the metadata in the metadata repository. The data delivery mechanism needs to be well understood, and the meta-data repository needs to either store the metadata in the proper format required or provide information about how to transform it. Data delivery is discussed in the next chapter, Chapter 8, which is appropriately entitled Business Metadata Delivery.

6. Lastly, you must create the metadata extraction as a repeatable process, and execute the transport, transformation, load into a repository, and automate its delivery.

# 7.5 Summary

This chapter surveyed many possible sources of metadata that may already exist in the digital environment, in electronic form. However, in order to be useful to the business community, technical metadata usually has to be translated in some way, into the language of the business, so that it can be readily understood. This chapter explored some of the ways to do so, such as extracting metadata components, resolving synonyms and homonyms, and finally stepping through the process of determining what metadata is useful to the business, how to find it in its technical form, and how to link it to where it will be helpful to users.

# Business Metadata Delivery

## 8.1 Introduction

In the last two chapters we discussed the capture of business metadata, both from existing data/metadata and from people's heads, both in groups and individually. All the capture in the world will do you no good, however, if you have no way to deliver it to people. The whole reason for bothering to capture business metadata is to make it useful to people and to help people do their jobs better and more efficiently. This chapter, therefore, presents various approaches to delivering business metadata directly to businesspeople, when and where it can make an impact.

**139**

## 8.2 Separating Business Metadata and Technical Metadata

Both business and technical metadata should reside in the enterprise metadata repository, but the two types of metadata should be logically partitioned. Business and technical metadata contain very different data. They are used in very different places in very different ways. The usage of business metadata, the focus of this chapter, is perhaps the main driving force for keeping the two logically separate. Figure 8.1 shows this separation.

As we shall see later in the chapter, however, the two kinds of metadata need to interact and interoperate with each other, so they have to be physically integrated. Sometimes you will need a business interpretation of technical metadata; other times you may want to take a technical action from business metadata, like generating a candidate data model from a business glossary or comparing a data-profiling result against business expectations, annotated in a glossary. Therefore, business and technical metadata must be logically separate but physically integrated.

## 8.3 Principles of Business Metadata Delivery

We need to cover a few basic principles of business metadata delivery before we discuss actual delivery mechanisms. These are guiding principles that will help you create your own delivery channels.

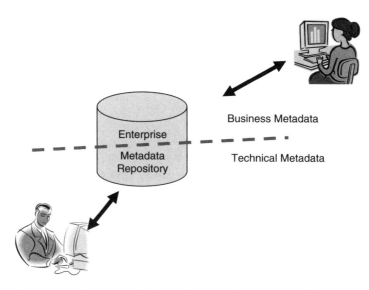

Business Metadata

Enterprise Metadata Repository

Technical Metadata

**Figure 8.1** Separating Business Metadata from Technical Metadata.

### 8.3.1  The Importance of Easy Access: Avoid the "Roach Motel!"

In Chapter 6, we discussed what a "roach motel" was. You can get data into a "roach motel", but you can't easily get it out. In that chapter, we talked about repurposing wiki data so that it can be used in another way; getting the data out of the wiki and into someplace else. The "roach motel" applies here in an even more basic way: If you capture the data, it does no good to anyone if he or she can't access it at all.

So the first principle is: Make sure the data has a use and can be accessed by the right audience. Moreover, the usage mechanism has to be easy for people. It can't be very complicated and require a lot of extra work; otherwise it will not be used!

### 8.3.2  Who Will Use It and How? Business Metadata Use Cases

Programmers have a technique for requirements gathering called Use Cases: It states the typical scenario under which the program will be used, who will be using it, and what business problems it is meant to solve.

The appropriate business metadata delivery mechanism will be highly dependent on these Use Case scenarios. Who needs this metadata, under what conditions are they likely to use it, and what is the best way for them to access it, given the business scenario? When do people need the clarity that business metadata can provide?

## 8.4  Indirect Usage of Business Metadata

The interesting thing about accessing metadata in general is that it is usually indirect; that is, somebody usually won't go into a metadata application and bring up the metadata he or she needs (although this is possible and is done in many environments, especially for metadata management). Instead, metadata's function is usually to support some task in an indirect way. Business metadata's function is to add context and clarity to data. This is why business metadata access is indirect; it is in conjunction with a larger task and is an adjunct to that task, not an end in itself.

Here are a few examples of indirect usage of business metadata:

✦ A user is viewing a document in a word processing program and encounters an acronym unique to the company and is not familiar with it.

✦ A user is analyzing an OLAP application (On-line Analytical Processing: cube or pivot table allowing quick access from summary to detailed data) and wants to know what the calculation is, where it came from, and what authority governs it.

✦ A user is entering data in a CRM (Customer Relationship Management) application and doesn't understand what is supposed to be entered into a specific field.

In each case, the user doesn't seek out business metadata for its own sake but instead wants clarity while performing a task. The usage of business metadata is not direct but indirect.

### 8.4.1   *Accessibility from Multiple Places*

We can therefore conclude that business metadata can be needed from anywhere, in all applications throughout the enterprise. One of the largest challenges of business metadata is the requirement that it be ubiquitous or accessed from anywhere. This is also a huge justification for a centralized business metadata repository or service-oriented delivery strategy, because the metadata often will need to be accessed from a different location from where it is stored. It is also very important that a strong architecture be established that plans for the capture, assimilation, and delivery of business metadata, because it needs to be accessible from many different places.

Here are a *few* of the environments that business metadata can be accessed from:

✦ Legacy application

✦ Intranet, enterprise portal

✦ External, customer-facing portal

✦ Web-based applications, both internal and external, both data entry and reports

✦ Reports

✦ Business intelligence (BI) reports and OLAP applications

✦ Wikis

✦ Word processing applications

✦ Spreadsheets

✦ Data mining applications

✦ Enterprise mashups

✦ Desktops

✦ Commercial Off the Shelf Software (COTS) packages

Innumerable places can access business metadata—so many that the possibilities are endless. Essentially, anywhere you need clarification of some kind, business metadata should be there to add that clarity.

### 8.4.2   Web Examples of Business Metadata Delivery

The Web is full of pages that utilize business metadata providing explanations and term definitions, which display either pop-up windows or a new page to clarify the terms used. For example, Figure 8.2 shows a page from dictionary. com with the definition of "osculate." If you hover over the blue underlined text called "pronunciation key," you will see the text "Click for pronunciation guide." Notice that the hover "help" text also shows up at the bottom left of the window.

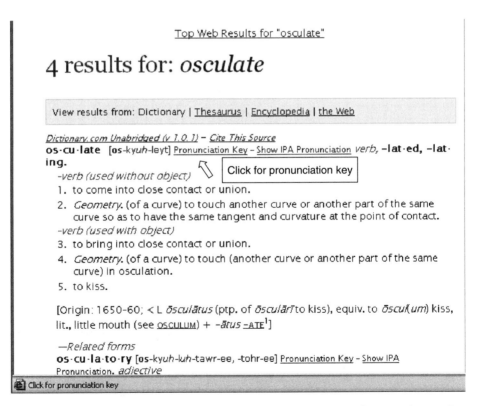

**Figure 8.2**   Hover Text Shown in the Box; Also Shows up at Bottom Left on Window Border.

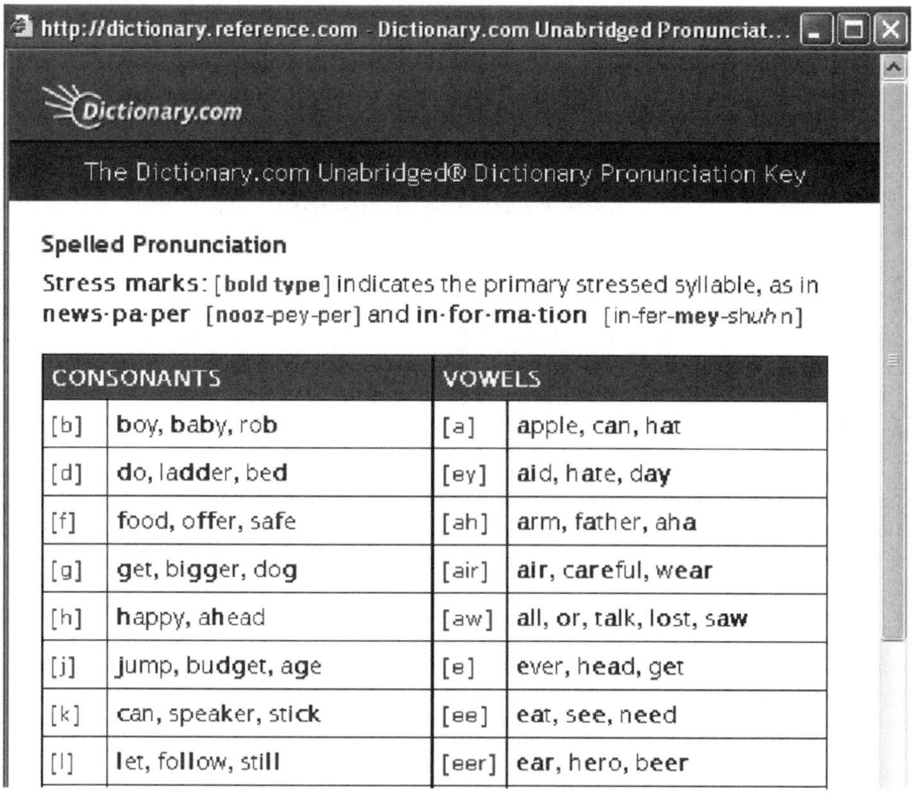
http://dictionary.reference.com - Dictionary.com Unabridged Pronunciat...

Dictionary.com

The Dictionary.com Unabridged® Dictionary Pronunciation Key

**Spelled Pronunciation**

**Stress marks:** [**bold type**] indicates the primary stressed syllable, as in **news·pa·per** [**nooz**-pey-per] and **in·for·ma·tion** [in-fer-**mey**-shuhn]

| CONSONANTS | | VOWELS | |
|---|---|---|---|
| [b] | boy, baby, rob | [a] | apple, can, hat |
| [d] | do, ladder, bed | [ey] | aid, hate, day |
| [f] | food, offer, safe | [ah] | arm, father, aha |
| [g] | get, bigger, dog | [air] | air, careful, wear |
| [h] | happy, ahead | [aw] | all, or, talk, lost, saw |
| [j] | jump, budget, age | [e] | ever, head, get |
| [k] | can, speaker, stick | [ee] | eat, see, need |
| [l] | let, follow, still | [eer] | ear, hero, beer |

**Figure 8.3** Pronunciation Guide Displayed in a Separate Window.

When you click on this text, the pronunciation guide comes up in a separate window, shown in Figure 8.3.

This technique can also be used to display definitions of important terms and expanded descriptions of terms. Web sites link to other Web sites with blue, underlined text. Similarly, it is common practice today to display terms that have definitions and descriptions/explanations using blue, underlined text; it is a de facto standard. The user clicks on this blue text, and it takes him or her to the page containing the term's definition. The blue text turns to magenta if the explanation text has been accessed before. Wikipedia also conforms to the blue text standard. It brings up another Wikipedia entry if underlined blue text is clicked from within any wiki entry. This blue text on the Web universally means there is descriptive text (business metadata) available; click here.

### 8.4.3    Business Metadata Delivery in an Interactive Report

The user should be able to access definitions of fields from any application in the environment. Figure 8.4 shows a report. The user should be able to highlight the name of a data element on the report, and the definition should be displayed, either as hover text (text that appears when needed, then disappears) or available with something like a right click.

What if more extensive business metadata is available and the user needs to choose which type to view? This more involved strategy is shown in Figure 8.5. Examples of different types of business metadata that could be available include:

✦ Where did the data come from, such as source systems, table names, and column names?

✦ What transformations have affected the data?

✦ When was the data last loaded successfully?

✦ What is the load history of the data?

✦ Who is the data steward for this particular data?

Figure 8.5 shows the progression of the user selecting the term and then choosing the type of business metadata desired.

Figure 8.5 shows an interactive exchange that can take place during the business analyst's normal workflow. For example, suppose that a business analyst is working in Business Objects:

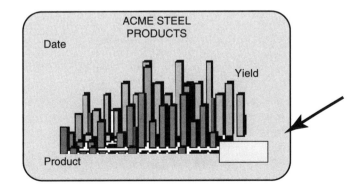

**Figure 8.4**    Report with Highlight Capability to Invoke Business Metadata.

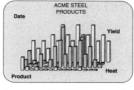
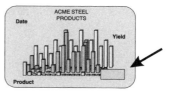

1 - an analyst is looking at
a screen or a report

2 - the analyst has a question about
some item found on the screen.
The analyst highlights the item

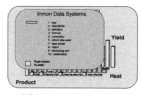
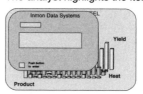

3 - IDS then asks the analyst
what information is desired

4 - IDS then returns the information
about the item

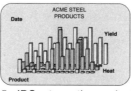

5 - IDS returns the analyst
to the original screen

**Figure 8.5** Business Metadata Delivery Based on Type of Metadata.

1. The business analyst sees a term that is of interest or that is questionable. This scenario is seen in (1) in the figure.

2. The business analyst highlights the text in question, as seen in (2).

3. The business metadata system then sends a pop-up menu to the analyst asking the analyst for what type of metadata the analyst would like to see about the text that has been queried. This is shown in (3).

4. Then the business metadata system displays the business metadata requested, as seen in (4).

5. When the analyst has found all the business metadata information that is needed, he or she can signal by a mouse click, which returns to the original screen, as seen in (5).

All of this interaction with business metadata is done while Business Objects is active. There is no need to leave Business Objects and have to return again. The net result of being able to access business metadata indirectly is that the analyst increases his or her analytical capabilities during the normal workflow of performing the analysis.

**Figure 8.6**   Portlet Entry Area for Business Metadata Reference.

### 8.4.4   Business Metadata Access from Applications

Some applications have the ability to invoke an outside application, sometimes called a "user exit," by the use of a hot key. Context-sensitivity, along with the hot key, provides access to the business metadata. However, caution should be applied when using this approach because it is always subject to change. The vendor can modify support of user exits in subsequent releases. Refer to your vendor's documentation for specific details pertaining to the particular software you are working with.

If this is not possible in your unique environment, you can always use portal software to achieve the same goal. You can create a portlet or small intranet application that calls up the business metadata by means of either manual user entry (typing it in) or cut and paste, if context sensitivity is not available. Obviously, the less a user has to enter the better, so context-sensitive invocation is always preferable, but a portlet window with entry area still gets the job done. Figure 8.6 shows a design of a very simple portlet that can be used for this purpose.

The best way to invoke this portlet is to have easy access to it for all users; for example, an icon can be placed in the user's tray at the bottom of the desktop, which can bring it up. The advantage of this approach is that no matter what application the user is in, the business metadata icon is available and can be accessed.

## 8.5   Business Metadata Delivery Use Cases

The following ideas and examples show how business metadata can be used in various ways in the enterprise.

### 8.5.1   Corporate Dictionary Example

One company created an internal corporate dictionary, which was especially helpful because the company had just gone through a major migration, replacing about a hundred home-grown systems with one ERP/Financials/CRM commercial off-the-shelf application. One of the side effects of this migration was the new vocabulary that the new application imposed on the business. The corporation, wanting to help the businesspeople get used to the new terms, saw the corporate dictionary as a way to facilitate this objective.

The corporation had an intranet portal, so it placed a small portlet resembling the one shown in Figure 8.9 on the main portal page, which allowed a user to enter a business term or phrase and press the lookup button. The main portal page resembled a newspaper, and we had the portal designers locate the dictionary portlet just above where most users would see the "crease," or default amount of screen shown on most windows without custom sizing. Figure 8.7 shows a stylized corporate portal main page with a dictionary portlet displayed on the right.

Most environments using a portal are set up by default to bring up the portal every time the user invokes its Internet browser as the home page. Of course, the user can change its home page to something else, but most users don't bother because this sort of customizing is low priority. This means that the dictionary can be accessed by simply invoking the Internet browser, which is very easy and requires no extra steps or extra thought. Invoking an Internet browser is part of a user's natural workflow, which conforms to our first principle of metadata delivery, as outlined in the first part of this chapter.

### 8.5.2  Business Metadata and Training

Another place where business metadata can make a huge difference is in helping new employees get acclimated to the corporate culture. The corporate dictionary mentioned in Section 8.5 can be extremely useful in this regard.

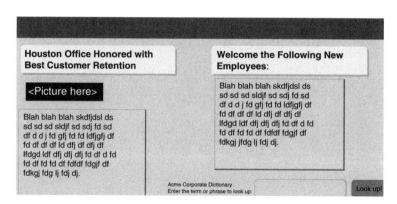

**Figure 8.7**  Dictionary Portlet Shown on an Intranet Portal Main Page.

In addition, if business metadata is collected as job tips, tricks, and helpful hints, it can be used in job training. These helpful hints can go far in getting a new employee up to speed quickly. Business rules can not only be used as a ready reference but can also assist in job training and helping new employees learn how the enterprise operates.

### 8.5.3  Business Metadata and Web 2.0: Mashups

As discussed in Chapter 6, a mashup is a composite application in which several different technologies and data sources are mixed together to form an integrated view.

Mashups have tremendous potential for business metadata delivery. We discussed previously how businesspeople themselves can use mashups to create their own business metadata. Mashups also empower IT to create vehicles through which information from various sources can be loosely integrated and comments or helpful hints can be added to deliver contextual data about reports. IT can create the mashup, which can include wikis for people to add comments themselves. Two or more reports can be tied together with pertinent information about how they relate; see Figure 8.8, which provides all sorts of background information on cases. The conglomeration can be thought of as business metadata, because the whole is bigger than its parts viewed separately. Notice in this screen how the acronyms are shown—more business metadata.

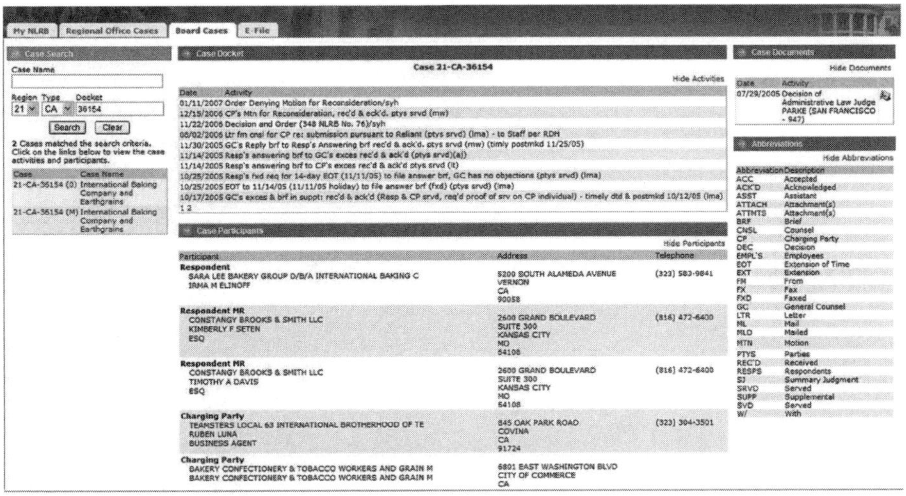

**Figure 8.8**  Mashup Reporting on Various Views of Case Information from Different Systems (Courtesy of Project Performance Corporation).

Social networks can be shown that point the user to experts in the area if they need to contact someone. Mashups are terrific for business metadata! See Chapter 6 for examples of mashups that users can create themselves. User-created mashups should then be available to provide useful insights for others. Mashups allow two or more separate applications to be tied together in one view.

Google has created and exposed an application programming interface (API) for Google Maps, and many mashups are being built that exploit maps and add commentary about locations. See Figure 8.9 for a mashup that shows a pushpin where each of the top 25 crimes took place, and an explanation of each from Wikipedia.

### 8.5.4   Visual Analytic Techniques

Business metadata can involve the use of visual analytic techniques to add a whole new view of the data. Figure 8.10 shows a three-dimensional (3-D) chart on crime incidents at taverns and bars. The data is easier to view because of the 3-D charts. Notice how the business metadata annotations make a difference in highlighting salient points in the chart.

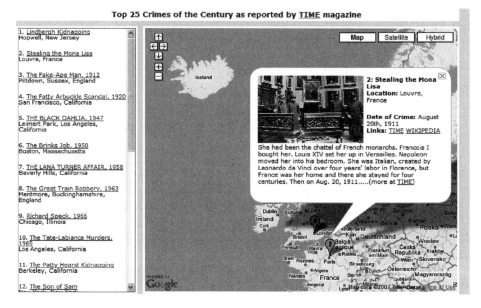

**Figure 8.9**   Mashup Showing Description of Crimes Based on Map Location.

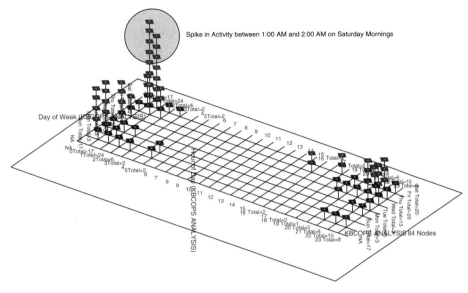

Bar/Tavern Incidents-April 2006

**Figure 8.10**   3-D Chart with Annotation. (Courtesy of Project Performance Corporation)

Figure 8.11 shows how an unstructured data tool (Inmon Data Systems) can display health problems based on how many times certain problems were referenced across all the records associated with a given patient.

Affinity analysis can be seen in social networking tools, as well as in general relationship depictions. Sometimes it may be important to track the various ways that people are related to other people in order to see if new connections can be found. In law enforcement, it is very important to cross reference people across cases and associated data about a person or a case. People may also play different roles across different cases. This data can be presented in a more effective manner graphically; see Figure 8.12.

One such software package used to author visual representations is a tool by Visual Analytics, Inc. (VAI) called VisuaLinks. Jordan Rose of Project Performance Corporation is a master at producing visual analytic applications. This one, and others in this chapter, represent some of his work.

### 8.5.5   *Technical Use of Business Metadata*

The main focus of business metadata is delivery of metadata in a useful form and language to business users. Interestingly, business metadata can be used by technical users as well.

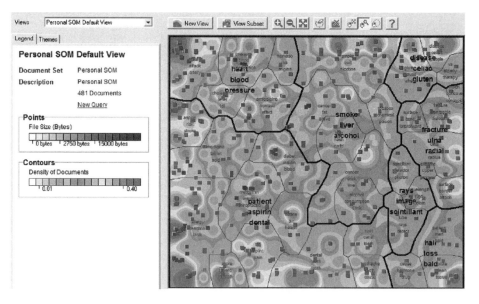

**Figure 8.11**   Heat Map Showing Document Concentration Based on Topic Area.

Corporate dictionary projects are often started by IT group members because they find that they themselves need a glossary to understand the business requirements better and to facilitate their communication with businesspeople. Terms can be seen as business concepts and can be reused across the enterprise as they are manifested in different systems.

Delivery mechanisms do not need to be customized as much for IT personnel as for businesspeople, because in general IT personnel are used to accessing specialized applications to get their jobs done. Thus, this kind of work is part of their normal workflow. However, a delivery mechanism geared toward technical personnel may want to make a special effort to display both business and technical metadata, so the user can easily translate between the two for themselves.

### 8.5.6   Delivery of the Integration of Business and Technical Metadata

A very creative delivery of integrated business and technical metadata can be seen in IBM's new integrated metadata repository. IBM has provided a business glossary, which has incorporated term life-cycle maintenance and stewardship

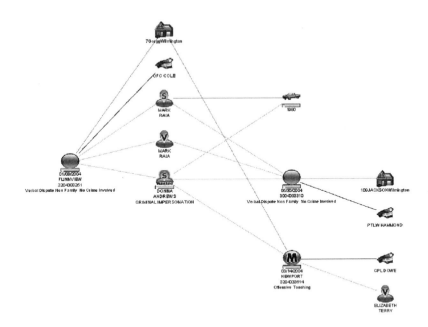

**Figure 8.12** Graphic Depiction of Affinity Analysis. (Courtesy of Project Performance Corporation)

(see Figure 8.13). This in itself is great business metadata delivery. But in addition, IBM has successfully integrated the business and technical metadata such that:

✦ You can actually generate a data model from the business terms (you do this through the categories and broad term/narrow terms you specify).

✦ You can perform impact analysis and see where a business term is used in the various enterprise system components (see Figure 8.13).

✦ You can analyze a business term's definition against data profiling performed against any and all data elements that are supposed to represent the term.

✦ You can see all the ETL jobs that involve the data elements representing that business term (shown in Figure 8.13).

Figure 8.13 shows IBM's integrated metadata repository in action, specifically all the linked occurrences (in this case 3) in the repository for the glossary term "First Name." It shows a database field and two objects from the ETL environment.

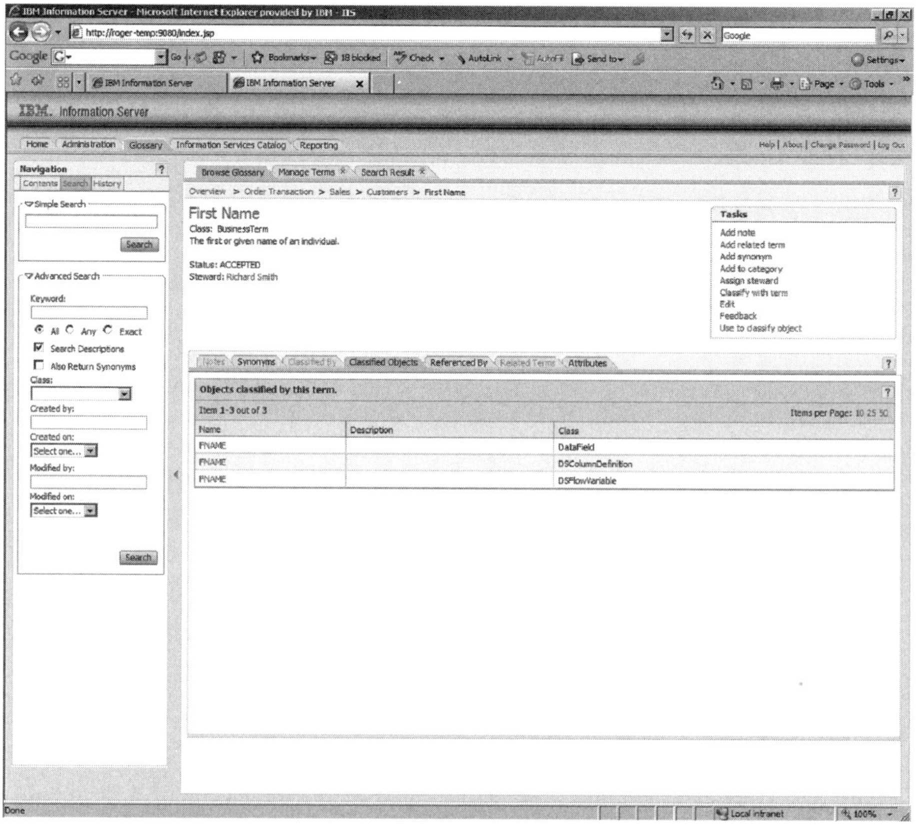

**Figure 8.13** IBM's Integrated Metadata Repository.

# 8.6 Summary

This chapter has presented several different kinds of delivery methods and channels for disseminating business metadata to users in order to enhance their normal work activity and help them perform their jobs better and more efficiently. However, designing delivery mechanisms is a creative exercise, and the reader will rapidly see that the possibilities for new and creative mechanisms are limited only by the imagination. The main point is to understand the users' needs, identify the type of metadata they feel will be helpful, and then devise a mechanism that interrupts their normal workflow very minimally or not at all.

# 8.7 References/Acknowledgments

+ Top 25 Crimes Mashup: http://www.mibazaar.com/top25crimes.html

+ Mashups from BEA: http://en.terpri.se/

+ IBM Information Server: http://www-306.ibm.com/software/data/integration/ info_server/

Thanks to Jeff Worthington at the EPA for emphasizing the importance of glossary/dictionary descriptions and definitions underlined and available on the Web with just a click; to Ajay Gandhi from BEA for all his help in understanding mashups and how Web 2.0 showcases business metadata; to Steven Totman from IBM who showed us the new release of Information Server, including their business glossary product and the integration of their metadata repository; and to all the great folks at Project Performance Corporation who got us screen shots at the last minute!

# Business Metadata Infrastructure

CHAPTER 9

## 9.1  Introduction

Numerous things need to be kept in mind when planning an infrastructure to support metadata, especially business metadata. This chapter addresses these considerations and will serve as a guide as you determine what kind of infrastructure best fits your current environment.

The chapter discusses what kinds of business metadata you may want to track and provides a data model as a guide. The metadata environment is shown to be like a data warehouse in many respects, requiring much of the same infrastructure components. Special tools are often required for both the capture and display of business metadata, and these are revisited from prior chapters for infrastructure consideration. Special integration and delivery mechanisms are discussed, namely, data federation and service orientation. Administrative sources of records and historical issues should also be considered in terms of structural and storage considerations. Lastly, the chapter covers the issues of buy versus build, with a third alternative in the mix: extend an existing product.

# 9.2 Types of Business Metadata

One of the first decisions concerning infrastructure that you must make is what sort of business metadata is important to the enterprise, as well as important enough to merit storage and management. Some of the major areas you will want to consider are:

- Business terms

- Business term definitions (Does a term have more than one definition? What about history?)

- Business rules

- Authority/governance/stewardship

- Origin: Where things came from (may be different from authority!)

- Scope: What is the scope or boundaries of authority?

- Organizations (both internal and external)

These are just a few of many different types of business metadata you may want to collect and manage. Remember, however, that data has costs; you can't just throw in everything. The Kitchen Sink metadata management strategy will be very costly, and we guarantee that it won't all apply to your specific business needs.

Figure 9.1 shows a high-level, conceptual metamodel that you can use as a guide to deciding what kinds of metadata to manage.

The model shows some of each type of metadata, business and technical. It is not intended to be an exhaustive model; in your environment you may come up with things unique to your business. Entities may have a lot of detail behind them, and when made into a logical model it will be larger. Each entity has a prefix indicating whether it is business (BMD) or technical (TMD) metadata. The model uses the Barker notation; you read each relationship as two sentences. For the purpose of aesthetics in the book, we have left the relationship

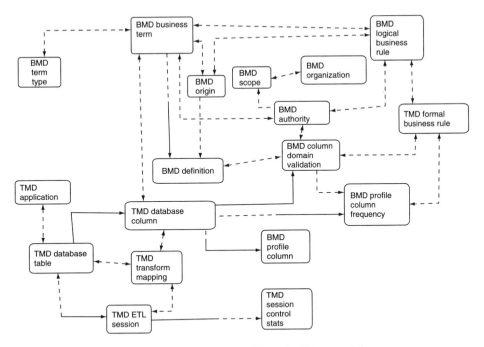

**Figure 9.1**  Business and Technical Metamodel.

names off of the diagram, so read each with a generic verb phrase such as "is associated with." A dotted line represents optional, solid is mandatory, and crow's foot is one or more. So the relationship between business term and definition would be read as follows:

✦ Each BMD business term may be associated with one or more definitions.

✦ Each BMD definition must be associated with one and only one BMD business term.

Just as you may create other entities that are not shown in this model (or omit some!), you may not agree with the relationships shown. For example, you may want to enforce a rule that mandates only one definition for every term. That is your choice. The model is included as a guideline only and is not to be interpreted as the only way to model metadata.

Note that the model includes technical metadata; this is for the purpose of integration, which we will explain in more detail later in the chapter. It is highly recommended that you be able to relate business and technical metadata together, to serve all sorts of purposes.

The data profiling metadata is indicated in the model as business metadata. It is actually both business and technical, but we refer to it as business because it enables the business to validate its definitions and data. Realize that it may have to be presented to the business user in a special format so that it can be understood more easily. However, many businesspeople are direct users of some profiling tools, especially Data Flux, because it is so easy to use and it creates wonderful charts and graphs. Businesspeople like charts and graphs! A picture is better than a thousand words, the old proverb says.

The model doesn't show some other interesting areas that you might want to consider:

+ Business context, including background information such as departmental history and corporate reorganizations

+ History and life cycle of the business metadata itself

+ Modification history (who modified the data, when, and why)

+ Aggregations, summaries, and formulas

+ Business process models

+ Business motivation

+ Images, including pictures of personnel

+ Geography

+ Weather

+ News feeds

## 9.3  The Metadata Warehouse

As we discussed in Chapters 6 and 7, business metadata is collected in various ways. The infrastructure therefore needs to support a variety of collection mechanisms including Web 2.0 technologies (see Chapter 6). Business metadata is also created through a transformation of technical metadata (Chapter 7). We have come to the conclusion that a good solution resembles a data warehouse architecture, but one designed specifically to handle metadata (see Figure 9.2).

This means that you must have all of the necessary components that you would need if you were building a data warehouse; the only difference would be the lack of a specialized delivery structure like you normally see in the BI

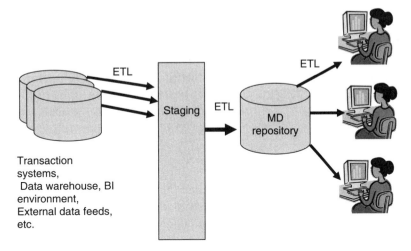

**Figure 9.2** Metadata Infrastructure, Metadata Data Warehouse.

environment (example: star schema or cube physical structure). You will still probably have to use ETL or common metadata bridges, as shown in Figure 9.2, because the metadata will have to be moved to the appropriate repository in the BI environment. Fortunately, many software and open systems firms provide metadata bridges or integration software that will help you accomplish the metadata ETL task. A quick search on the Internet for "metadata integration" will yield hundreds of responses for you to select from.

A special structure like a star scheme is not required because metadata in general and business metadata in particular do not require analytics. One possible exception is data quality statistics. Most business metadata is semi-structured textual content; some is unstructured comment text or even images. Business metadata adds context to the data, and it usually does so with textual descriptions. Obviously, textual descriptions cannot be "sliced and diced" like numbers can. Therefore, the data delivery side of the equation, though fraught with its own challenges, is usually easier than data warehousing and does not require a specialized physical data structure. We will, however, discuss a few exceptions.

### 9.3.1 Business Metadata Differences

The main difference between the infrastructure required for a data warehouse and that required for business metadata is the type of content. Business metadata usually consists of text. Now, however, we are beginning to see images as business metadata, and even really simple syndication (RSS) feeds, maps, and weather data. Some of these new data sources become links and do not go through ETL at all. A traditional ETL strategy and software may not be able to handle some of these types of objects, and even if they could, special hardware requirements would need to be considered, owing to their large size. The same can be said for the staging area, which in data warehouse architectures is usually a dedicated set of tables or separate database. The staging area that houses business metadata may end up being a combination of structures, including both flat files and a database. The enterprise metadata repository may also end up being a combination, consisting of a content management system and database. Databases are not the best technology to manage large documents and images/multimedia. Just as in data warehousing, the overall data architecture strategy for your metadata repository environment may be centralized or federated. The choice for the architecture will be largely dependent on the capabilities of the technology tools selected and the organization's funding capabilities, which were discussed in Chapter 5.

## 9.4    Delivery Considerations

In Chapter 8, we introduced some creative ideas for the delivery of business metadata to users. From an infrastructure perspective, it is important to note the general requirements for the possible delivery strategies.

### 9.4.1    *Delivery in the Legacy Environment*

You may want to deliver contextual information to legacy applications, like business term and/or form field definitions. Legacy environments were generally not created using open technology, so you may have to get very creative. First, are your applications home grown (developed in-house), or are they commercial off-the-shelf software (COTS)? Obviously, you have a better chance of modifying the applications directly to display business metadata like term definitions if the application was internally developed in-house. You may even be lucky enough to have someone still around who understands how this might be done!

Commercial products, on the other hand, are usually very closed systems. Some may provide extension options, but watch out! Sometimes commercial products will void their warranty or service agreement if you tinker with their internals.

### 9.4.1.1 Getting Creative

There may be a way to creatively deliver descriptive metadata in the transaction environment by not having to interface with the legacy applications—by using a portal.

We created a corporate dictionary/glossary for a client, which was using the AquaLogic portal set of tools. We created a very simple glossary search portlet that looks like Google's one fill-in-the-blank text box with a "Go!" button to the right (shown in Chapter 8). We placed the portlet on the intranet home page, so that it was available anywhere. An even better mechanism that we looked into (but did not implement because it required too much work) is to have an icon on the tray for the dictionary search mini-application. The problem with either method is that they are not context-sensitive; they do not recognize where the mouse or insertion point is at any given point in time.

If your home-grown application was developed fairly recently (in the last 5 to 10 years), then it may have a context-sensitive help mechanism built in. This mechanism can be hijacked for the purpose of business metadata. However, the downside to this arrangement is that someone has to write it, and this process sounds like "documentation." Neither users nor programmers get excited about this! There is a better way, as will be described later. First, however, we need to describe business metadata in the conventional BI environment.

### 9.4.2 Infrastructure Required for BI Environments

BI tools like the Cognos suite of products usually come with a means of delivering some descriptions to the user. For example, when browsing the tree of the business element names, hover text is available. In other words, when your mouse hovers over the business element name, it can display a definition or description that you provide. Cognos, however, has its own metadata repository and requires that this hover text be referenced from its repository. This means that if you have an enterprise metadata repository, you will have to build ETL to move the definitions from the enterprise repository into the tool's specialized repository.

### 9.4.3 Graphical Affinity

Special infrastructure may be required for certain delivery mechanisms—for example, graphical affinity and visual analytic tools. In Chapter 8, we illustrated several of these tools and discussed how they can enhance the display of both data and metadata to add clarity that only pictures can provide. "Heat maps" show the concentration of documents clustered around specific topics using colors like degrees of red and blue. Affinity diagrams can show how one person is tied to various cases or events in the system, and different roles can be indicated with different symbols.

In these cases, special tools such as IDS Visualization, Seepower by Compudigm, and VisuaLinks by Visual Analytics, Inc. may be needed, and expertise in these tools may also be required. Consultants like Jordan Rose, mentioned in Chapter 8, who have expert knowledge in a specific tool can jump start your project and get it up and running faster, because you don't need to factor in the learning curve. Companies like PPC specialize in development of the visual analytic application and also mentoring your personnel, so when new views of the data are required, your staff can create them.

### 9.4.4   New Web 2.0 Technology: Mashups!

A very exciting method is now available that can capture and deliver business metadata at the same time: mashups. Mashups are integrated Web applications that usually consist of a collection of different types of components and data, all displayed together on the same Web page. The really cool feature of these new tools that have recently been released is their ability to allow ordinary users—not just programmers—to create their own mashup, with no programming.

For example, BEA has released AquaLogic Pages, a product that provides all the infrastructure, toolkit, and plumbing needed to allow users to design and create their own conglomeration of components—from fetching rows directly from a database to calling a Web service, accessing an RSS feed, or even creating their own data table or publishing a preexisting Excel spreadsheet. On the same Web page, the user can link objects together so that they feed data to one another, also with no programming[1]. For example, the user, while analyzing a BI report showing declining sales in the month of January, can access a weather report for the dates in question, and place a comment on the page stating the reason for the decline in sales: It was a series of major snowstorms in that geographical area. In a similar manner, the same technique can be used to dynamically adjust inventory: A snowstorm is predicted for a certain geographic area, and a hardware retailer can stock up on sand, rock salt, and shovels to accommodate an influx of sales in the affected stores—all within the mashup. See Chapters 6 and 8 for more specifics on mashups.

---

[1]In order for this system to work, a developer is required in the beginning to develop templates that the users can plug and play. The template will have the "hooks" built into it that allow it to connect to other components to get/receive data. Once these templates are built, the users can link them together with other components, allowing them to send and receive data from these other components.

# 9.5 Integration

### 9.5.1 Business and Technical Metadata Integration

In order to manage the entire metadata environment, business and technical metadata must sometimes be integrated. Business changes will affect the technical environment, and the faster IT can respond to change, the more effectively the business can compete in the ever-changing marketplace. One of the first places that changes can be spotted proactively and managed is in the metadata environment.

Here is a hypothetical flow of events in the metadata environment:

✦ In a wiki on Marketing's portal, someone makes a comment that a new field is needed in one of Marketing's key applications. Marketing has determined that a new measure of ad campaign performance is needed that will help the department determine the effectiveness of campaigns move efficiently and respond faster.

✦ The Marketing Rep proposing the change creates a new business term in the glossary and provides the formula required in the definition to compute the measure.

✦ IT determines where the data currently resides through analysis of technical metadata, using the formula entered in the glossary as a reference; the metadata repository is used to find the data elements that are tied to the business terms used in the definition's formula. IT creates a new mashup, displaying a database query showing examples of the actual data and posing questions on the wiki, seeking verification that the data is correct.

✦ Meanwhile, Marketing itself has created a mashup, accessing data from the Marketing application and creating the required field. This not only answers the immediate need, but also helps IT further understand the requirements of the field, as well as be able to pose more sophisticated questions regarding the source data used as input for the computation.

✦ IT is then able to gather requirements in an asynchronous way, the requirements are recorded in the conversation back and forth, and clarity can be reached more rapidly. Meanwhile, Marketing is not held hostage while IT develops the field, because Marketing uses its own field on the mashup.

The integration described here is quite complex:

✦ It requires that users understand what the data in their source systems mean, which dictates that definitions exist for data elements (the data dictionary, which defines system data elements, is not the same thing as a business glossary, which defines business terms).

✦ It requires that impact analysis be performed from a business metadata description.

✦ It requires software that helps businesspeople to create their own mashups.

✦ It may even be possible, providing the right integrated infrastructure exists, to generate a data model from well-placed business terms in the glossary.

### 9.5.1.1 Example of an Integrated Metadata Repository Tool

Tools are now starting to become available that provide the integration necessary between business and technical metadata, and also promote a reasonable way to store some business metadata. IBM, like many companies, has embarked on an acquisition frenzy in order to be the first on the block with a truly integrated metadata repository across many tools. The following pieces are now integrated in their metadata repository, out of the box:

✦ Business glossary

✦ Data profile data

✦ ETL

✦ Data quality data

✦ Data models (and data element definitions)

✦ Physical schema

A data analyst can look at the glossary and display a list of data elements that represent that business term in the systems throughout the enterprise. Data profiling results for a given data element can be shown side by side with the business definition in order to determine whether the data accurately reflects what the definition indicates. In the same way, a data warehouse field can be compared with the business term definition, and if they are not synchronized, ETL jobs can be examined to determine what the problem might be. Although most of this analysis will be done by technical people, the business is the ultimate beneficiary of this integration, because they will be able to directly benefit from more accurate data, and more transparent analysis with better traceability. See Chapter 8 for what this integration looks like in IBM's Information Server.

### 9.5.2 Integration and Administrative Source of Record: Conflict Resolution

Metadata resides all over the enterprise, in many different places throughout the Corporate Information Factory, as we have discussed throughout this book. Just as in a data warehouse, conflicts may arise when metadata is extracted from multiple sources. One type of metadata may have different values, but it is supposed to be the same piece of metadata. This happens in the context of master data management (MDM) projects all the time, when Customer data is located in five different systems; which is the best? Which is the "Gold Copy"? In the case of metadata, would all values go in the metadata repository or only in the "Gold Copy"?

Data elements are an example of this situation. Suppose you have a data element called "Recognized Revenue," which shows up in three different systems, each time with a different definition. Which definition is correct? As you can imagine, these three data elements may actually represent entirely different concepts, which is another issue that your metadata repository must be able to handle. But suppose they really are the same thing; which definition is the best one? Which do you use?

The usual solution to that problem is for you to include each definition along with each data element, but the universal data concept will need its own definition.

But what about stuff that is supposed to be the same metadata, which shows up in different places, and one gets updated and all the other locations are not kept in synch? Definitions maintained in an Excel spreadsheet are one example. The definitions are supposed to be created in the spreadsheet and copied to the database design tool, but a new data modeler joins the staff that doesn't know anything about the spreadsheet. She maintains the definitions in the database design tool. The same situation often happens across tools; the definition may be created and maintained in both Cognos and the database design tool. Which takes precedence?

One way to help resolve this problem is to create a CRUD (Create Read Update Delete) matrix illustrating tools and files that maintain metadata objects. See Table 9.1 for an example.

We have included a file entitled "Metadata system of record table example" on the Web site for this book, www.mkp.com/businessmetadata, as an example of a table that can be used to define the creation and maintenance life-cycle processes and tools for a set of metadata objects.

### 9.5.3 Integration Technologies

We have compared the metadata environment to a data warehouse and discussed the use of a physical metadata repository. This approach, like the data

**Table 9.1** Metadata system of record matrix

| Meta Object | Strategic Modeling Tool | Tactical Modeling Tool | DBMS Tool | Data Integration Tool | Reporting Tool |
|---|---|---|---|---|---|
| Entity Name | C | | | | |
| Entity Type | C | | | | |
| Entity Definition | C | U | | | R |
| Entity Scope | C | | | | |
| Entity Active Ind | C | U | | | |
| Entity Logical Business Rule | C | U | | U | R |

warehouse, has many advantages, such as the existence of a single physical source of record that can be always counted upon to be up-to-date. Here is another possible integration strategy.

### 9.5.3.1   Federated Metadata

Another approach to integrated metadata management is virtual integration, known as "Federated." In this approach, a user requests metadata and an integration engine, using conflict resolution rules and source information, goes out in real time, sources the requested data, and reconciles it on the fly. Federated tools—MetaMatrix, for example—have the ability to interface with tools in both directions: get and receive metadata. For example, these tools would be able to get data definitions from the database design tool and feed them to the Cognos repository for display when viewing a data mart, all virtually with no need for a physical repository.

### 9.5.3.2   Business Metadata as a Service

Software services, or Service-Oriented Architectures, are becoming a popular way to obtain integrated data. A data service, in this case a metadata service, is invoked, data is obtained, and all the mechanics are done by the service, independent of hardware or software platform. Services can be invoked by software programs internally or by businesspeople if an interface is provided to them.

Business metadata service delivery can be used either with or without a metadata repository; it is a data delivery mechanism. If services are desired, the appropriate infrastructure, centralized or federated, must be in place to support the delivery of the service.

# 9.6 Administrative Issues

This section addresses a few of the administration issues that will have infrastructure ramifications.

### 9.6.1 Administration Functionality Requirements

The metadata infrastructure must account for how the metadata environment will be managed and administered. These issues include:

+ How security will be managed both for the access of metadata and the access to the reporting environment

+ How the operational activities of metadata governance, acquisition, configuration, versioning, change management, and the like, will be administered

+ How workflow and metadata quality checks, audits, and errors will be administered

+ How the program code will be managed and upgrades or new releases will be managed

+ How the metadata will be duplicated/replicated, how it will be backed-up, and the processes to support disaster recovery

+ How the programs will be operationally scheduled, monitored, and debugged if necessary

Use cases are an effective means of documenting the requirements and the actions that will need to be monitored to administer the metadata environment. These issues may result in additional hardware, software, or resource requirements.

### 9.6.2 Do You Keep History?

Should you maintain history on each metadata object? The answer will probably vary, depending on the type of business metadata. For example, you may want to keep history of business term definitions. The most obvious type of business metadata that you definitely want to keep are data profiling statistics, because they show how data quality is showing improvement or degradation over time.

Those familiar with data warehouse development will recognize that the same set of issues that are used to address "Slowly Changing Dimensions" apply here as well. Those issues include:

✦ Is the requirement to only keep and report the latest value for the metadata object? In this case we "overwrite" the value of the metadata and thus, only the most recent value can be communicated.

✦ Is the requirement to keep a limited number of values for the metadata? This may be the case where the need is to keep the current version and one previous version of the metadata value. In this case, we must copy the current value and overwrite the previous value, and then we must also overwrite the current value with the new value of the metadata.

✦ Is the requirement to keep all values for the metadata? In this case, we must keep all the "history" of the values for the metadata object. The requirement to keep history on the changes to metadata is often critical to business processes and communications. However, the ability to achieve this requirement will be directly dependent on the capabilities of the hardware and software infrastructure.

# 9.7  Metadata Repository: "Buy or Build"

The first question a CIO asks very early in the planning process is, "Do we buy or build it ourselves?" Acquiring the licenses to achieve many of the things we have discussed in this chapter is easily a mid-six-figure endeavor. However, the software licensing price for some products can be less than five figures, or less than $10,000. So how do we make the decision and arrive at an answer to the question? Some of the issues that impact the decision can be funding availability and organizational/cultural-related. Organizations that normally purchase software solutions will have a natural tendency to consider the "buy" alternative. Conversely, organizations that tend to develop software internally will tend to consider the "build" alternative. In either case, we recommend that the organization fully define its metadata integration requirements prior to making the decision. For example, in the beginning of the chapter, we provided a data model to help you hone in on the specific business metadata you are interested in tracking. We have developed some tools to help you determine your metadata requirements on our Web site: www.mkp.com/businessmetadata.

### 9.7.1 Considerations in Making the Decision

Some organizations know they don't have the capital funds available, and they also know that the metadata project must begin. In that case, the decision should be easy; having no capital allocation of funds means we must build it. Funding and timeframe pressures often force the buy or build decision to be easier.

The following is by no means an all-inclusive list, but the decision to buy or build can include these considerations:

✦ Are the capital funds available for a purchase?

✦ Does the organization prefer to purchase solutions, or does it prefer to build solutions to fit their specific needs?

✦ Does the organization have the skills and resources to complete a build solution? This can be a challenge for most organizations attempting metadata at an enterprise level.

✦ Can a compromise be achieved that limits the project scope so that the resources of the organization can achieve a successful build solution?

✦ Does a solution have to be implemented in a timeframe that can only be achieved with a buy solution?

✦ Are there buy solutions available that are within our funding capabilities and closely match our functional requirements?

Note that even if the decision is to buy, a model of the desired metadata is essential to evaluate each particular package.

### 9.7.2 Special Challenges of Business Metadata

Throughout this book we discuss the special challenges of business metadata. Hopefully, by now the reader understands that business metadata is primarily unstructured and has complex relationships that are far closer to a network model rather than a relational model. When you evaluate commercially available products, you will need to realize that most, if not all, of these products do not support all business metadata out of the box. Thus, these products may not even have structures to contain and maintain business metadata. Even IBM, which is farther along in terms of an integrated business and technical metadata repository, doesn't support business rules (to our knowledge, at this writing). Therefore, when you purchase a product, you will most likely have to extend the repository to support business metadata objects and life cycle. However, in order to technically integrate business metadata with your technical metadata, a common integration structure must exist. Again, having a data model of your requirements is crucial to this process.

# 9.8 The Build Considerations

Building an integrated metadata solution is a significant and complex custom software development project. These efforts can be the equivalent of a significant data warehousing project (addressing data rather than metadata). However, business dictionary, ontology, or taxonomy build projects can have considerably less complexity and risk.

We have included an example project plan for the build option on the Web site for this book. Although good books have been written concerning how to build technical metadata solutions, you should realize that none of these books focuses on business metadata. It is recommended that you refer to these books to get a good working knowledge of the task at hand, realizing that you may have to accommodate some of the complexities we have discussed in this chapter. We have included these publications in our list of recommended reading.

# 9.9 The Third Alternative: Use a Preexisting Repository

There is a third alternative in addition to buy versus build: Use a repository from an existing tool. For example, many data warehouse tools use their own repository to get their jobs done:

- ETL tools (Informatica, IBM, Ab Initio, etc.)

- BI tools (Cognos, Business Objects, etc.)

- Data profiling tools (Informatica IDE, SAS Data Flux, etc.)

- Enterprise Information Integration (EII) tools (Metamatrix, Composite, etc.)

- Enterprise Application Integration (EAI) tools and Service Oriented Architecture (SOA) tools (BEA, IBM WebSphere, Tibco, etc.)

This solution can be a workable one because since a repository already exists, you don't have to build it from scratch. However, you must remember that when you build any extension to a preexisting product, you must be careful because the product is subject to change. It is always recommended that you use the APIs (such as database views) provided by the vendor and not link your structures directly with the underlying structures of the product's database. In addition, it is advisable that you isolate your structures in some way from the product's structures in order to minimize the impact of upgrades and prevent your structures from being destroyed. For example, if you are using Oracle, put your structures in another schema and use a dblink (database link) to link your structures to the product's structures.

# 9.10 Summary

There is no "one size fits all" infrastructure for metadata, especially business metadata. You must pay close attention to your specific requirements and focal areas, and select an infrastructure that supports your needs. Requirements gathering is always a best practice, regardless of which option you choose.

We have discussed different issues that an overarching metadata infrastructure must address. These issues include delivery methods and specialized delivery requirements. We have also laid out some guidelines for evaluating and selecting an approach to the metadata repository, outlining three alternatives:

+ Buy a commercially available product.

+ Build your own repository.

+ Retrofit an existing product.

All along the way, we have pointed out some of the special considerations that business metadata presents, and we have highlighted the fact that even if you choose to buy a product, you will still most likely have to end up extending it in some way to support business metadata. At this writing, commercially available product support for business metadata is just emerging; please check our Web site, www.mkp.com/businessmetadata, for updates as new products become available.

# Data and Information Quality as Business Metadata

## 10.1 Introduction

Data and information quality, by its very nature, must involve both business and technical metadata. Business metadata is needed to communicate with the business-people and to provide the business with barometers as to where they are in the data quality spectrum at any point in time. Consequently, technical metadata is necessary to carry out the mission of the data quality initiative and implement the plan. In this chapter, we focus mainly on the business metadata part of data quality but also touch upon technical metadata as it bears on the business metadata. We will see that it is very important that business and technical metadata work together to deliver information quality.

We will cover several other topics concerning information quality, notably the importance of a business dictionary in ensuring quality data, and how an information quality methodology becomes part of business metadata, in addition to its guiding the production of work products, which are also themselves business metadata. Lastly, the delivery of information quality metrics results is critical business metadata, and this chapter will illustrate several techniques for this delivery.

# 10.2   Definition and Purpose of Data and Information Quality

Data quality has been an important information management concern for the last several decades. In recent years, some high-profile data quality incidents have brought the agencies involved some unwanted attention and even notoriety in the national and international news—for example:

+ The bombing of the Chinese Embassy: Out-of-date map

+ Mars Lander: Wrong unit of measure

Data quality metrics should be considered a type of business metadata: It is information about the data. The data quality metrics will tell the businessperson about that data's quality and reliability. However, before we discuss whether data quality is business metadata, we need to set out some definitions.

The following definitions come from a glossary authored by the International Association for Information and Data Quality (IAIDQ), a nonprofit "professional society of people passionate about improving information and data quality" (IAIDQ, July 20, 2006).

## 10.2.1   *Distinction between Data and Information*

Data, as we pointed out in Chapter 1, is raw representation of facts; it needs metadata to supply the context for it to be useful. Here is IAIDQ's definition of data:

**Data:** (1) Symbols, numbers, or other representation of facts; (2) the raw material from which information is produced when it is put in a context that gives it meaning. (IAIDQ, December 25, 2006)

Information, a closely related concept, is data in context. Here is IAIDQ's definition of information:

**Information:** (1) Data in context, i.e., the meaning given to data or the interpretation of data based on its context; (2) the finished product as a result of processing, presentation and interpretation of data. (IAIDQ, December 25, 2006)

Clearly, information is data plus metadata, and perhaps it is specifically business metadata that adds the context. Therefore:

Information = Data + Business Metadata

### 10.2.2  Adding Quality

Next, we can add the quality component. Interestingly enough, "data quality" is not in IAIDQ's glossary; only "information quality" is listed there. If you consider data to be raw facts, it makes more sense to discuss information quality than data quality. Information takes into account the context of data, and quality makes sense only in regards to a context. Remember our discussion in prior chapters, especially Chapter 1, about the number 7. Without any context, it is just a number, and a number by itself has no quality associated with it. Therefore, although "data quality" is a common term used in the discipline of data management, this chapter will hereafter refer to "information quality."

Here is IAIDQ's definition of information quality (three separate definitions are given, one having two components):

**Information quality:** (1) Consistently meeting all knowledge worker and end-customer expectations in all quality characteristics of the information products and services required to accomplish the enterprise mission (internal knowledge worker) or personal objectives (end customer). (2) The degree to which information consistently meets the requirements and expectations of all knowledge workers who require it to perform their processes. (Larry English, noted data and information quality expert and author)

**Information Quality:** The fitness for use of information; information that meets the requirements of its authors, users, and administrators. (Martin Eppler, co-founder of IAIDQ)(IAIDQ, December 25, 2006)

The notion of "meeting business requirements" is common to all three of these definitions. The business ultimately defines the information quality requirements.

## 10.3  Information Quality as Business Metadata

If the purpose of information quality is to meet business expectations, then it is important that the business should be kept apprised of information quality and its progress toward meeting the requirements set by the business. Therefore, there is an ongoing obligation of information delivery. However, there is an even more basic information component: The businesspeople need to agree on the information quality requirements, and communicate these requirements in such a way as to translate them into executable checks and actionable plans.

Chapter 4 discussed the importance of clear communication and made the case that business metadata can help clarify things and enhance the communication with rigorous definitions and contextual information. Chapter 11 will discuss the human/computer interaction and note how an extra layer of complexity is created owing to both having their own set of semantics. Figure 10.1 illustrates the barrier in communications between human and machine.

The translation is very important here. First, as stated earlier, the business has to state the information quality requirements clearly and unambiguously, once the requirements have been agreed upon (which in and of itself, is a daunting task and is certainly not for the faint at heart!). Then, these requirements have to be translated into test criteria (technical query language) to gauge how much of the data is noncompliant. Lastly, a plan has to be determined for showing how to fix the data, keeping in mind the business processes that generate the data in the first place.

As you can see, this process is laden with translation challenges back and forth:

+ What are the requirements? (Business)

+ How much of the data is "bad"? (Technical, then translates back to business)

+ Plans should be made to fix the data quality to meet the requirements for quality (It starts out as business and then involves both business and technical aspects.)

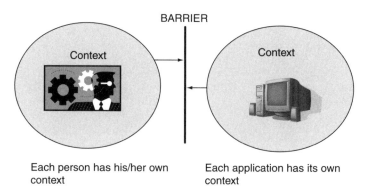

**Figure 10.1** Human/Computer Communication Barrier.

### 10.3.1 The Interaction of Business and Technical Metadata

As you can see, both business and technical metadata are required for information quality. Information quality requirements start out as business metadata, but usually the sleuthing and discovery work done beforehand consists of technical metadata; this is research into how bad the data is. Next the current state of affairs needs to be translated back to the business so business analysts and executives can understand its business ramifications. Business then needs to determine what is an acceptable level of information quality and this can then be translated back to technical validation routines. These routines need to be run periodically and reported back to the businessperson, in terms that the businessperson will understand—for example: "How are we doing in reaching our goals?" "Are we making progress in a positive direction?"

Technical and business metadata therefore work hand in hand in producing the results of information quality expectations, goals, monitoring, and achieving the goals over time. In order to achieve better information quality, both business and technical metadata are required; you cannot have one without the other. Furthermore, they must work in concert; if they do not, an important part of the equation will be missing. If you have too much emphasis on the technical metadata with no translation back to the business, then you will ultimately lose the support and sponsorship of the business: Why should the business fund the information quality effort? To them it can be a black hole if they don't know what is going on and what it is being achieved for the business. On the contrary, if no technical metadata is involved and there is no technical measurement and monitoring, no one will know how bad it is or whether any progress is being made. Therefore, a partnering of both technical and business metadata should be set up in order to accomplish anything in information quality.

#### 10.3.1.1 Technical Metadata: The Role of Data Profiling

The first step is to see what you have, what the baseline condition of the data is, so that you can create intelligent requirements. A technique called data profiling can be used for this purpose. Data profiling is a methodical, repeatable, and metrics-based evaluation of data. Typical measurements included in such an assessment are:

✦ Number of rows examined

✦ Number of unique values found (which can tell us business rule violations)

✦ Percentage of uniqueness (which indicates the presence or absence of a unique identifier)

✦ Domain analysis

✦ Minimum and maximum values found (which is an early indicator of anomalies in the field, since bad data are often "outliers")

✦ Size of the field

✦ Number and percentage of null values

✦ Datatype of values in the field

✦ Pattern of the data (numeric, uppercase/lower case, etc.)

Figure 10.2 shows the first report that data profiling provides for a table. It can be regarded as a 25,000-foot view of the data, an overview of data in a table.

This overview can be very helpful and can help you pinpoint possible difficulties in the data; it can also help you figure out which columns will require the most analysis and will likely present your greatest problems. For example, in Figure 10.2, notice that the zip field is shown and that the minimum value is not a zip code. This detail tells you right away that you will probably have trouble with this field.

But this report is not very friendly to the businessperson. For example, take the number of distinct values in a given column. When you see 100% distinct values in a specific field, you have an indication that the field is a primary key. Most nondata modelers don't understand this, but you can explain it by saying

| | Attribute | # Distinc | # Record | Distinct Ratio | Documented | Inferred Data Typ | Data Type Flag | Documen | Inferred N | Inferred Min Value | Inferred Max Value |
|---|---|---|---|---|---|---|---|---|---|---|---|
| 1 | op_oper_nbr | 19058 | 19066 | 0.9996 | CHAR(6) | INTEGER | Incompatible | Null OK | Not Null | 21000 | 498441 |
| 2 | om_name1 | 16824 | 19066 | 0.8824 | CHAR(20) | VARCHAR(20, 0) | Convertible | Null OK | Not Null | "C" PUNCH RANCH | ZZZ RESVERED |
| 3 | om_name2 | 3712 | 19066 | 0.1947 | CHAR(20) | VARCHAR(20, 0) | Convertible | Null OK | Null OK | "BUDDY" AND BARBARA | ZOILA |
| 4 | om_auth_rep | 6463 | 19066 | 0.3385 | CHAR(20) | VARCHAR(20, 0) | Convertible | Null OK | Null OK | % RUSS MILLER | ZWICKER, ELDON |
| 5 | om_c_o_name | 5778 | 19066 | 0.3031 | CHAR(20) | VARCHAR(20, 0) | Convertible | Null OK | Null OK | # 414 | ZX LAND & CATTLE |
| 6 | om_prnt_appl | 2 | 19066 | 0.0001 | CHAR(1) | CHAR(1) | Identical | Null OK | Null OK | N | Y |
| 7 | om_prefer_cd | 3 | 19066 | 0.0002 | CHAR(2) | SMALLINT | Incompatible | Null OK | Not Null | 3 | 15 |
| 8 | om_adr_stret | 12456 | 19066 | 0.6533 | CHAR(20) | VARCHAR(20, 0) | Convertible | Null OK | Null OK | # 25 LAFAYETTE LOOP | YOST ROUTE |
| 9 | om_adr_city | 2435 | 19066 | 0.1277 | CHAR(20) | VARCHAR(20, 0) | Convertible | Null OK | Null OK | ..... | ZZZ RESERVED |
| 10 | om_adr_st | 45 | 19066 | 0.0024 | CHAR(2) | CHAR(2) | Identical | Null OK | Not Null | AK | WV |
| 11 | om_adr_zipe | 2783 | 19066 | 0.1460 | CHAR(5) | INTEGER | Incompatible | Null OK | Not Null | 0 | 99999 |
| 12 | om_adr_zipb | 770 | 19066 | 0.0404 | CHAR(4) | SMALLINT | Incompatible | Null OK | Null OK | 0 | 9999 |
| 13 | om_phone | 10363 | 19066 | 0.5435 | CHAR(12) | VARCHAR(12, 0) | Convertible | Null OK | Null OK | (208)3-62012 | ~ |
| 14 | om_eff_dt | 1697 | 19066 | 0.0890 | CHAR(8) | INTEGER | Incompatible | Null OK | Not Null | 1011993 | 12311999 |
| 15 | om_exp_dt | 1282 | 19066 | 0.0672 | CHAR(8) | INTEGER | Incompatible | Null OK | Null OK | 1011996 | 12312010 |
| 16 | om_pl_retnd | 2 | 19066 | 0.0001 | CHAR(1) | CHAR(1) | Identical | Null OK | Not Null | N | Y |
| 17 | om_undef_1 | 481 | 19066 | 0.0252 | CHAR(6) | VARCHAR(6, 0) | Convertible | Null OK | Null OK | * | YUMA |
| 18 | om_undef_2 | 394 | 19066 | 0.0207 | CHAR(6) | VARCHAR(6, 0) | Convertible | Null OK | Null OK | #4531 | YES |
| 19 | om_undef_3 | 439 | 19066 | 0.0230 | CHAR(6) | VARCHAR(6, 0) | Convertible | Null OK | Null OK | &14546 | ~~ |
| 20 | om_perm_prt | 2534 | 19066 | 0.1329 | CHAR(8) | DATETIME YEAR T | Convertible | Null OK | Null OK | 1979-01-22 00:00:00.00 | 2000-10-31 00:00:00.00 |
| 21 | om_base_lse | 497 | 19066 | 0.0261 | CHAR(8) | DATETIME YEAR T | Convertible | Null OK | Null OK | 1995-02-28 00:00:00.00 | 2000-01-02 00:00:00.00 |
| 22 | om_graz_nbr | 20 | 19066 | 0.0010 | CHAR(2) | SMALLINT | Incompatible | Null OK | Null OK | 1 | 98 |
| 23 | om_appl_prt | 1098 | 19066 | 0.0576 | CHAR(8) | DATETIME YEAR T | Convertible | Null OK | Null OK | 1980-01-04 00:00:00.00 | 2000-10-27 00:00:00.00 |
| 24 | om_bill_cnt | 101 | 19066 | 0.0053 | CHAR(2) | SMALLINT | Incompatible | Null OK | Null OK | 0 | 99 |
| 25 | om_perm_hol | 1 | 19066 | 0.0001 | CHAR(1) | CHAR(1) | Identical | Null OK | Null OK | Y | Y |
| 26 | om_chg_dt | 0 | 19066 | 0.0 | CHAR(8) | | | Null OK | Null OK | | |
| 27 | state | 10 | 19066 | 0.0005 | CHAR(2) | CHAR(2) | Identical | Null OK | Not Null | AZ | WY |
| 28 | office | 63 | 19066 | 0.0033 | CHAR(3) | SMALLINT | Incompatible | Null OK | Not Null | 10 | 90 |

Not a zip code!

**Figure 10.2** Data Profiling Table Report.

it provides a means to single out a given row of data and know for sure that the data belongs to a specific instance. If the table doesn't have a field with 100% distinct values, it has integrity problems.

Data profiling tools further enable you to drill down and get reports on each column, like pattern analysis and a value/frequency report (see Figure 10.3). This particular report is sorted by frequency, showing the most numerous values first.

| | Value | Frequency | % Distribution |
|---|---|---|---|
| 1 | RESERVED NUMBER | 548 | 2.8742 |
| 2 | ZZZ RESERVED NUMBER | 31 | 0.1626 |
| 3 | HOLDING NUMBER | 12 | 0.0629 |
| 4 | NATURE CONSERVANCY | 10 | 0.0524 |
| 5 | RESERVE NUMBER | 10 | 0.0524 |
| 6 | RAFTOPOULOS BROTHE | 8 | 0.0420 |
| 7 | BYNER CATTLE COMPAN | 7 | 0.0367 |
| 8 | RUMPH RANCH PARTNER | 7 | 0.0367 |
| 9 | ALLEN, EDWIN "BUD" | 6 | 0.0315 |
| 10 | CHASE FARMS | 6 | 0.0315 |
| 11 | SIMS LIVESTOCK | 6 | 0.0315 |
| 12 | BAIRD, JOHN | 5 | 0.0262 |
| 13 | DENNY LAND & CATTLE | 5 | 0.0262 |
| 14 | HUNT OIL COMPANY | 5 | 0.0262 |
| 15 | INDIAN CREEK RANCH | 5 | 0.0262 |
| 16 | MACKAY, DONALD AND | 5 | 0.0262 |
| 17 | MARLEY, MARK | 5 | 0.0262 |
| 18 | NATURE CONSERVANCY | 5 | 0.0262 |
| 19 | NAVAJO NATION, THE | 5 | 0.0262 |
| 20 | ROSS, WARREN | 5 | 0.0262 |
| 21 | SANFORD, NORMAN AN | 5 | 0.0262 |
| 22 | SMITH, KENNETH P. | 5 | 0.0262 |
| 23 | THOMAN PRIMARY TRUS | 5 | 0.0262 |
| 24 | TRANEL, NED | 5 | 0.0262 |
| 25 | ANDERSON, JAMES | 4 | 0.0210 |
| 26 | ANIMAS FOUNDATION | 4 | 0.0210 |
| 27 | AXTELL RANCHES LLC | 4 | 0.0210 |

**Figure 10.3**    Value Frequency Report.

But what do these statistics have to do with the business? First, they can tell the businesspeople at a glance if the data is reasonable. Do the columns in the table really represent the data they are supposed to represent? Second, they can help the businesspeople see which columns are not compliant with business expectations and they can act as a springboard to defining the information quality requirements.

But the big question is, can you hand a businessperson the reports in Figures 10.2 and 10.3? Probably not. In fact, we recommend a working review session to provide context, both business and technical metadata, to the reviewers of the profiling report. This is an example of technical metadata that needs to be transformed into business metadata; that is, some interpretation is necessary.

### 10.3.1.2   Translating Technical Metadata into Business Metadata

The results of data profiling need to be explained in business language. What do these reports mean to the business? Here a means of translation is required.

The following is an excerpt from an actual report representing a translation of data profiling output for one column in an overall table report. The column is called "cmty_code," which stands for "community code." The report begins with a definition of the field, supplied by the current system that contained the data. As you can see, the quality of the definition is not great; this is typical.

---

**Cmty_code**

**Overall Field Summary**

It is not clear what this field represents or what a proper format for this code should be. The majority of this field's data profile report is about discovery of what this code is supposed to look like: What is the valid domain for this data?

---

**Definition**

At the Survey level, the common community code used with CMTY_CLASSIF_CODE to link to a plant community in ISMS_CMTY_TYPES.

**Additional Description**: Use GIS or Vegetation Data. If not available, use best judgment based on a field examination. See Additional Description for Overstory_size_class field regarding survey areas and significant differences in habitat areas.

## Null/Data: Not Available Counts

| Value | Frequency | %Distribution |
|---|---|---|
| Multiple Communities | 23 | 0.5262 |
| Other | 1 | 0.0229 |

| Unspecified | 2722 | 62.2741 |
|---|---|---|

This field seems to have 62% of the data representing "Data Not Available" or "Unknown/Unspecified." The field does not allow NULLs (which is the usual way to represent unknown values in a database), but there are three values that might represent an unknown value or a "catch-all" classification. Note that there is only one occurrence of "Other."

## Range of Values

| Inferred Minimum Value | Inferred Maximum Value |
|---|---|
| CAC111 | WFR |

Since it is difficult to determine the definition of valid data in this field, it is also difficult to look at the minimum or maximum value in this field and detect if there exists any invalid data. The minimum and maximum values show the different formats of the data; most of the data begins with one or more uppercase letters, followed most of the time (but not all) by one or more digits. This is further shown in the Patterns section which follows.

## Patterns Identified

The pattern that appears the most is reflective of one distinct value "Unspecified," which is in mixed case. It appears that most other values are in uppercase and usually (but not always) followed by a digit string.

| Pattern | Primary | # Matches | % Conforming |
|---------|---------|-----------|--------------|
| X(11) | Primary | 2722 | 62.27 |
| UUU999 | | 967 | 22.12 |
| UU | | 349 | 7.98 |
| UUU | | 134 | 3.07 |
| UUU9(5) | | 63 | 1.44 |
| U(6)99 | | 43 | 0.98 |
| UU9UUU99 | | 35 | 0.80 |
| X(8)bX(11) | | 23 | 0.53 |
| UUUU | | 18 | 0.41 |
| UUUU9U99 | | 12 | 0.27 |

This is the single value "Unspecified" occurring 62% of the time

The Inferred Patterns shown above use the following special symbols:

✦ X=Upper or Lower case character

✦ U=Upper case character

✦ L=Lower case character

✦ C=Any character (including digits)

✦ b=blank

✦ (7)=number of times the previous character repeats; for example U(7) represents the occurrence of 7 characters of either upper or lower case.

✦ 9= Any digit character 0–9

## High/Medium/Low Frequency Values

| | Value | Frequency | %Distribution |
|----|-------|-----------|---------------|
| 1 | Unspecified | 2722 | 62.2741 |
| 2 | CH | 222 | 5.0789 |
| 3 | CHS125 | 141 | 3.2258 |
| 4 | DFR | 99 | 2.2645 |
| 5 | CF | 96 | 2.1963 |
| 6 | CHS124 | 61 | 1.3956 |
| 7 | CHC221 | 56 | 1.2812 |
| 8 | CDO00000 | 54 | 1.2354 |
| 9 | CHS351 | 43 | 0.9838 |
| 10 | CHS117 | 42 | 0.9609 |
| 11 | CDS521 | 34 | 0.7779 |
| 12 | CDC521 | 33 | 0.7550 |
| 13 | CHS352 | 32 | 0.7321 |
| 14 | CDOHMA11 | 31 | 0.7092 |
| 15 | CDS522 | 31 | 0.7092 |
| 16 | KMC | 29 | 0.6635 |
| 17 | CDC421 | 28 | 0.6406 |
| 18 | CWS525 | 28 | 0.6406 |
| 19 | Multiple Communities | 23 | 0.5262 |
| 20 | CDH524 | 22 | 0.5033 |

Mixed case

No digits after the upper case characters

Includes a string of zeroes

Three upper case characters followed by digits

The table above shows the top 20 most frequently occurring values. Again, this report shows this field's lack of format standardization. Is this reasonable, from a business perspective? The code seems to mostly consist of two or three uppercase characters followed by several digits, but sometimes it consists of an uppercase character string only with no digits following. Some codes are mixed case. Some codes have a string of zeroes at the end.

Many values only occur once, and they reflect the same inconsistent format as the highest occurring values (see table below). The value "Other" occurs only once, and may not be useful.

| Value | Frequency | %Distribution |
|---|---|---|
| CHS521 | 1 | 0.0229 |
| CHS609 | 1 | 0.0229 |
| CLC521 | 1 | 0.0229 |
| CMC221 | 1 | 0.0229 |
| CMS215 | 1 | 0.0229 |
| CMS354 | 1 | 0.0229 |
| CPP00000 | 1 | 0.0229 |
| CR | 1 | 0.0229 |
| CSF121 | 1 | 0.0229 |
| CWC721 | 1 | 0.0229 |
| CWF541 | 1 | 0.0229 |
| CWS521 | 1 | 0.0229 |
| HO | 1 | 0.0229 |
| HTO00000 | 1 | 0.0229 |
| Other | 1 | 0.0229 |

### 10.3.1.3  Analysis of the Report

The report has various sections explaining facets of the profiling data. Generally, these areas include:

- **Definition:** What the field means. This can be obtained from the system documentation, but its quality will vary

- **NULL/Data not Available Counts:** This examines data representing "unknown" or "not available." NULL counts are included, as well as any other special codes or text values like N/A that probably mean the same thing as "not available." In a numeric field, zero or a string of nines (9999) often mean the same thing as NULL. For example, in the report, the value "Unspecified" occurred in 62% of the data. This is a high percentage; is it reasonable?

✦ **Range of Values:** Often, outliers exist in the minimum or maximum value spectrum of the data and can represent anomalies in the data, for example, a code like 9999 in a numeric field often shows up as a maximum value in a field. The example provided in the report shows no particular outliers. However, some choice ones are shown in Figure 10.2: As we pointed out earlier, look at the zip code field called om_adr_zipa. Notice that neither the minimum nor maximum values are valid zip codes: the minimum is 0 and the maximum is 99999.

✦ **Patterns Identified:** Sometimes data validity can be spotted by looking at the pattern or format of the data. For example, phone numbers that are not in one of several formats like (999)999-9999 or 999-999-9999 are probably not valid.

✦ **High/Medium/Low Frequency Values:** Data profiling tools can show a frequency analysis of all distinct values and the number of occurrences of each. This is helpful in determining specific anomalies and showing how pervasive the problems are. In the report, the inconsistency of format is shown for the top 20 values, and the question is posed to the business: Is this reasonable, or is the code supposed to have a set format like three alpha characters and three digits? If the latter is true, then much of the data has problems.

The report interprets the profiling results and turns the technical metadata into business metadata, so the businesspeople can quickly pinpoint where the problems lie. Profiling by itself does not indicate where the problems are; it must be interpreted into business language, and then the business can apply its business acumen to the raw data and determine the level of quality that exists.

## 10.4 Setting Expectations for the Data: The Dictionary's Role

Good, unambiguous, understandable and robust definitions are at the heart of information quality. It is easy to see why: If you haven't clearly defined each field, how do you know what the contents of that field should be? The sample report interpreting profiling results in the last section shows this very clearly.

Definitions should adequately set the expectations for what data should exist in the field. Sometimes definitions should reference a specific domain or range of valid values. For example, Project Status Code is defined as a code that indicates the state of the project in a specific moment of time; valid states are: I-Initiated; P-Pending; F-Funded; A-Active; C-Closed; S-Suspended; X-Canceled. This definition sets the standard for what is expected in the field, and if any value other than the ones specified is found in the field, then it can be considered problem data that does not conform to business expectations.

Sometimes there may be complex interdependencies between fields. When this occurs, the dependencies may or may not be spelled out in the definitions. In this case, business rules will often dictate the dependencies, which will be the key for determining information quality. But the large majority of anomalous data can be detected by simply comparing the profile results with the definitions for each field. This is why the definition of each field should be included in the profile report to the business user. If the definitions are not clear, this will become evident right away because the comparison between the definition and the profile results will be inconclusive. It will also bring home to the businessperson the importance of good definitions!

# 10.5 Information Quality Methodology

This is a book on business metadata, and not on information quality. Even so, we felt it was important to discuss briefly the role of an information quality methodology in the context of business metadata. Any sort of data management strategy or plan should be considered business metadata, because it should involve the business. After all, if information is a valuable asset to the enterprise, the management of that asset involves both the business and IT, and business metadata is at the core of managing information quality. As we saw earlier in this chapter, only the business itself can define what high-quality information looks like, in the context of its individual business. So the methodology, strategy, and plan for turning poor quality data into valid, accurate, consistent, complete, timely, accessible data with integrity are by necessity business metadata.

The purpose of an information quality methodology is to outline the procedures for performing information quality analysis and mitigation efforts, independent of any specific technology. It provides a repeatable technique that can be used for many different kinds of information quality problems throughout the enterprise.

Figure 10.4 shows an example of an information quality methodology called The Cornerstones of Data Quality™ by Westridge Consulting.

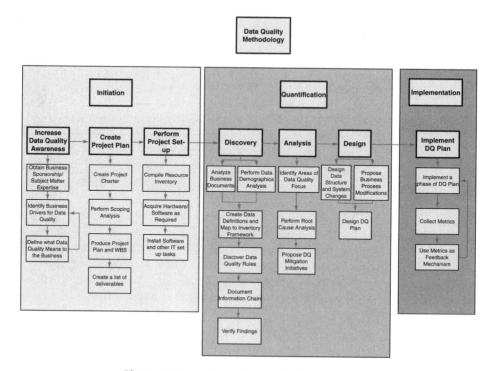

**Figure 10.4**  Information Quality Methodology.

The methodology itself is business metadata because it is a framework for conducting information quality tasks. However, each box in the diagram represents a task, and each task has certain deliverables produced in the performance of the task. The deliverables and any other documentation created while performing the task also become business metadata. Perhaps the most important business metadata that is produced are the quality metrics, both before and after mitigation. It is important that this business metadata, which traces the efforts at mitigation of specific data elements, be linked to the data elements themselves so that a business user can get information about the information quality plan underway and its progress.

# 10.6  Information Quality Business Metadata Delivery

Presentation methods vary and need to be tailored to the correct audience. Senior executives respond better to less detail and more pictures, with drill-down capability if they want to see the detail as verification. Line managers, on the other hand, appreciate the details. Usually, charts are effective for all audiences.

The following examples are from an advertising/Yellow Pages company that wanted to beef up its Internet presence and offer maps showing the locations of its advertisers, so patrons could find them and conduct business with them. The following several examples show different presentation methods for displaying similar data: they illustrate the problem of how data quality issues were thwarting their ability to display advertiser maps. Geocodes are used on maps to pinpoint a specific location; granularity of geocode, indicated by rooftop (best) and centroid (not very precise), refers to how close on a map you can get to the actual location.

The first presentation option in Figure 10.5 shows the data only, with a little explanation (but not much!).

The lack of any visual representation leaves the person looking at these statistics with the feeling of "so what?" What is the point? Is this bad or good? Some business metadata is lacking.

The next option, shown in Figure 10.6, is a little better; it shows a pie chart. But still the missing business metadata leaves one with a distinctly uncomfortable feeling: Is this good or bad?

| Count of businesses with addresses | 3,701,543 |
|---|---|
| Percentage with Geocoded address | 80 |
| Percentage with Rooftop Geocode | 65 |
| Percentage with Centroid Geocode | 15 |
| Percentage Failed Geocode | 20 |

**Figure 10.5** Data Quality Presentation Option: Data and Some Explanation.

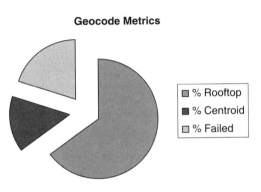

**Figure 10.6** Pie Chart Illustrating Data Quality.

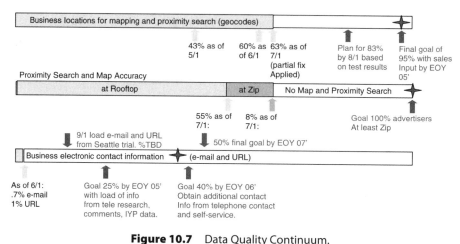

**Figure 10.7**   Data Quality Continuum.

The next presentation option, shown in Figure 10.7, shows each type of metric as a continuum, along with the current condition and progressive goals, leading to the final goal indicated by a star. This option is very clear, because it is obvious what is "bad" and "good" and how far we have to go to get to the end state.

The last option in Figure 10.8 shows a rather whimsical piece of Swiss cheese, with each hole labeled with a specific information quality problem. The Swiss cheese diagram is clear about one thing: all the holes are "bad."

This graphic turned out to be very effective; all the managers were clamoring with "Okay, so what are we going to do about this terrible state of affairs?" We then pulled out the graphic with the continuum shown in Figure 10.7 and demonstrated that we had a plan. It created the case very vividly.

Another way to present data quality is to use traditional business intelligence report types, like dashboards and performance meters. Then, of course, you can always use the usual charts and graphs; just make sure the line going up is labeled carefully so that it is clear what trend you are trying to show. Are you trying to show that the number of errors/defects is going down or up? Is data quality getting worse or better? Figures 10.9 and 10.10 are from Data Flux, and show the traffic light analogy for the scorecard display. You always know what is "good" and "bad" with this display!

Data Flux is one of the only data profiling tools that can function as a workbench for data stewards, data-savvy business people. Figure 10.11 shows how data can be shown in conjunction with graphs to communicate the story behind the data.

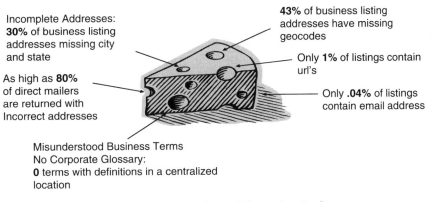

Incomplete Addresses: **30%** of business listing addresses missing city and state

As high as **80%** of direct mailers are returned with Incorrect addresses

**43%** of business listing addresses have missing geocodes

Only **1%** of listings contain url's

Only **.04%** of listings contain email address

Misunderstood Business Terms No Corporate Glossary: **0** terms with definitions in a centralized location

**Figure 10.8**   Swiss Cheese Information Quality.

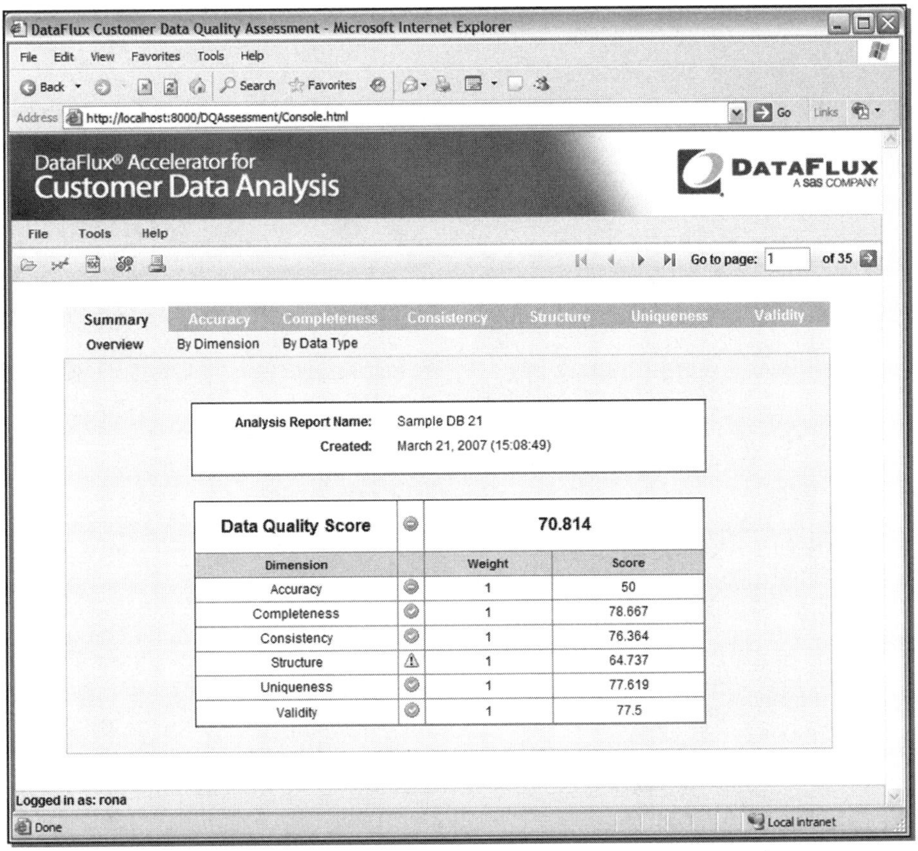

**Figure 10.9**   Data Flux Data Quality Scorecard for Business People.

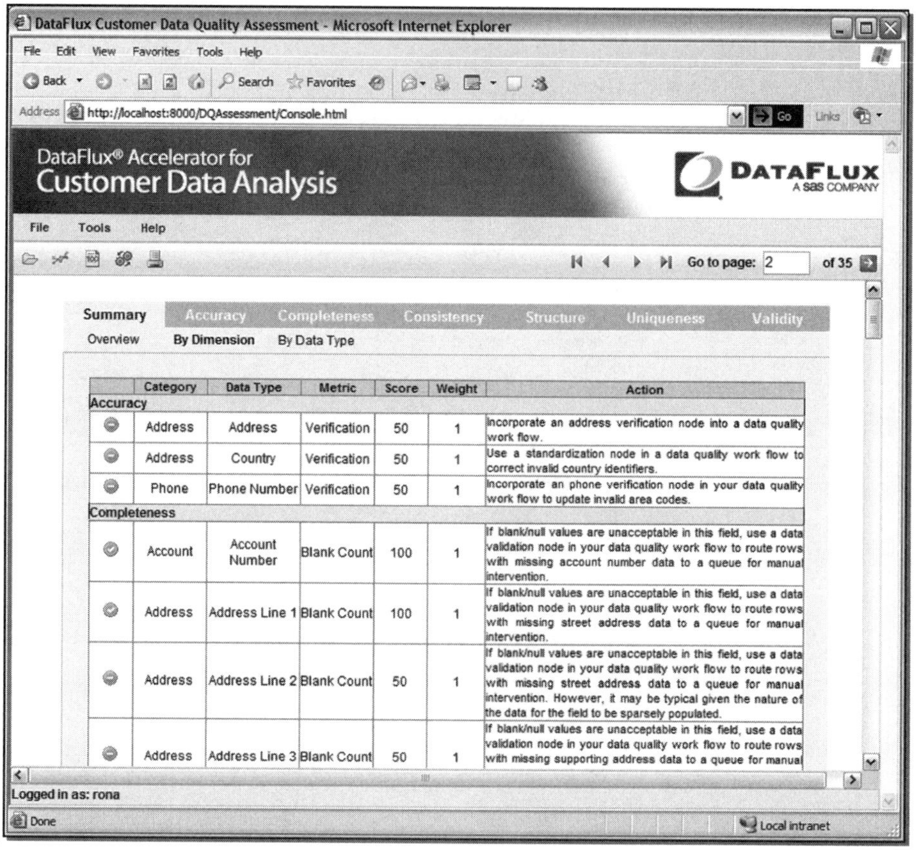

**Figure 10.10**　Drill Down into Details of Data Quality Dimensions Using Scorecards.

# 10.7 Summary

This chapter has made a case for making information quality and quality metrics an important part of business metadata, providing context to data: indicating the level of reliability and trust ability of the data. Those organizations that are not measuring information quality metrics are missing a critical type of business metadata.

First, we made a distinction between data and information, and observed that when we refer to "data quality," we really should be using the term *information quality* because it is only in reference to context that quality can be measured, and information is defined as data plus context.

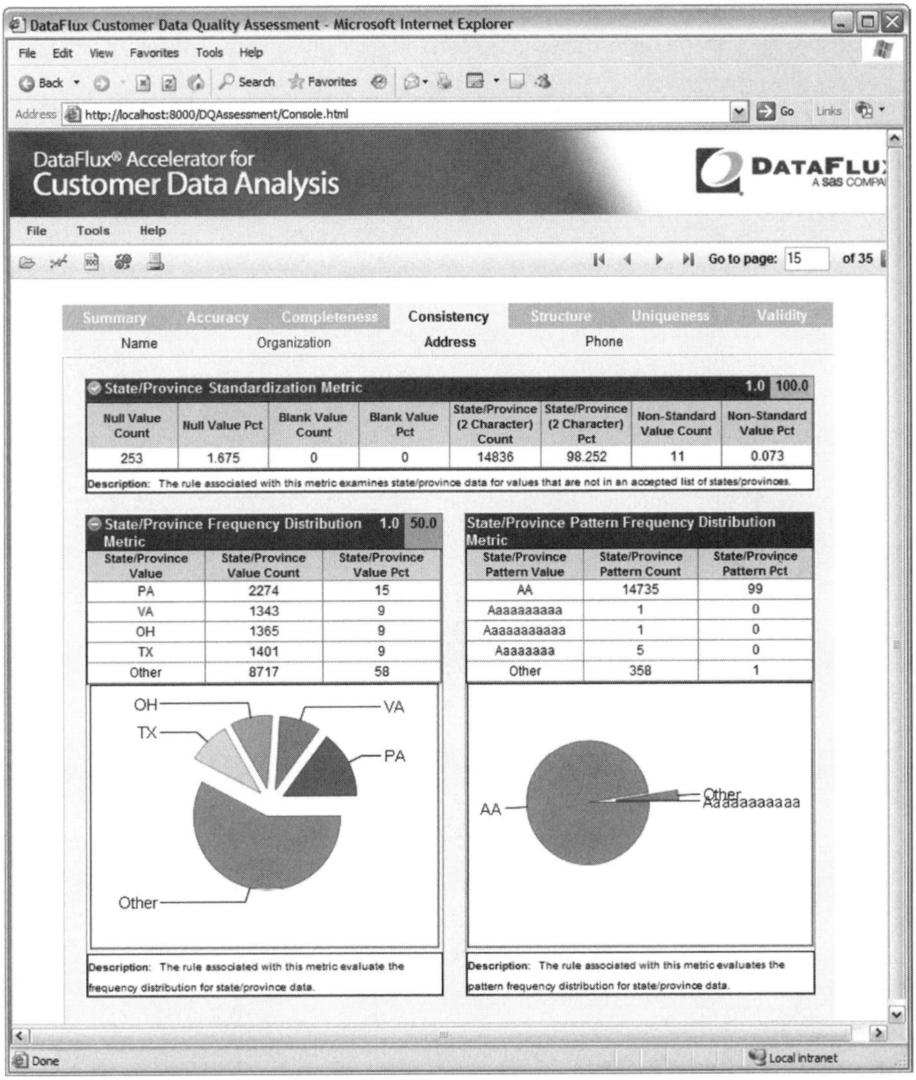

**Figure 10.11**    Data and Graphics Together Help Businesspeople.

Then we discussed how information quality is usually measured on a technical level, but there is a need to translate the technical findings into business metadata, in the language of the business, so that businesspeople will understand what the information quality issues are, and, more importantly, their ramifications to the business. In the process of this discussion, we revisited the human/computer communication problem that we discussed earlier in

Chapter 4 and will amplify in Chapter 11. We used data profiling as an example of technical metadata and showed how the results of data profiling can be presented and explained to businesspeople so that they can understand the issues uncovered in the profiling process.

We discussed the role of the dictionary in terms of setting expectations for information quality. It is nearly impossible to talk about data element quality without the help of a dictionary describing what these elements are supposed to represent. Next, we focused on how an information quality methodology fits as business metadata and pointed out that both the methodology itself and the artifacts created in the process of using it are business metadata. Lastly, we illustrated several ways to present information quality results to businesspeople as business metadata.

# 10.8 References

+ Eckerson, Wayne. "Data Quality and the Bottom Line." *TDWI Report Series*.

+ Fryman, Lowell. "Taking Data Quality Metrics to the Boardroom: A Case Study." *Rocky Mountain Oracle User Group Training Days Proceedings*, February 16, 2006.

+ IAIDQ. "About IAIDQ." July 20, 2006. http://www.iaidq.org/main/about. shtml

+ IAIDQ. "IQ/DQ Glossary." December 25, 2006. *http://www.iaidq.org/main/ glossary.shtml*

+ O'Neil, Bonnie. *Cornerstones of Data Quality™: A Data Quality Methodology*. Westridge Consulting, 2001 and 2006.

# Semantics and Business Metadata

## 11.1 Introduction

Semantics, a subject that has great depth and breadth, can only be viewed here in very broad overview, focusing specifically on semantics as a type of business metadata. After a brief survey of semantics and semantic technology, we will cover the relationship of semantics and business metadata.

## 11.2 The Vision of the Semantic Web

Tim Berners-Lee envisioned the idea of the "semantic web," wherein intelligent agents would be truly intelligent.

In his vision the computer would know exactly what "booking a restaurant reservation" meant, as well as all the underlying tasks associated with it. For example, you could ask the computer to book a reservation at an Indian restaurant on the way home from work, and the computer would find an Indian restaurant located directly on your way home, book a reservation for you, and put it automatically on your calendar, all without human intervention.

In the context of searching for documents, a semantic web would be able to understand what the documents contained. Today, we rely mostly on document titles and tagging. Tagging is usually done manually either by the document author, someone else charged with tagging after the fact, or through a folksonomy like del.icio.us. But a true semantic web could decipher document contents on its own.

On a smaller scale, the semantic web means distinguishing between word senses: when there are two or more senses of a word, the user is asked, "***Did you mean...?***" For example, we have used the word "mole" throughout the book to illustrate word sense. Google can now distinguish between spelling variations and probable errors. However, if Google were semantically enabled, it would be able to distinguish between the different word senses of mole, and Google would either ask the user which sense he or she wanted or, better, would display results based on each sense. Both intelligent agents and semantically aware queries involve understanding the meaning of things. Berners-Lee's example bases actions on meanings and is able to combine several different tasks automatically due to what making a reservation means. In the simpler example of the semantically aware query, it translates into returning query results differently based on different meanings. In either case, the basic notion is the same: the goal is to codify meaning so that computers can "understand" and take useful action based on that meaning.

# 11.3   The Importance of Semantics

The term *semantics* is derived from ancient Greek philosophy. In ancient Greece, as is the case even today on college campuses, it was—and still is—the study of meaning. The definitions, context, assumptions, and rules surrounding a business concept are its semantics. In our information systems throughout the years, we have done a poor job at capturing semantics. In Chapter 4, we pointed out that humans are, by nature, poor communicators, but we are even worse at writing things down. (Remember how we all absolutely *hated* to do documentation?! Now it's coming back to bite us!)

Two very important items that encapsulate the semantics of a business are the definitions of its terms and its business rules. Therefore, one way to help the business articulate its semantics is to build repositories that store these critical semantic components. Out of necessity, these repositories are usually home-grown, because as of this writing, the traditional repository tools don't store business rules or any type of business metadata very well, beyond that found in Entity/Relationship (ER) models. (Check our Web site for product updates: www.mkp.com/businessmetadata.) We discuss these two semantic elements elsewhere in the book: under the heading Definitions in Chapter 4 and the heading Business Rules in its own chapter, Chapter 13.

The present chapter explores semantics in several areas:

◆ How do we express semantics so that it can be communicated?

◆ How is the nature of semantic communication different between human and human, human and computer, and computer and other computers?

Semantic technologies are covered briefly here. However, semantic technologies typically aren't working to solve the same problem that business metadata sets out to solve. We will cover these two different approaches, and we will highlight how business metadata concerns itself with semantics. The goal of business metadata is to make data understandable to businesspeople; therefore, the chapter is about delivering semantics to the businesspeople.

### 11.3.1  *Semantics Are Context-Sensitive*

Every industry has its own unique language, a fact we might not notice if we work in that specific industry. A consultant who doesn't know the industry and its jargon can get confused very fast. Likewise, we have all experienced going to work for a new company and being abruptly confronted with the company's language: the acronyms, abbreviations and business terms that are uniquely its own. Even within the organization, each department usually has its own language; often, formulas or calculations mean different things in different divisions. For example, the term *revenue* can be ambiguous and usually means different things in different groups, such as Sales or Finance.

Therefore, it is safe to say that semantics is highly dependent on the context. The meaning of a term or phrase can vary depending on the group of people using the term (see Figure 11.1). We each have our own context, based on our unique background and circumstances, as well as on which organizational division we belong to.

#### 11.3.1.1  *Each Information System Has Its Own Context*

In a similar fashion, each information system has its own set of semantics, showing what data elements mean in the context of that system (see Figure 11.2).

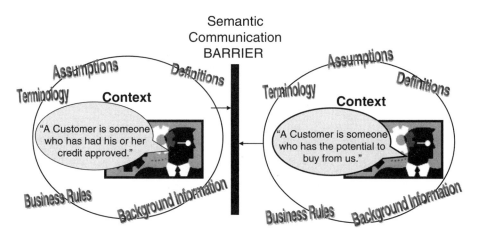

**Figure 11.1** Each Person Has His/Her Own Context.

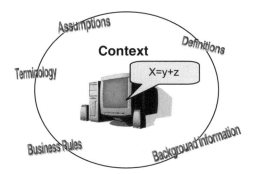

**Figure 11.2** Each System Has Its Own Semantic Context.

The problem is that the semantics of each system are poorly documented. Some systems don't have any documentation at all, and if you are lucky enough to have the documentation, it is usually of shoddy quality. The state of data definitions in most systems is deplorable. Most definitions are tautologies ("a unicorn is a beast with one horn" defines the term by itself; it adds no new information. The word "unicorn" means one horn: uni = one, corn = Old English for horn). A very common tautological definition that is seen in most systems is "Customer ID is the ID of the Customer."

### 11.3.1.2 *Each System Has Its Own Semantics, and Semantics Are Not Shared*

Each system is a semantic island: The semantics for any given system hold true for that system only, and all bets are off that the same semantics apply to any

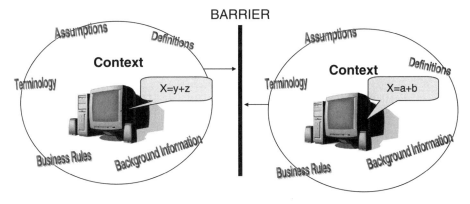

**Figure 11.3**    Each System Has Its Own Context, So How Do They Share Data?

other system (see Figure 11.3). This begs the question: How can two or more systems really share data if the semantics are different?

For example, suppose a firm has a sales database that tracks Customers. However, the Sales Department most probably does not define Customer in the same way that the Shipping Department has defined it in its database. The Sales Department's Customer database almost certainly contains prospects, and the Shipping Department's database almost certainly does not; it is highly unlikely that they are shipping anything to someone who has not bought it (unless they have a "try it, you'll like it" policy). This problem is even true of information systems within the same department, because different systems are usually developed by different people, in a different situation, to solve different business problems. Individual developers leave or get transferred and new ones come in. Unfortunately, the semantics of business systems have been largely overlooked and ignored. Everyone just "assumes" that Customer is the same across the organization, because it is called the same thing. Assumptions are very dangerous!

The discipline of semantics, therefore, is all about becoming aware of these definitions, assumptions, and the contextual nature of data. It is also about trying to capture this information so that data can be more understandable and also can be easily shared, across the enterprise and even externally to the enterprise, when appropriate.

### 11.3.1.3   Human to Computer: No Shared Semantics

Semantics, as it is communicated to humans, is a type of business metadata, which leads us to the next problem. The context problem is further complicated by the human/computer interaction; how do we know for sure if the human's context is the same as the one the system has?

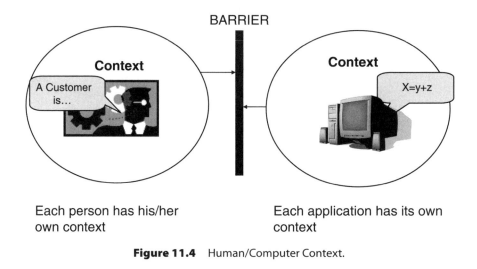

Each person has his/her own context                Each application has its own context

**Figure 11.4**   Human/Computer Context.

# 11.4   Attempts to Capture Semantics: Semantic Frameworks

Various attempts have been made to capture semantics. Lee Orbs, for example, has created the Semantic/Ontology Spectrum, and it has been enhanced in Mills Davis's paper entitled "The Semantic Wave" (see Figure 11.5). Note that the terms in this figure are explained below.

Figure 11.5 shows ways that technology has endeavored to collect semantics, leading to richer forms of knowledge representation and toward the goal of knowledge being able to create new knowledge in the form of reasoning. Some of these concepts, such as taxonomy and glossaries, have been covered in other chapters, especially in Chapter 4. Most of these frameworks are geared toward the machine part of the equation and often leave the humans confused, which means they are ignoring business metadata.

### 11.4.1   *Controlled Vocabulary*

A controlled vocabulary (CV) provides a means to restrict term usage to those terms specified in the controlled vocabulary. A CV often includes "preferred terms" that should be used instead of the referenced term. Preferred terms keep search engines from having to reference all terms and can therefore add speed. One of my clients, going through a very lengthy and painful migration to a new CRM system, wanted to phase out all the legacy terms used before the

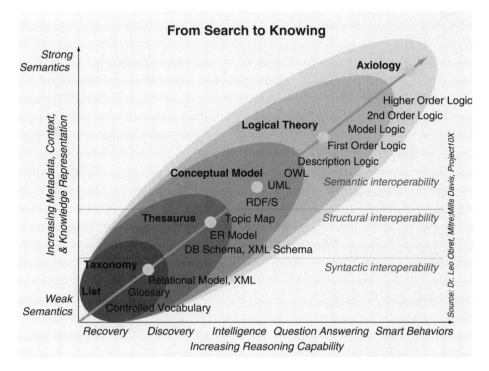

**Figure 11.5** Semantic Spectrum.

migration and adapt "cold turkey" to the terms used in the new system. One way this can be done is to provide a list of the old terms with a reference to the preferred term next to each legacy term. Controlled vocabularies have both human and machine utility, but they are very simple in terms of elucidating meaning.

## 11.4.2 Glossary

One major building block of good codified semantics is a good dictionary. Dave Hollander of Contivo, a semantic integration tool vendor, stresses that a good definition takes a lot of work to create, and it should be "set complete." This hearkens back to set theory, in which a set is "complete" when it is well-defined and it is very clear what constitutes membership in a set. Getting businesspeople to specify good, "set-complete" definitions is difficult to do because we have not trained ourselves to be precise and the language we use actually encourages ambiguity. The rules of well-formed definitions are covered in Chapter 4. The glossary or dictionary is at the heart of any business metadata solution, since it is geared mainly toward humans.

### 11.4.3 Taxonomy

A taxonomy is a classification scheme that adds organization in the form of a hierarchy to the terms and relates them to one another in a parent/child or broad term/narrow term relationship. For example, a fork is an eating utensil; dinner forks and dessert forks are examples of special kinds of forks. The broad term is "eating utensil" and the narrow term is "fork"; the narrow terms for "fork" are "dinner fork" and "dessert fork" This is the foundation for expressing good definitions and semantics and is an excellent starting place to capture meaning. A taxonomy is a step beyond a dictionary or controlled vocabulary because it goes beyond just definitions; it adds the hierarchy on top of the list of defined terms. Many industries have taxonomies that have been created by standards groups. Taxonomies are used to classify things like products and geography, as well as to facilitate enterprise search. We covered taxonomies in detail in Chapter 4 because they are very useful in optimizing search. The classic example of a taxonomy is the one used to identify species in the animal kingdom (see Figure 11.6). A taxonomy helps both humans and machines organize information, and so a taxonomy can be considered business metadata.

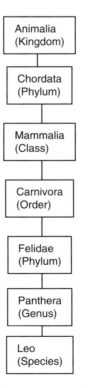

**Figure 11.6** Part of the Taxonomy of the Animal Kingdom. (Adapted from McComb, 2004, p.52).

### 11.4.4 Entity/Relationship (ER) Model and Thesauri

#### 11.4.4.1 Thesauri

Both entity/relationship (ER) models and thesauri provide relationships between terms. Thesauri have been used for many years by authors to locate words that mean relatively the same thing to color one's writing. This book has certainly benefited from the Microsoft Word thesaurus! Thesauri can also be used by machines, though in a limited way. It could be argued that a thesaurus only provides the synonym relationship, whereas an ER model can express a richer vocabulary of relationships, along with providing cardinality and optionality. Therefore, the ER model should be ahead of the thesaurus in the spectrum.

#### 11.4.4.2 The ER Model

Figure 11.7 shows a very simple ER model.

The "flavor" of ER modeling shown in Figure 11.7 is called Barker Notation because it was invented by Richard Barker while he was at Oracle. It is arguably the best notation for displaying relationship semantics because it provides a richer, more robust means of semantic expression. An ER diagram always generates two unambiguous relationship sentences that express business rules, along with cardinality and optionality. The diagram in Figure 11.7 is interpreted as follows:

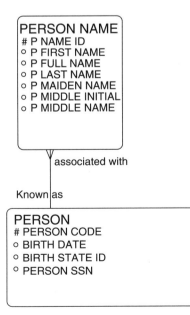

**Figure 11.7** Entity/Relationship Diagram (ERD), Using Barker Notation.

◆ Each Person Name must be associated with one and only one Person.

◆ Each Person must be known as one or more Person Names.

These sentences are in fact business metadata that can communicate clearly to businesspeople, even those that don't have an affinity for diagrams.

Other ER model "flavors" do not express as much semantics as the Barker Notation, and therefore most practitioners of data modeling do not address the semantics of the relationships effectively. Consequently, the usefulness of an ER diagram to communicate to nontechnical businesspeople has been hotly debated. Noted author and data modeler extraordinaire David Hay is fond of emphasizing the importance of ER models (as are the authors of the present volume) and credits the Barker Notation for much of this communication facilitation. For more detail in this regard, see his book *Data Model Patterns: Conventions of Thought*[1]. It is therefore the consensus of the authors that an ER model constitutes business metadata because it communicates relationships between concepts in both a graphical and linguistic way. Parenthetically, ER models are also used to generate technical metadata (database schema), and to communicate relationships between data elements to technical people: database designers, database administrators (DBAs), and developers.

### 11.4.5 Conceptual Model, RDF and OWL, Topic Map, UML

#### 11.4.5.1 Conceptual Model

The techniques we have just discussed (glossaries, thesauri, and data models) are used to capture business metadata in ways that can be understood by human beings. Conceptual models also provide business metadata to humans. A concept model provides the ability to represent each individual concept; then data elements can be mapped to them to show where each business concept is stored in all systems. There can be more than one data element in an enterprise representing a single concept, and sometimes vice versa (although a good modeler will argue that this only happens when fields are overloaded—a model will never intentionally permit this!). Therefore, a concept model is not the same thing as a data model.

#### 11.4.5.2 RDF and OWL

Resource Definition Framework (RDF) and Web Ontology Language (OWL; letters scrambled around to form OWL) are modeling languages used to express

---

[1]Dorset House Publishing, New York NY, ISBN 0-932633-29-3, 1995.

concepts and relationships in ways that can be processed by computers. OWL in particular provides a very rich vocabulary of possible relationships. However, these languages do not express business metadata; a human is not expected to be able to read and understand OWL or RDF.

### 11.4.5.3 Topic and C-Maps

A topic map (see Figure 11.8) represents topics (or concepts), associations between the topics, and occurrences, which are relationships between the topic and information about that topic. There is an ISO standard for topic maps: ISO/EIC 13250:2003. A Concept Map (C-map) is a variant of the topic map.

RDF constructs are called "triples" because they are made up of concept-relationship-concept. RDF triples could easily be expressed in a topic map or C-map. See Figure 11.9 for a very simple RDF triple, represented as a C-map.

### 11.4.5.4 UML

UML is comprised of a standard set of models created by the Object Management Group (OMG). UML is based on Object Oriented (OO) design, using class hierarchies. It has 12 different model types, and it is meant to be platform-independent

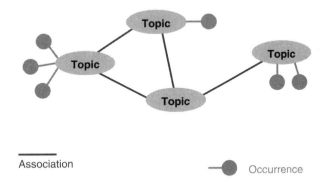

**Figure 11.8** Example of Topic Map Format (from Wikipedia).

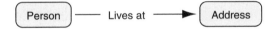

**Figure 11.9** RDF Triple.

and technology-agnostic. The OMG also intends it to support Model-Driven Architecture (MDA), allowing for models to generate code directly. UML is much more effective than ER models in generating software applications, but it can be argued convincingly that UML is misplaced in the chart showing it to be on the same level as RDF and OWL. Its ability to capture semantics is restricted by a hierarchical design. More germane to our purposes, UML models are geared to a technical audience, and businesspeople would have a hard time deciphering them. Although UML models can provide a more efficient means to generate applications, the bottom line is that they do not express semantics to businesspeople, and therefore are not useful as business metadata.

### 11.4.6   Description Logics and Other Forms of Logic

Logic provides the ability to reason and to create new knowledge from existing knowledge. For example, if I know the following:

+ A sister relationship exists between two females who share the same parents.

+ Mary and Sue have the same parents.

+ A woman (Person A) is said to be an aunt of another person (Person B) when Person B's mother is a sister of Person A.

+ A cousin relationship exists when one person is the son or daughter of the other person's uncle or aunt.

+ John is Mary's child.

+ George is Sue's child.

New knowledge can therefore be inferred:

+ Mary and Sue are sisters.

+ Mary is George's aunt.

+ Sue is John's aunt.

+ John and George are cousins.

Logic is able to make the connections in the knowledge base. I can infer the cousin relationship between George and John based on all the other facts provided. The term *Description Logics* (DL) refers to a family of knowledge representation languages that use formal logic and can be translated into first-order logic (FOL). FOL is a system of deductive reasoning. One of the flavors of OWL is called OWL DL, and it is based on description logic.

### 11.4.7 Ontology

In philosophy, ontology is the study of being or existence. In computer and information science:

> an **ontology** is a <u>data model</u> that represents a set of concepts within a <u>domain</u> and the relationships between those concepts. It is used to <u>reason</u> about the objects within that domain. Ontologies are used in <u>artificial intelligence</u>, the <u>semanticweb</u>, <u>software engineering</u>, and <u>information architecture</u> as a form of <u>knowledge representation</u> about the world or some part of it.

> (From Wikipedia, accessed March 10, 2007)

An ontology is therefore a way of representing knowledge, including relationships and classifications. An ontological classification scheme can be represented as a graph or a network diagram; topic maps or C-maps can be used to represent ontologies. Ontologies typically add more detailed relationships than can be expressed in ER models or UML, however it can be reasonably argued that an ER model is an ontology. OWL is considered to be an ontology language (as mentioned earlier, this is what the "O" in its name stands for) and has many built-in relationship types that add to its inferencing capability.

# 11.5 Semantics as Business Metadata

Semantics is all about meaning, and business metadata is about adding meaning to data. Making meaning explicit is adding context to data. Thus, any way we can capture the semantics of data and be able to display this meaning to a business user to add clarity to data, we are delivering business metadata to them.

The simplest way to capture meaning in a way that can add clarity to a business person is to provide definitions of terms used in applications, formulas or calculations, and so on. This business glossary provides the meaning of an individual term or data element on the spot to a user viewing data in an application, and can also provide immediate clarification. For example, it would be helpful to present definitions of possibly confusing fields in a web form.

However, as Dave McComb points out in his excellent book, *Semantics in Business Systems*, "Definitions Are Not Enough" [McComb, 2004, p. 49]. Dictionaries typically do not provide the relationships between terms that are so critical to understanding. Therefore, we need to capture relationships between terms and to deliver them as business metadata as well. In our web form example, it may be helpful to provide business rules about the field in question, clarifying the relationship between the term in question and other data.

Expressing relationships can get very tricky: There is a continuum of richness, as depicted in the Semantic Spectrum. Taxonomies offer broad term/narrow term expression, which provides a basic, rudimentary hierarchical relationship. However, many things don't fit neatly into hierarchies, so a more flexible relationship structure is needed. Humans can grasp C-maps, and depicting concept relationships in a network model may be helpful to businesspeople.

The Semantic Spectrum illustrates the need for the richness of expression that moving upwards in the spectrum provides. However, the tools we have today for communicating these concepts to humans are severely limited. A nontechnical person usually finds it difficult to decipher the tools and languages that offer semantic richness. While the semantic vendors are attempting to tackle the more difficult problem of computers being able to reason with the end goal of offering more useful solutions to humans, we still have much work to do on the human side of the equation. We must continue to work on effecting more precision in communication, and we must be able to distinguish nuances of dialects and different usages or meanings of the same word, or vice versa, when two different words mean the same thing. As we will next see, concept modeling can help in this endeavor.

### 11.5.1   *Semantic and Conceptual Models*

A concept or conceptual model is a model that conveys individual concepts and their relationships to one another, independent of implementation. A concept is different than a business term because terms can often express more than one concept, or more than one term may be expressed in a single concept (in other words, there is a many-to-many relationship between term and concept). Dave McComb states that the difference between a semantic model and a conceptual model is "the effort spent on resolving meaning" (McComb, 2004, p. 77). Therefore, a semantic model attempts to be more rigorous in the expression of meaning for each concept.

#### 11.5.1.1   *Delivering Definitions and Relationships*

A conceptual model can therefore be used to express each atomic concept and its relationship to other concepts. An ER model can be used to represent relationships between concepts. (See Figure 11.7 earlier in this chapter for an example of a very simple conceptual model of Person and Person Name expressed as an Entity/Relationship Diagram [ERD].) Data modelers distinguish between three levels of ER models: conceptual, logical, and physical. Good modelers disagree on the boundaries between conceptual and logical, but all will agree that a physical model includes implementation details that are not pertinent to the other two. A conceptual model is meant to focus on the main concepts required to do business.

Alternatively, Concept Maps can be used, which allow for more flexibility in relationship expression. See Figure 11.10 for an example of a C-Map.

The C-map is not constrained by the rules of OO, which force hierarchies. It also does not have the problems of relational modeling, which does not allow hierarchies. The lack of these constraints is both good and bad.

For example, even though the relational model does not represent hierarchies well,[2] it does provide rigor and certain rule enforcement (such as cardinality, optionality, and relational integrity).

One of the known problems in the semantic modeling technologies available today is their lack of visual modeling approaches. This is rapidly changing; a good example of a nice visual tool is Top Braid, by Top Quadrant. The use of the C-Map and its extensions also allows us to have both semantic richness and visual models.

### 11.5.2   Business Metadata Expression

As we have already mentioned in this chapter, the problem with OWL (and many semantic languages or modeling techniques) is that, although it is a rich, robust modeling vocabulary, it is not easily translatable into business language; it is expressed in XML syntax. If the goal of your project is to create a purely business metadata environment for the delivery of data explanations to businesspeople, then OWL, at this stage of its evolution, is not the right way to go;

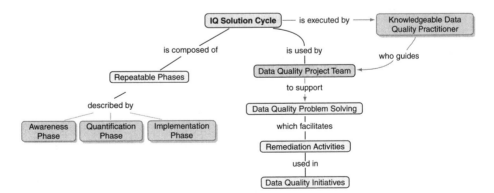

**Figure 11.10**   Example of a Concept Map (C-Map).

---

[2]Various ER database design methods have added extensions that handle hierarchies such as IDEF1X and Barker Notation, but both have problems when physical, relational models are generated from them.

well-formed definitions are the appropriate vehicle. English-language explanations of rules and relationships can be added as enhancements to definitions. Another alternative is to use a combination approach with both a dictionary and C-Map or ER model to express the concept model because some users like graphical models. When the user is looking at a data element in a system and wants its definition, a hot key or button can be pressed. If he wants more detail, like all the relationships between other business concepts, another mouse click or "details" button can be pressed. Not everyone will probably want this grain of detail, and the definition may be all that's needed at first, but the detail is available right there if required.

However, OWL goes a long way toward solving one part of the equation: the computer's understanding and reasoning capability. Go back to Figure 11.4, which depicts the man/machine communication problem. OWL helps the computer side of the drawing. This will assist the businessperson behind the scenes, because it will provide the building blocks and the infrastructure needed for automated reasoning, more intelligent search, and intelligent agents (see the next section). But one must still communicate back to the human in a reasonable way, which is the basic concern of business metadata. Therefore, semantic technologies, while full of promise and paving the way for the future, do not at present provide much business metadata.

### 11.5.3  Exposing Semantics to the Business

We have established the need for semantic expression and delivery of business metadata to communicate context, and we have also provided a quick survey of the semantic landscape and the current semantic technology state of the art. How can we use business metadata to deliver contextual information and semantics to businesspeople in order to enhance their understanding of the data if the expression of semantics is only in a technical representation?

Today's technology necessitates writing a business translation alongside any technical representation of semantics, if one exists. Apparently, the main link is the dictionary or glossary. If OWL is used, one can attempt to generate fact statements from the relationships, or use a C-map. Glossaries and thesauri can be used to serve up definitions, along with synonyms and broad/narrow term relationships, and can also reference ERDs. As discussed earlier in the chapter, the delivery of the definitions needs to be as ubiquitous as possible, no matter what application is being used. Definitions should be made universally available throughout the Corporate Information Factory (CIF) and the entire IT environment. This can be done by invoking a definition as a Web service, using a portal, or any number of other ways. If you are ambitious, you can add business rules and business processes into the mix. Therefore, when the user gets the definition of the data element, he or she can click a details button and be able to view business rules, process diagrams, and other specifics. If the user likes diagrams, you can even display a relevant portion of the ERD. Although this takes some infrastructure and architectural planning, it generally doesn't require purchase of additional hardware or software, because if you are clever you can get it done with "Bonnie's Law," or "Use whatever is lying around." (For more information on creative delivery strategies, see Chapter 8.)

In addition to definitions, it is wise to do semantic modeling and create an enterprise conceptual model, as described earlier, and map all systems' data elements to this model. Unlike some semantic technologies, semantic models such as an enterprise concept model can be used directly by analysts and businesspeople, providing the following benefits to the enterprise:

✦ A semantic and physical inventory of data elements throughout the enterprise

✦ A systematic way to determine data redundancy and put plans in place to manage it

✦ Two data elements that represent the same concept, reusing the same definition

✦ The foundation for data sharing, both internal and external to the organization

✦ The foundation for an enterprise data quality initiative

Such a system can then be used to track associated contextual information for each concept, including business rules, allowing this business metadata to be made available wherever it is needed. Although tools are helpful, they are not necessary; it is possible to create this as a homegrown solution. See Chapter 8 entitled Business Metadata Delivery for ideas on delivering business metadata to the businesspeople.

# 11.6 Semantics in Practice

## 11.6.1 Integration, Web Services, SOA, and Semantics

Data sharing is difficult both internally and externally in part because of the lack of semantic understanding of the data. The major role of semantics in integration is to clarify meaning so we can be assured we are integrating two or more elements that mean the same thing. We have to do a better job of deciphering the underlying semantics of the data, so that we can get the integration accurate and match apples with apples.

Another traditional system integration barrier is the point-to-point interface. In the past whenever one system needed to share data with another system, a separate interface was built, without regard for other interfaces that might be in place between the two systems. As these interfaces are proliferating, systems are becoming increasingly brittle; one small change might affect hundreds of interfaces (see Figure 11.11).

What is needed is a more broker-oriented type strategy for interfaces. Imagine the following architecture, using a registry. Suppose there were services—mechanisms to provide data and information to the requester. Whenever data was needed, a service would be called, and the service would be invoked, providing the data to the requester. Where the provider goes to obtain the data is hidden from the requester, so point-to-point interfaces would not be necessary (see Figure 11.12).

"A service is a unit of work done by a service provider to achieve desired end results for a service consumer" (He, 2003) Web services act as a broker, ensuring that requesters and providers can work together, independent of implementation details.

A Web service works as follows: There is a service broker that maintains a registry of available services. The services are registered using WSDL (a variant of XML). The requester sends XML (using SOAP, which is an envelope for XML) to the service provider, and the provider sends the desired results back, also using SOAP. Figure 11.13 shows Wikipedia's diagram of Web services.

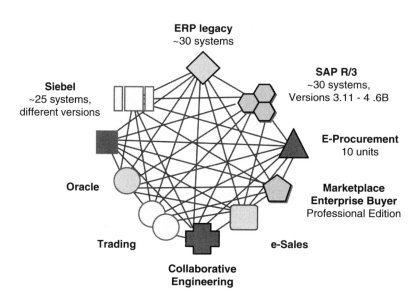

**Figure 11.11** Point-to-Point Interfaces (courtesy of Contivo).

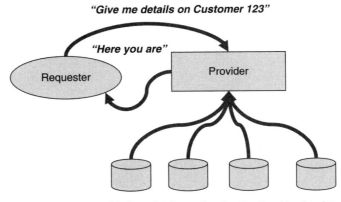

**Figure 11.12** Services Broker.

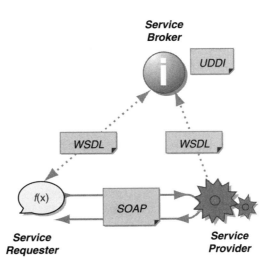

**Figure 11.13** Web Services (courtesy of Wikipedia).

Web Services works because it uses XML and its variants, which in itself is platform-independent. It therefore can hide all of the technological integration details from the requester. XML is also standards-based, allowing it to be used by everyone.

Web Services has come into the forefront to assist with eliminating direct, point-to-point interfaces, hiding the underlying technology, and making connections between systems reusable.

(It should be noted that the default behavior for Web Services is point-to-point; but its real power is in breaking free of the point-to-point and enabling true Service Oriented Architecture).

### 11.6.2 Service-Oriented Architecture (SOA)

Sometimes the term *SOA* is misused; what it really refers to is the architecture necessary to make Web Services possible. It takes a lot of planning and infrastructure to set up Web Services, not the least of which is common semantics across the enterprise. It is very important to reach a common understanding of each service's meaning and the data delivered by the service (and, of course, the data needed as parameters that are fed to the service).

#### 11.6.2.1 Business Metadata and SOA

There is therefore a huge need for both a data and terms dictionary and a services dictionary. As SOA matures, the same searchability problem will exist as that outlined in Chapter 4: "What is the name of that service that does X?" What is needed is a semantically aware search paradigm that can locate similar services if a synonym is used.

Yet, semantics is the most neglected area of SOA, on both the integration (back-end) side and the definition of the services themselves (front-end). At the very least, robust, unambiguous definitions of both data and services need to be captured and exposed to both providers and requesters. Adding definitions to services will provide greater understanding of the services to both technical people and businesspeople.

All this may sound very technical, applying only to developers. However, the semantics behind the service (i.e., what constitutes a Customer) needs to be exposed to the businesspeople, so that they know what their application is providing. Therefore, service definitions, assumptions, and context are all business metadata.

### 11.6.3 An Extensive Semantic Vocabulary Implementation

Probably one of the most extensive semantically aware vocabulary management efforts is the implementation ongoing at the National Cancer Institute (NCI). In its fight to cure cancer, the NCI has created a business vocabulary and metadata registry that permits semantic interoperability: the registry ensures that all cancer centers use the same nomenclature for diseases and other medical terminology. In the medical community and especially in cancer research, maintaining a common, unambiguous vocabulary is key to making sure that the same disease is being referred to when data is shared. The NCI's business goals are:

✦ To create a world wide web of cancer research, widely shared and available

✦ To facilitate the delivery of innovations in cancer prevention and treatment

The NCI's technical goals are to create sharable data that convey "semantic, syntactic and lexical meaning" (Warzel, 2006), are both machine and human understandable but place an emphasis on machine understandable, and make the data "semantically interoperable, widely and publicly accessible" (Warzel, 2006). In order to do so, the NCI built its own infrastructure and tools, using "Common Data Elements" or a conceptual model. Its solution to the problem of providing a common vocabulary was constructed using several different standards, to make it sharable:

✦ UML

✦ OWL

✦ ISO 11179

The NCI built its solution using a controlled vocabulary and thesaurus, including relationships between terms. However, the NCI Thesaurus is not "just" a thesaurus; it uses OWL and is description logic based, also using a concept hierarchy organized into trees. The terms were stored in a 11179 registry, and the registry metadata was mapped to UML structures from the Class Diagram. The solution includes three main layers:

✦ Layer 1: Enterprise Vocabulary Services: DL (description logics) and ontology, thesaurus

✦ Layer 2: CADSR: Metadata Registry, consisting of Common Data Elements

✦ Layer 3: Cancer Bioinformatics Objects, using UML Domain Models

The NCI Thesaurus contains over 48,000 concepts. Although its emphasis is on machine understandability, NCI has managed to translate description logic somewhat into English. Linking concepts together is accomplished through roles, which are also concepts themselves. Here's an example:

Concept: <u>Disease</u>: ALD Positive Anaplastic Large Cell Lymphoma

Role: Disease_Has_Molecular_Abnormality

Concept: <u>Molecular Abnormality</u>: Rearrangement of 2p23 (Warzel, 2006, p.18)

NCI's toolkit is called caCORE, and it includes objects that developers can use in their applications. In this way, local cancer centers and research facilities can develop their own applications and use the objects created by NCI to interoperate and share data with all other cancer research centers that share NCI's vocabulary. Here are the components of its extensive toolkit:

+ Terminology browser

+ Common Data Element (CDE) browser

+ Form Builder to create user-specified collections of CDEs

+ Sentinel Tool to generate alerts triggered by metadata changes

+ caCORE SDK to create semantically integrated applications, including:

    + Semantic integration workbench

    + Code generator, which takes UML model and creates Java

    + UML Loader, which transforms UML model into data element metadata

### 11.6.3.1    NCI Conclusion

NCI had to build an extensive infrastructure because semantic technology is still in its infancy. It spans the whole Semantic Spectrum in Figure 11.5. It includes both business and technical metadata, and it enables humans to be confident that terminology is being used consistently and data is being shared responsibly. After all, cancer research is a matter of life and death. It is comforting to know that this type of solution is being employed in such a critical area.

Although most organizations lack the resources to create such a comprehensive solution, we can take heart from this example that, hopefully, software vendors will notice and will begin to provide the plumbing and infrastructure for these types of solutions so that it won't have to be reinvented for it to be implemented.

# 11.7 Summary

The quest to provide meaning to data is inherent in business metadata, and therefore semantics plays a large role. There are two facets to the delivery of meaning:

+ To the human

+ To the computer

Thus far, the emphasis in the semantic technology community has been on the computer facet, forgetting the human. The rationale behind this emphasis was that, in trying to figure out how to codify meaning, perhaps the computer issue was the more difficult of the two. As the thinking goes, when this problem is solved, resolution of the human/semantic problem may follow easily. However, we are finding that all our attempts to codify meaning using semantic technology is leaving humans more and more confused. OWL code and XML, after all, are not really human-friendly.

Yet the problem remains: how to best communicate the meaning and context behind the data and how to enhance businesspeople's understanding of the data. The answer to our quest, given the state of today's technology, can be summarized as follows:

✦ Good, unambiguous, robust definitions of business concepts (and mapping terms and data to these concepts)

✦ A method of representing relationships between concepts that allows for different kinds of relationships (perhaps C-maps or topic maps are the most promising, but Barker Notation ER models do a good job too)

The National Cancer Institute's amazingly extensive solution for delivering vocabulary to the cancer research community includes business metadata: a browsable metadata repository for researchers, in addition to the technical infrastructure required. However, the technical infrastructure was necessary to ensure that the vocabulary shared with all the cancer research centers was always consistent (semantic interoperability). Even though the NCI's mammoth effort is unlikely to be replicated in many organizations because of the extraordinary amount of work that was undertaken, we should be optimistic about the future. As technology evolves, perhaps tool vendors will begin to offer this infrastructure so that others can create similar solutions. Then we will begin to see how semantic technology will enable computers to reason and become more useful. At the same time, semantics will be able to add clarity and deliver business metadata to the businesspeople directly. In the meantime, homegrown solutions will continue to develop and will become more sophisticated as we learn from each other and build on our learning as we attempt to capture more semantics in our systems.

# 11.8  References

✦ Bolloju, Narasimha, and Leung, Felix S.K. "Assisting Novice Analysts in Developing Quality Conceptual Models with UML." *Communications of the ACM* 49, No. 7 (July 2006).

✦ Davis, Mills. "The Semantic Wave 2006, Part 1: Executive Guide to Billion Dollar Markets." *Project10X*, January 2006.

✦ He, Hao. "What Is Service-Oriented Architecture?" O'Reilly XML.com, September 30, 2003. http://www.xml.com/pub/a/ws/2003/09/30/soa. html

✦ Hollander, Dave. *Contivo Vocabulary Management Solution*, referencing Hasso Plattner Keynote Address at SAP Tech Ed, Los Angeles, 2001.

✦ Institute of Human Machine Cognition Web site: http://cmap.ihmc.us/

✦ Komatsoulis, George A. "caBIG™ Interoperability: Technology, Process and Progress." DAMA International Symposium and Wilshire Metadata Conference, April 2006.

✦ Majumdar, Arun K. SOA or SOS? Rationale for a Semantic Service-Oriented Infrastructure. Cutter Consortium, *Enterprise Architecture,* 9, No. 1 (2006).

✦ McComb, David. *Semantics in Business Systems*. San Francisco: Morgan Kaufman, 2004.

✦ Warzel, Denise, with De Coronado, Sherri, Fragoso, Gilberto, and Chilukuri, Ram. "The NCI's caCORE: Leveraging Standards and Business Vocabulary for Semantic Interoperability." Semantic Technology Conference, March 2006.

✦ Wikipedia. "Web service." http://en.wikipedia.org/wiki/Web_services, accessed on December 15, 2006.

# Unstructured Business Metadata

**CHAPTER 12**

## 12.1 Introduction

Most IT professionals think of metadata as existing in and relating to the world of structured information. Most business professionals understand that business metadata also exists in another world, that is, in the unstructured environment. This chapter discusses the importance of unstructured business metadata and describes the major benefits that managing it in an organized, systematic way can bring to the enterprise.

## 12.2 Structured Data and Unstructured Data

The world of structured data is a world of transactions, reports, updates, and databases.

Typical technologies for the structured environment include:

- ✦ UDB/DB2
- ✦ Oracle
- ✦ Teradata
- ✦ SQL Server

The structured environment is the backbone of most businesses. Here are some examples of structured processing:

- ✦ Bank teller transactions
- ✦ Manufacturing control
- ✦ ATMs
- ✦ Airlines reservations

But there is another world of information , and that world is the one of unstructured data and processing. In the unstructured world, unlike the structured world, there is no format, no structure. Anything can be said in any way in any language. Typical unstructured applications include:

- ✦ E-mail
- ✦ Telephone transcriptions
- ✦ Spreadsheets
- ✦ Text files
- ✦ Document files
- ✦ Reports

Typical technologies found in the unstructured world include:

- ✦ Microsoft Outlook
- ✦ IBM Lotus Notes
- ✦ Microsoft Excel

Figure 12.1 shows these two worlds.

Interestingly, the two worlds do not intersect to any great degree. Technology and applications are either structured or unstructured, but not both. A world of promise would open up if a real intersection of the two environments could be effected.

Typical unstructured technology is shown in Figure 12.2.

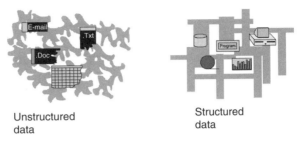

The world has two major processing environments

**Figure 12.1**   Two Types of Data.

Figure 12.2 shows that e-mail, text files, .doc files, and transcripted telephone conversations become the source of unstructured data. Indeed, there are many other sources of unstructured data, including:

✦ Adobe Acrobat (.pdf) files

✦ PowerPoint (.ppt) files

### 12.2.1.1   *Main Distinction between Structured and Unstructured Data*

In the world before PCs or the Web, database search was the primary method used to find electronic data. Most data was fielded or stored in a database structure. Each field was supposed to hold a single piece of information (database designers called it "overloading" when users would try to cram more than one piece of information into a single field). Searching structured data was relatively easy with database query tools: The instruction "Find me all the transactions where someone purchased Product X" was accomplished by either typing Product X into a single parameter entry area or specifying the field name and the value in two entry areas on a screen.

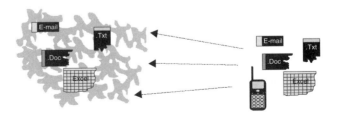

Some typical sources of unstructured data

**Figure 12.2**   Typical Sources of Unstructured Data.

### 12.2.1.2 Enter Unstructured Data

Unstructured data is not so easy to find because its contents have not been fielded in the same way as structured data. For example, the request "Show me all the proposals that the company has produced in the last 5 years that have something to do with Semantic Technologies" is not so easy to fulfill, because proposals don't have a field called "Category" that can be searched. As we all know, the information explosion of documents has created a huge glut: How do you find anything in the morass of unstructured data that exists everywhere, from corporations' shared drives to individuals' laptops?

### 12.2.1.3 Semistructured Data

Some data traditionally labeled "unstructured" is actually semistructured. A corporate glossary, for example, is semistructured: It has some structure, depending on how it was constructed. At the bare minimum, it has a term name and a definition. It may also have other components such as synonym, abbreviation, and/or acronym. Other types of semistructured data include the following:

- ✦ E-mail, which has the following components:
  - ✦ Sender
  - ✦ Recipient
  - ✦ Date
  - ✦ Subject
  - ✦ Relative importance
- ✦ Spreadsheet files, which are usually called "workbooks" and consist of:
  - ✦ Individual spreadsheets (the tabs)
  - ✦ Cells
  - ✦ Print area
  - ✦ Labeled or named area

For that matter, it could be argued that all files are semistructured because they all have the following components or attributes:

- ✦ Title
- ✦ Author

✦ Date Created

✦ Date Modified

✦ File Type

✦ Size

As we saw in Chapter 1, the Title of a document is a very important piece of business metadata. All knowledge workers (creators) need to be trained to name files carefully. However, it is very difficult to understand and glean (and classify) the contents of unstructured data because these files contain lots of text. A way must therefore be devised to peer into the contents of these files and discover what they contain, so that documents can be classified and ultimately found by businesspeople when they are needed. Only then can these documents be useful to the enterprise.

# 12.3 Text

The content of unstructured files that is relevant to metadata is text. In one form or the other, text becomes the basis for examining the content of unstructured data. In order to make unstructured data useful, the textual contents of these files must be extracted and understood electronically. Figure 12.3 shows that text is pulled from the unstructured sources.

The text is pulled by using one of several interfaces—third-party interfaces, interfaces provided by the vendor, or interfaces provided by the in-house programmer. However the interfaces are done, the text is read and is available for processing.

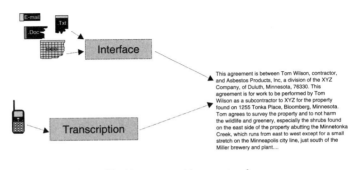

Text is accessed by means of
a transcription or an interface

**Figure 12.3** Extracting Text from Unstructured Data.

### 12.3.1  A Distillation

Once the text is pulled from the unstructured file, the text can be examined. The starting point for an examination of the text—a distillation of unstructured text—is to pull recognized words out of the file. Figure 12.4 shows this extraction of words.

Once the words are pulled out of the file, they are separated into two categories—words that are business relevant and those that are not relevant. Only words that are business relevant are of interest to the developer building the infrastructure.

A further distinction can be made as to whether the words should be classified as business metadata.

Figure 12.5 shows the separation of business-relevant words from the collection of all the words.

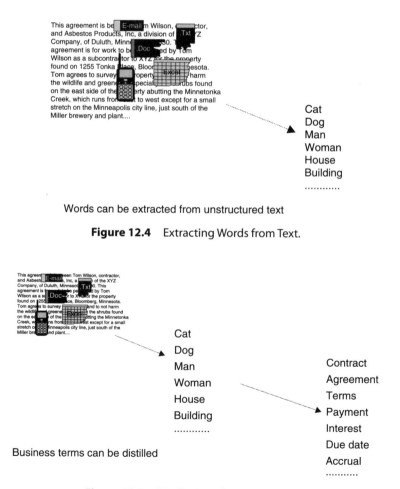

Words can be extracted from unstructured text

**Figure 12.4**  Extracting Words from Text.

Cat
Dog
Man
Woman
House
Building
............

Contract
Agreement
Terms
Payment
Interest
Due date
Accrual
..........

Business terms can be distilled

**Figure 12.5**  Distillation of Business Terms.

### 12.3.1.1   Extraneous Words

After the business-relevant words are extracted, a further distillation can be made: Extraneous words can be removed. Sometimes these extraneous words are called "stop" words. They are words that don't add any context, such as "a," "an," "the," "with," "for," "that," "which," "and," "to," and "up." Figure 12.6 shows the removal of extraneous or "stop" words.

### 12.3.1.2   Stemmed Words

Now the remaining business-relevant words can be "stemmed," which is the process of reducing words to a common stem. Take the following words, for example:

+ payment

+ paid

+ payee

+ pays

+ paying

These words all share a common stem—"pay." For further processing, the stems of words are used for analysis, rather than the literal word itself. Figure 12.7 shows the stemming of business-relevant words.

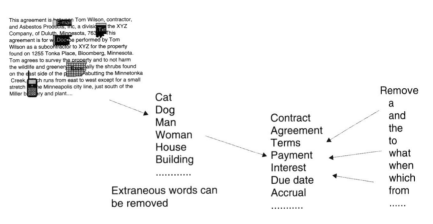

**Figure 12.6**   Removing Extraneous Words.

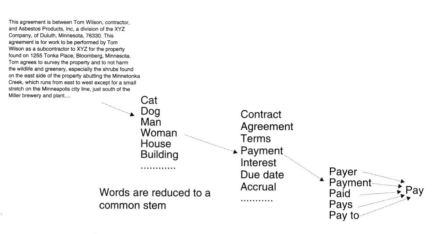

**Figure 12.7**   Reducing Words to a Common Stem.

### 12.3.1.3   Counting the Words in a Document

The words can now be grouped and counted for each document based on their frequency of occurrence. The inference is that the more frequently a word stem occurs in a document, the more likely the document is to be about the word. The ability to count the word stems of business-relevant words provides the capability of determining what a document is about. Figure 12.8 shows the counting of word stems.

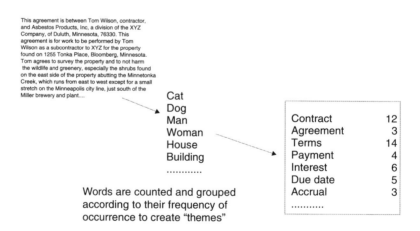

**Figure 12.8**   Counting and Grouping Words Forming "Themes".

### 12.3.1.4 Industrial Recognition

Another technique for determining what a document is about is the so-called industrial recognition approach. In this approach, the metadata found in the business-relevant words is passed against a dictionary of categories of business subjects, such as accounting, marketing, and sales. Many industries have a standardized dictionary, sanctioned by an association or standards group, for that specific industry. In addition, some companies have begun to market industry-specific classification schemes, taxonomies, or ontology that can help businesses in these industries to organize their data and Web sites. Based on the content of these industry-recognized words and phrases, unstructured documents can be characterized as being relevant (or not relevant) to different aspects of business.

Figure 12.9 shows the passing of unstructured text against industrially recognized dictionaries and/or ontology.

The distillation process that has been described is one of refining unstructured data into a manageable and comprehensible format. The result of the distillation process that has been described is the extraction and identification of business metadata from unstructured text. Once the business metadata is distilled, a lot can be done with it.

### 12.3.1.5 Business Metadata Terms

Each occurrence of business metadata can have its own descriptive information. For example, the following descriptive information can be recorded for the business metadata term *payment:*

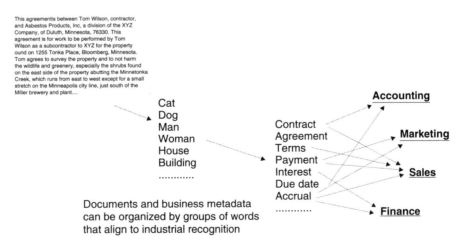

This agreementis between Tom Wilson, contractor, and Asbestos Products, Inc, a division of the XYZ Company, of Duluth, Minnesota, 76330. This agreement is for work to be performed by Tom Wilson as a subcontractor to XYZ for the property ound on 1255 Tonka Place, Bloomberg, Minnesota. Tom agrees to survey the property and to not harm the wildlife and greenery, especially the shrubs found on the east side of the property abutting the Minnetonka Creek, which runs from east to west except for a small stretch on the Minneapolis city line, just south of the Miller brewery and plant....

Cat
Dog
Man
Woman
House
Building
............

Contract
Agreement
Terms
Payment
Interest
Due date
Accrual
............

**Accounting**

**Marketing**

**Sales**

**Finance**

Documents and business metadata can be organized by groups of words that align to industrial recognition

**Figure 12.9**   Organizing According to Word Groups.

 ✦ The definition of payment

 ✦ Payment aka (also known as)

 ✦ Payment formula

 ✦ Who owns the term *payment*

 ✦ Where else the term *payment* is found, and so forth.

Figure 12.10 shows that once the business metadata is distilled, other descriptive information about the business metadata can be collected.

A further refinement of the distilled business metadata involves the process of defining relationships between the different occurrences of business metadata. Figure 12.11 shows just one of those relationships that can be created.

### 12.3.1.6 Recognizing Relationships

Figure 12.11 shows that a group of business metadata terms have been distilled. After the distillation, the words can be further refined into a relationship, or series of relationships. The figure also shows that a contract is another name for an agreement. A contract can have terms, payments, interest, due dates, and accruals.

Many types of relationships can be recognized, including:

 ✦ Belonging to

 ✦ Type of

 ✦ Is the same as (synonym)

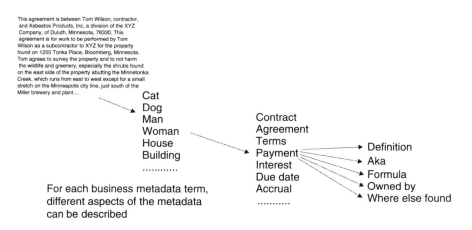

**Figure 12.10** Descriptions of Each Business Metadata Term.

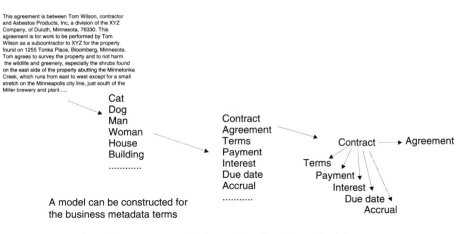

**Figure 12.11**   Business Metadata Terms Model.

+ Is related to

+ Is used for (function)

+ Is in the same family as

Different types of classification are further described in Chapters 4 and 11.

### 12.3.2   Linking Unstructured with Structured Data: Bridging the Gap

As discussed in several places in this book, information systems have grown up around structured data and structured systems. The structured environment:

+ Is made up of data that has fields, columns, tables, rows, and indexes

+ Centers around transactions

+ Has reports, audits, and definitions of words

The unstructured environment is very different from the structured environment, which is characterized by a high degree of predictability and order. The unstructured environment has no particular order to it; it consists of freeform text, which is found everywhere in diverse types of documents—medical reports, warranties, contracts, e-mail, and spreadsheets. Most often the text has no rules governing its creation or usage. It has no keys, no indexes, no columns, no attributes. The text is truly free form and is disorderly.

As mentioned earlier, the worlds of structured data and unstructured data seem to operate in parallel universes that do not intersect. With few if any exceptions, there is no bridge or interface between the two worlds. The worlds are as alien to each other as Mars and Earth. However, if a bridge between the two worlds is finally created, the construction of entirely new kinds of systems will be possible.

The world of structured systems is inhabited mostly by technical metadata, whereas the world of unstructured systems is inhabited mostly by business metadata. (*Note*: This is not a perfect subdivision; some business metadata can be found in the structured environment and vice versa.) But almost all the division is separate and clean.

### 12.3.2.1    Integration

If unstructured data is to be used in the structured environment, it must go through an integration process. This process is similar to the integration process used for legacy systems data as it passes into the data warehouse environment. However, the integration process used for unstructured data is very different in kind: it requires a systematic determination of the semantic and linguistic content of the text. We discussed the first part of this process in the last section. After text distillation, the unstructured data must be matched with structured data so that it can be used to create truly integrated solutions. Following textual distillation and analysis, it can be moved to the structured environment, where the text can be placed in a standard relational database and be accessed, analyzed, and linked to structured data by standard database software.

Finding keys to match unstructured data with the structured data may be a challenge, however. The relational world works by means of relationships between tables, matching a primary key in the "parent" table with a foreign key in the "child" table. How do you know, for example, that the John Smith referenced in a specific e-mail should be linked with the John Smith who works in Engineering?

Probabilistic matching algorithms can be used to come up with suggested matches. Data quality tools such as First Logic (now Business Objects) and Trillium have been using sophisticated algorithms for years to perform this function. Tools vary in their complexity, but a variety of tools are available that can find probabilistic matches.

### 12.3.2.2    Abstraction

The business metadata that lives in the unstructured environment is in the form of abstractions. As an example, consider the following cases.

✦ The Chrysler building is a form of a building.

✦ Tom Cruise is a movie star.

✦ Chicago is a city.

✦ *Building the Data Warehouse* is a book, and so forth.

In fact, a lot of text is nothing but abstractions, and *every* abstraction is a form of business metadata. However, not every abstraction in the textual environment is treated as metadata. Instead, a selective abstraction process is needed that can be applied to the unstructured environment. In some cases, large generalizations are considered the basis for metadata. Examples of large generalizations include:

✦ Profitability

✦ Expenses

✦ Happiness

✦ Peace

✦ War

✦ Love

But there are other bases for metadata in the textual environment. The analyst can create what can be termed *external categories* to identify particular abstractions. Alternatively, ontology, glossaries, and/or taxonomies can be created to ferret out the important abstractions from the large body of possibilities found in text.

### 12.3.2.3 Examples of Useful Bridging Applications

Linking the two types of disparate data can create extremely powerful applications in a wide range of businesses, from health care to homeland security. Here are a few examples.

#### 12.3.2.3.1 Disease Control
The Centers for Disease Control (CDC) has a database containing various diseases and their common symptoms. Imagine the reports coming in from various news feeds, shown in Figure 12.12.

Linking the unstructured data (various symptoms) with disease data can help the CDC to detect the breakout of disease and to control it before it becomes an epidemic. Figure 12.13 shows the screening of the data using external categories.

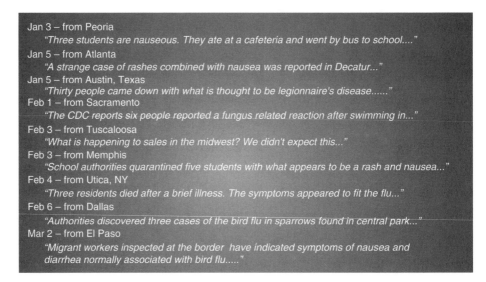

**Figure 12.12** News Feeds: Unstructured Data.

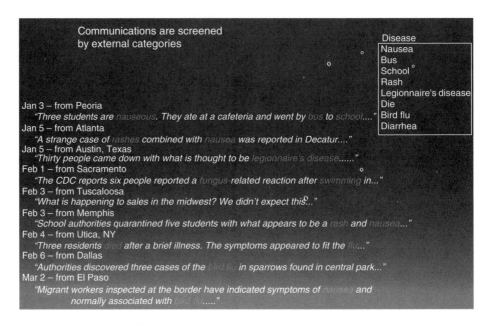

**Figure 12.13** Screening Using Categories.

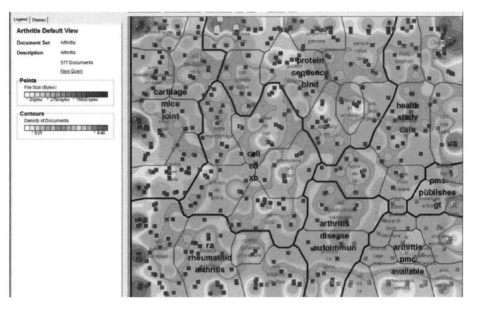

**Figure 12.14**  Self-Organizing Map.

### 12.3.2.3.2  Healthcare

Imagine a personal profile that can be accumulated about an individual, based on a complete medical history and coupled with personal habits, medications, exercise, and the like. A personal profile can be mapped to different parts of the body; such a profile can provide an integrated report showing areas where a person is vulnerable, and a plan can be created with the health of the whole person in mind. Self-organizing maps can be created that visually show the person's areas of greatest vulnerability (see Figure 12.14).

## 12.4  Summary

The world of data and associated metadata is divided into two major types of technology: structured and unstructured. Unstructured technology consists generally of text. In order to make sense of the text, a distillation process occurs, which encompasses the following steps:

✦ Words are separated into business-relevant words and nonbusiness-relevant words.

✦ Extraneous words are removed.

✦ Words are reduced to a common stem.

✦ Themes of words are created for a document for the purpose of understanding what the document is about.

✦ Industrial recognition of the words can occur by classifying documents according to their content.

Once the text has been distilled, the remainder is business metadata. The business metadata can then have its own metadata, such as

✦ Description

✦ Definition

✦ Aka

✦ Formula

✦ Business rules

The recognition of the world of unstructured data has spawned a new class of technologies aimed at capturing and managing the unstructured data and associated business metadata in our environment. These technologies can add significant value to the business metadata and provide increasing opportunities to expand our business capabilities.

# Business Rules

## 13.1 Introduction

Business rules, like business metadata in general, are not well documented but are nevertheless important and have value to the business. Business rules would have even more value to the enterprise if they were written down and it was determined where in the business systems they were enforced. This would enable the organization to verify whether or not the rules were being universally enforced. As we will see in this chapter, the promise of business rules is the maintenance of the rules by businesspeople themselves. Lastly, we will discuss some of the issues involving tools and practical implementation concerns.

## 13.2 What Are Business Rules?

A business rule, simply defined, is a constraint upon the business that the business puts upon itself (i.e., it is self-inflicted). It clarifies what the business allows and what it prohibits. Another way to express this definition is to say that rules provide guidance to the business.

Ron Ross, considered the "father of business rules," describes a business rule in this way:

> A business rule is simply a rule that is under business jurisdiction. Under business jurisdiction is taken to mean that the business can enact, revise, and discontinue their business rules as they see fit. If a rule is not under business jurisdiction in that sense, then it is not a business rule. For example, the laws of gravity [*sic*] is obviously not a business rule. Neither are the "rules" of mathematics. (Ross, 2005, pp. 75–76)

This description is clear, stating unequivocally that the business has control over its rules. At the same time, it raises a question about external authorities or agencies that impose rules on the business. For example, Sarbanes-Oxley, Basel II, and other regulations come to mind. Aren't these business rules, even though they have been externally imposed on the business? It is obvious that the enterprise has to abide by these requirements.

This issue touches on the matter of compliance, which is covered in Chapter 14. Suffice it to say here that the external regulation in and of itself is not a business rule; it is the means of enforcement that the enterprise chooses to adopt that is the business rule. The company can choose to abide by the rule, or it can take the risk incurred by ignoring it. The company can decide to interpret the rule in different ways, which may also prove risky. In any case, it is not the external regulation itself that is the business rule; rather, it is how the organization chooses to enforce the regulation in its environment that is the rule. And in this case, the compliance action conforms with Ron Ross's definition.

Ross informally began the business rules movement in the late 1980s– early 1990s, with contributions from a number of people like Barbara von Halle. (Halle's column in *Database Programming and Design*[1] helped give momentum to the movement.) The purpose of the movement was to make business rules equally understandable to both businesspeople and computers, allowing a businessperson to change a rule. This method would give a business complete agility, allowing it to respond quickly to change without the need for programming, completely bypassing and eliminating the typical barrier of IT backlog.

The movement spawned a variety of tools, most notably business rule engines optimized for rule-firing performance. Although some rule engine tools include a rule management facility to help businesspeople create and modify rules, a few other tools exclusively provide this facility and some can even be "bolted on" to engines as a management layer.

---

[1]*Database Programming and Design* is now a defunct publication, and has been replaced by *Intelligent Enterprise*. Some back issues are available at http://www.dbpd.com/vault/archives.shtml

### 13.2.1 Business Rules as Business Metadata

Business rules obviously fit into our category of business metadata. From the start business rules have been primarily about expression of rules in business language. The rules governing or constraining values allowed for a data element are business metadata. Therefore, there is a natural affinity between business rules and business metadata.

# 13.3 Where Are Business Rules Found?

Business rules are ubiquitous. When they are written down, they are most commonly found in policy and procedures manuals and in system documentation as well. However, the most common business rule repositories are the people themselves: Most business rules are buried in people's heads. Therefore, all the techniques we discussed in the knowledge capture chapter (Chapter 6) apply to the mining of business rules

Since business rules are not found in just one area but are everywhere, it may be difficult to find them, capture them in an easy to understand format, and then expose them where they can be useful.

Documented business rules can be collected from the following places:

◆ Policy and procedure manuals

◆ Program code

◆ Workflow applications

◆ System user documentation

◆ Memos

◆ Guidance documentation

◆ E-mails

◆ Government regulations and compliance documentation (although probably not the business rules themselves; the real business rules are the organization's responses to these regulations)

◆ Legal documentation

◆ Sales and Marketing procedures, including special discounts and rewards to high-volume customers

These are just a few of the obvious places where the business analyst will find rules. The astute analyst will also discover some nonobvious places when he or she starts to dig deep.

Business rules are frequently written in technical jargon and therefore are not easily decipherable by nonexperts. This observation is definitely true of business rules buried in code. The word "code" is used for a reason; most businesspeople don't speak in Java or C#. (Indeed, many business people might think that C# is a musical key signature and not a programming language.)

### 13.3.1  Business Rules and Managing the Business

Even though business rules are seldom written down, they are usually active behind the scenes. They help constrain the business by keeping it on track and verifying or validating that the business runs smoothly. But if they are not centrally located and documented, how do you know that they are universally enforced throughout the enterprise? It is essentially the same problem as the universal confusion over the meaning of data that we discussed in other chapters, reinforcing the importance of a glossary and a conceptual data model (or semantic model). In addition, imagine having a thorough understanding of your business rules and where they are enforced. This would provide impact analysis for change, and it is a step in the direction of the overarching dream of flexible systems and changing the business rules with no programming.

Business rules can be extremely effective tools in managing the business, once you have captured them and made them available to businesspeople. It is possible to do diagnostics on a rule to determine whether it is having the desired effect. Is the Loyalty Program having the desired effect of customer retention and repeat buying, or are we just giving away too much? What if the rules for what constitutes a "Premier Customer" were changed? What are the discounting policies and rules? What if they were to be changed—would heavier discounting bring in more business, or would it be just money lost? By isolating the rule and making it available to the businessperson to change, it makes systems more flexible and able to respond more quickly to changing market conditions.

There is another advantage in digging the rule out of its usual habitat of being buried in code: even if you are not using a rules system, you can expose the rule both in technical jargon (if the users are technical) and in plain English to provide users with the context of the data at any time. This is the classic role of business metadata.

#### 13.3.1.1  Are Business Rules Worth the Trouble of Capturing and Managing?

The question that arises with any IT initiative is whether it is worth the money it costs to produce the system. Business rules, being extremely amorphous and ubiquitous, are costly to gather and capture, and they are also costly to manage over time. Is the effort worth it?

Often, the answer seems to be "no" because the business doesn't see the value that managing business rules brings, or, alternatively, the business might understand that it does have value, but not enough, or that the value is hard to measure and apply to business management.

If rule management could really be turned over to businesspeople, and they could tweak the rules if they were given the power and authority to do so, then would business rule systems be worth it? They might be because as a result the business would be much more adaptable to market conditions. However, do businesspeople really want to perform maintenance? After all, that is what the technical people have never wanted to do, so why should the businesspeople want to do it? However, businesspeople are always complaining that IT is not fast enough to respond to feature and change requests. If maintenance was in the hands of the businesspeople, they wouldn't have anyone to blame (or maybe that's what they are afraid of!).

### 13.3.2  Business Rule Systems

Several products now on the market allow business rules to be created and managed by savvy businesspeople. Of course, these products require setup by technical people. The following examples are from Blaze Advisor™, a product of Fair Isaac Corporation. Other companies offering products of note in this family include:

- ✦ ILOG
- ✦ Corticon
- ✦ Versata
- ✦ Haley Systems
- ✦ Pega Systems

Many of these products offer different ways of creating rules, whichever way suits the type of rule. For example, some rules are simple if/then rules. These can be entered by using a simple syntax and predefined keywords (seen in yellow in Figure 13.1).

Most rule tools provide different ways of entering rules; For example, if a set of rules represents a lookup table, then it can be expressed more easily as a decision table. Figure 13.2 shows an example of a decision table, and Figure 13.3 presents the same decision table, viewed three different ways. (If you are familiar with business intelligence tools such as Cognos or Business Objects, you will recognize these display differences.)

Decision trees can also be helpful in representing rules like these in a more visual format. See Figure 13.4 for Blaze Advisor's decision tree format:

If at least 2 children satisfy age < 8
then set discount to 0.25.

If product's ID does not start with "SPX"
then the PromotionStatus of the Product is False.

If the name of the custome is unknown
then print("Please enter your name").

If order's purchase Date is earlier than 'January 1, 2002'
then print("Your purchase is no longer eligible for return").

SeniorMale is any customer such that (age > 65 and gender is male).

**Figure 13.1** Simple If/Then Rules [Fair Isaac].

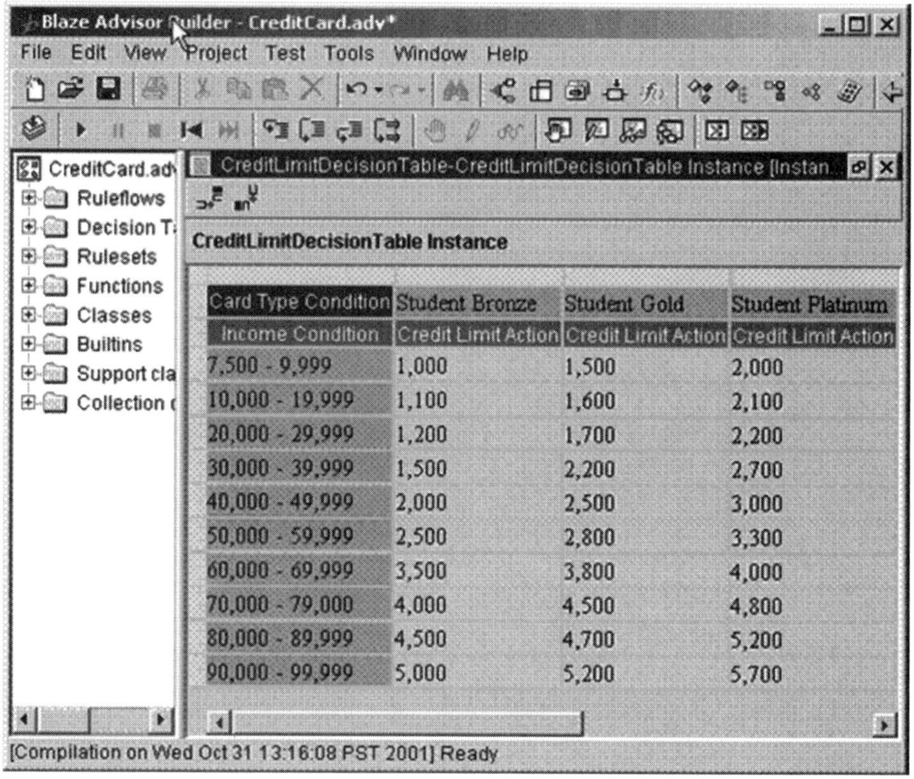

Blaze Advisor Builder - CreditCard.adv*

File   Edit   View   Project   Test   Tools   Window   Help

CreditCard.adv
- Ruleflows
- Decision T.
- Rulesets
- Functions
- Classes
- Builtins
- Support cla
- Collection

CreditLimitDecisionTable-CreditLimitDecisionTable Instance [Instan...

**CreditLimitDecisionTable Instance**

| Card Type Condition | Student Bronze | Student Gold | Student Platinum |
|---|---|---|---|
| Income Condition | Credit Limit Action | Credit Limit Action | Credit Limit Action |
| 7,500 - 9,999 | 1,000 | 1,500 | 2,000 |
| 10,000 - 19,999 | 1,100 | 1,600 | 2,100 |
| 20,000 - 29,999 | 1,200 | 1,700 | 2,200 |
| 30,000 - 39,999 | 1,500 | 2,200 | 2,700 |
| 40,000 - 49,999 | 2,000 | 2,500 | 3,000 |
| 50,000 - 59,999 | 2,500 | 2,800 | 3,300 |
| 60,000 - 69,999 | 3,500 | 3,800 | 4,000 |
| 70,000 - 79,000 | 4,000 | 4,500 | 4,800 |
| 80,000 - 89,999 | 4,500 | 4,700 | 5,200 |
| 90,000 - 99,999 | 5,000 | 5,200 | 5,700 |

[Compilation on Wed Oct 31 13:16:08 PST 2001] Ready

**Figure 13.2** Business Rule Decision Table.

| Income | 25,000 - 34,999 | 25,000 - 34,999 | 25,000 - 34,999 | 35,000 - 44,999 | 35,000 - 44,999 |
|---|---|---|---|---|---|
| Card Type | Poor | Good | Excellent | Poor | Good |
| Credit Limit | 2,500 | 3,000 | 4,000 | 3,000 | 3,500 |

| Income | Card Type | Credit Limit |
|---|---|---|
| 25,001 - 35,000 | Student Bronze | 2,500 |
| 25,001 - 35,000 | Student Gold | 3,000 |
| 25,001 - 35,000 | Student Platinum | 4,000 |
| 35,001 - 45,000 | Student Bronze | 3,000 |
| 35,001 - 45,000 | Student Gold | 3,500 |
| 35,001 - 45,000 | Student Platinum | 4,500 |
| > 45,000 | Student Bronze | 4,200 |
| > 45,000 | Student Gold | 4,700 |
| > 45,000 | Student Platinum | 5,200 |

← **1-Axis Vertical**   **1-Axis Horizontal**   **2-Axis Grid**

| Card Type | Student Bronze | Student Gold | Student Platinum |
|---|---|---|---|
| Credit Rating | Poor | Good | Excellent |
| Homeowner? | false | true | true |
| Income | Credit Limit | Credit Limit | Credit Limit |
| 25,001 - 35,000 | 2,500 | 3,000 | 4,000 |
| 35,001 - 45,000 | 3,000 | 3,500 | 4,500 |
| > 45,000 | 4,200 | 4,700 | 5,200 |

**Figure 13.3** Decision Table Displayed Three Different Ways: A Different Way to Represent Rules.

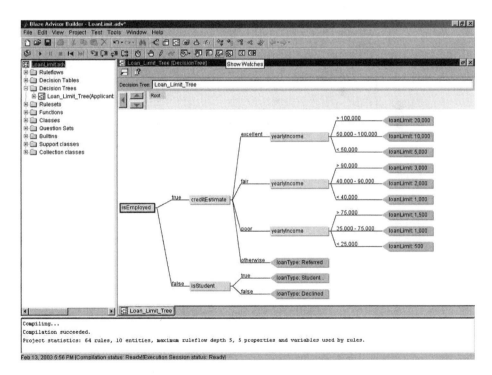

**Figure 13.4** Business Rule Decision Trees.

Decision tables are useful when the business rules are based on a small number of conditions, with each rule corresponding to a particular combination of data values or value ranges. Common examples include rate tables, pricing charts, discount schedules, and so on. Decision trees allow you to trace a chain of conditions to a single appropriate action. Looking at branches coming from a decision point (or "node") in the tree lets you quickly confirm that all applicable possibilities have been accounted for. A ruleset that has rules sharing many initial conditions and that result in a single outcome can be represented very effectively as a decision tree, such as a diagnostic tree.

Many tools allow for a special interface to be created for businesspeople and nontechnical users to maintain the rules. Figure 13.5 shows a rule maintenance application screen that can be used for this purpose.

The real power behind these tools lies in the execution of the rules. Rules are stated in a nonprocedural way, and the rule engine figures out the most appropriate order to fire the rules at execution time. Because some rules do require more control over the order of execution, Blaze Advisor provides a ruleflow utility. See Figure 13.6 for an example of a ruleflow.

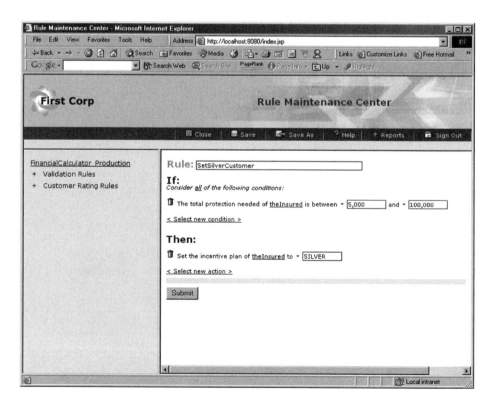

**Figure 13.5**   Rule Maintenance for Nontechnical Users.

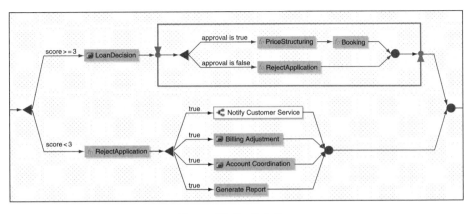

**Figure 13.6**   Ruleflow.

Some rule engines offer powerful conflict resolution features; they can help determine whether addition of a new rule will conflict with any existing rules already in the system. Some tools also include inferencing, which means creating new knowledge from existing knowledge (e.g., if I know that Sue and Mary are sisters, and Mary has a child named John, I can then infer that Sue is John's Aunt).

### 13.3.3   Rule Management

Business rule engines automate the enforcement of business rules in an IT system. However, many of these tools lack the level of business metadata support that would be helpful. For example, wouldn't it be nice if business rules were linked to the terms that they use, so that you could click on the term and get its definition? And wouldn't it be nice to link the data stewards in charge of the rules to the rules themselves, so that if people had a question about the rule, they could know who to go to? Business rule engines focus on the enforcement of rules, making them executable, with varying degrees of business friendliness in the areas of creation and modification. As of this writing, however, they generally don't focus on the business parts of the problem, such as stewardship and business clarity/background information.

Rule management products provide these features and more. An example of an elegant rule management product is Rule Express, offered by RuleArts. This class of product provides the business metadata behind the rules so that they can be managed effectively in the business, with appropriate stewardship programs and processes. It is necessary to have both a rules engine and a rules management tool. Using today's products (as of this writing), you will probably have to accomplish this goal with more than one tool.

### 13.3.4 Business Rules and the Metadata Repository

Support for business rules at the time of this writing in traditional metadata repositories is spotty. Sometimes the tool will include a business rule object but will not provide all the possible relationships that you would like to have. Some provide only one business rule object; you need at least two—one to express the rule in "business speak" and another to express the rule more formally.

It is possible to extend a traditional metadata repository tool to support business rules, but it can get tricky. The trouble is that most (if not all) business rules relate to more than one data element, and repositories usually are oriented toward data elements, meaning that they allow business rules to be entered as context to an individual data element but not as a repository element in their own right. As seen in Figure 13.7, business rules are related to data elements in a many-to-many fashion.

An example of a simple rule would be:

> A professor is only allowed to teach upper division courses in his or her degreed field.

The relevant data elements referred to in the rule are:

+ Professor

+ Course

+ Attribute of course: upper division

+ Attribute of professor: subject of degree held

+ Attribute of course: subject

The rule above then refers to several data elements. Undoubtedly, there are lots of other rules pertaining to these elements, so the relationship is many-to-many.

Most repositories provide the means to be extended, so this feature can be added, and a new repository element called Business Rule can be created and linked to data elements. Be careful when repository products are extended, however; for example, make sure you follow the vendor's instructions meticulously to make sure your object is in the right place in the metamodel (parent/child). Vendors often vary in the level of support their front-end browser and reporting

**Figure 13.7** Business Rule to Data Element: Many-to-Many Relationship.

tools have for user extensions. We have seen this to be true in the past, but with today's more advanced products the past limitations concerning front-end display of repository extensions are less likely to be a problem.

### 13.3.5  Business Metadata about Business Rules

As we have seen, business rules are business metadata as long as they are expressed in the language of the business. Business rules provide the context behind the data: They indicate the rules that are tied to the data elements. But business rules also have their own associated business metadata: information about the rules themselves, such as the authority behind the rule (who says that it's a rule?), terms used in the rule, the source of the rule, and so on. We have described several ways that metadata about the rules can be captured, notably by using a rules management product or a traditional repository. The third option, which is always a possibility, is to build your own metadata repository. Constructing your own repository in the context of business rules becomes a little trickier than it would be for usual business metadata, if the intention is to use a business rules engine. You will have to figure out a way that your homegrown repository will relate to the rules in the engine. For example, which product will be used to create the rules? If you create them in the repository, you will need a transport mechanism like ETL to extract and load them into the rules engine. If it is the other way around, you still have the same problem, only in reverse. You will have to verify whether the rules engine product has an API to import or extract rules. However, going to this trouble and building such a facility will provide 360-degree visibility into your business metadata and all the business rules.

## 13.4  Summary

In this chapter we have surveyed the rise of business rules, both as a discipline (just documenting rules is useful to the business) and as a new approach to writing applications (isolating business rules so they can be maintained by business people). We have seen that business rules, by their very nature and purpose, are business metadata. The chapter used one business rule engine product as an example and illustrated some of the features of rule engines. In addition, rule management products were discussed, which link the rules with data element definitions, stewardship information, and so on. A few suggestions were provided in terms of implementation so that the end result will be a 360 degree view of both business rules and their associated data elements (and vice versa), along with other important business metadata.

## 13.5 References

- ✦ Fair Isaac. "Fair Isaac Blaze Advisor: How It Works." April 2006. http://www.fairisaac.com/NR/rdonlyres/8CCEDAB8-25C4-4579-8F14-D08DE332C5A5/0/HowAdvisorWorks61WP.pdf

- ✦ Ross, Ron. *Business Rule Concepts: Getting to the Point of Knowledge*. Business Rule Solutions, LLC, Houston, TX, 2nd edition, 2005, ISBN 10-094104906x.

# Compliance and Business Metadata

## 14.1 Introduction

The world of today is one of regulation and compliance to information standards and statutes. Once there was freedom of information, but after it was abused by several corporations, government and other regulatory bodies created standards and statutes designed to regulate the flow and use of information. Compliance has become extremely pervasive and costly to most businesses. Sarbanes-Oxley is the regulatory compliance issue most often discussed in the corporate environment. Business metadata can help compliance efforts in many ways, and several examples will be introduced in this chapter.

A number of important compliance initiatives have been introduced in recent years. This chapter dives into Sarbanes-Oxley in some detail to serve as an example of compliance efforts.

# 14.2    Compliance Standards

The four most prominent compliance standards are Sarbanes-Oxley, HIPAA, Basel II, and the Patriot Act. This chapter describes Sarbanes-Oxley because it so widespread: It applies to all publicly traded corporations. Other regulations are more industry-specific: HIPAA applies to organizations working in the health-care arena; Basel II applies to financial institutions; and the Patriot Act requires, among other things, the monitoring of foreign students.

### 14.2.1    Sarbanes-Oxley Provisions

Wikipedia outlines the main provisions of Sarbanes-Oxley as:

+ Creation of the Public Company Accounting Oversight Board (PCAOB)

+ A requirement that public companies evaluate and disclose the effectiveness of their internal controls as they relate to financial reporting, and that independent auditors for such companies "attest" (i.e., agree, or qualify) to such disclosure

+ Certification of *financial reports* by *chief executive officers* and *chief financial officers*

+ Auditor independence, including outright bans on certain types of work for audit clients and precertification by the company's *Audit Committee* of all other nonaudit work

+ A requirement that companies listed on stock exchanges have fully independent audit committees that oversee the relationship between the company and its auditor

+ Ban on most personal loans to any executive officer or director

+ Accelerated reporting of *trades by insiders*

+ Prohibition on insider trades during *pension fund* blackout periods

+ Additional disclosure

+ Enhanced criminal and civil penalties for violations of *securities law*

+ Significantly longer maximum jail sentences and larger fines for corporate executives who knowingly and willfully misstate *financial statements*, although maximum sentences are largely irrelevant because judges generally follow the *Federal Sentencing Guidelines* in setting actual sentences

✦ Employee protections allowing those corporate fraud *whistleblowers* who file complaints with the Occupational Safety and Health Administration (<u>OSHA</u>) within 90 days to win reinstatement, back pay and benefits, compensatory damages, abatement orders, and reasonable attorney fees and costs. (Wikipedia, referenced in October 2006)

The law's main areas of concern to IT, and to organizations in general, involve a focus on "internal controls," monitoring of financial transactions, and reporting of "material events," which may have a significant impact on an investor's decision to purchase the company's stock. Section 409 expands the definition of material events and requires extensive disclosure of these to the general public.

The focus on controls highlights IT governance, which is discussed in Chapter 3. There are obvious possibilities for usage of business metadata in helping to track the organization's governance of information. Some of the information entails traditional business metadata such as who is the steward for this data. However, questions such as "What are the business rules concerning modification of this type of transaction?" hearken to business metadata. Business rule compliance is very pertinent to the management of compliance information. (The topic of metadata relative to business rules is covered in Chapter 13 of this book.)

## 14.3   Types of Compliance

There are two basic types of compliance—financial compliance and communications compliance (see Figure 14.1).

### 14.3.1   Financial Audits

Financial transactions are those activities that have resulted in the exchange of money for some purpose. Compliance to financial transactions implies

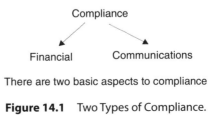

There are two basic aspects to compliance

**Figure 14.1**   Two Types of Compliance.

- ✦ The audit of the amount of the transaction

- ✦ The completeness of all transactions that have transpired

- ✦ The classification of transactions

- ✦ The verification of the parties involved in the transaction

- ✦ The date of the transaction, and so forth.

### 14.3.1.1  Metadata and Financial Transactions

Traditional metadata can be very useful for financial audits and can provide some basic traceability for the transaction, covering items such as:

- ✦ Who entered the transaction

- ✦ When the transaction was entered into the system

- ✦ When it was modified

- ✦ Who modified it

But why and how did the transaction occur? Why was the transaction modified? Having the capability to answer questions like those is the concern of business metadata. Often, systems do not provide a way to track the rationale behind a transaction other than having an unstructured comment field.

It is possible to extend transaction systems to permit a user to enter the rationale behind transaction edits, or the reasons why a transaction was modified. However, it is very important that users understand the importance of entering in a "rational rationale"—that is, a rationale that makes sense and is real. All of us are familiar with information systems and automated forms that force an entry in a field. If we don't know what to enter, we enter nonsense just so we can get past the field. For example, timesheet applications often require that you fill in a text box if you modify an entry. It is possible to enter "blah blah blah" and the application will accept it; you just need to enter something. Therefore, it is important that users are trained to enter a real reason, and not just a meaningless phrase. Of course, many business process and performance challenges are associated with asking business users to enter this data. How long does it take, and is the data important enough to the organization to justify the time and cost involved in this entry? How do we reward the staff doing the data entry for complete and accurate data? Many solutions to the issue are possible since it is not at all new to governance data.

### 14.3.1.2  Financial Transaction Background Activities

A whole host of activities may occur prior to the financial transaction; for example:

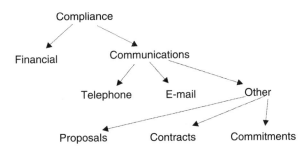

There are many facets to communications

**Figure 14.2**  Many Facets of Business Communications.

+ A negotiation has occurred.

+ Promises and proposals have been made.

+ Commitments have been made.

+ Arrangements for payment have been negotiated.

The transaction represents the culmination of all of its background activities. However, the business transaction generally does not occur until after all of the above activities have been completed.

### 14.3.2   Communications Audits

All of these background activities are captured in communications—e-mails, letters, telephone calls, memos, and so forth. All of these communications are subject to compliance, as are financial transactions. Figure 14.2 shows that communications encompass the different prefinancial aspects of corporate activities.

#### 14.3.2.1   Compliance Words and Phrases

In order to achieve compliance at the business metadata level, it is necessary to identify the words and phrases to which the different compliance standards are sensitive. Figure 14.3 presents a sample list of these words and phrases.

## 14.4   Screening Communications

Once the list of sensitive words and phrases is collected, the next step is to create a "screen" or a "sieve" of these words and phrases. Such a screen is shown in Figure 14.4.

| Sarbanes Oxley | Basel II | HIPAA |
|---|---|---|
| - promise to deliver | - account | - patient |
| - contingency sale | - account management | - episode of care |
| - executive loan | - fiduciary | - provider |
| - commitment | - rate of return | - payment |
| - SPV account | - risk | - coverage |
| - off the books | - put | - carryover coverage |
| - revenue recognition | - call | - treatment |
| - proposal | - long | - outcome |
| - ..................... | - short | - diagnosis |
| | - churn | - disease |
| | - ................. | - .............. |

Some business metadata terms relevant to
different forms of compliance

**Figure 14.3**  Business Metadata Terms Pertaining to Regulation.

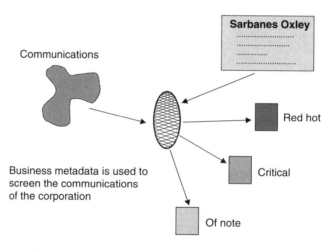

**Figure 14.4**  Screening Corporate Communications.

In Figure 14.4, it is seen that the communications of the corporation in text form are passed through the screen. The screen consists of words and phrases that have been deemed important to compliance. Although the figure presents a list of words and phrases for Sarbanes-Oxley, the same list could be used for HIPAA, Basel II, or other regulations.

### 14.4.1   Sorting Through the Words and Phrases

The text is then passed through the screen. When a word or phrase is found to appear on the compliance list, it is pulled out. Based on the criticality of the word or phrase, the word or phrase is sent to one of three places. If the word or phrase is a "normal" word or phrase, it is placed in the simple index list. An index can then be created if there is a further need for investigation.

If the word or phrase is critical, it is placed in the context list. An index is then created, and the text before and after the word or phrase is captured. In this way, an analyst or auditor can scan the context of the word or phrase before deciding to investigate further. This method of indexing words and phases has been termed *meta tagging* and has been used for a decade in content management systems. The best practice is to divide words into different classes of compliance concern: the "normal" class—the audit class; the critical class; and the "red hot" class, where important conversations and discussions are recorded in their entirety.

The third possibility is to collect the entire message. This is done only when one encounters a word or phrase that is almost certain to spell trouble. In this case, the entire message is lifted and placed in the message list. Should someone erase the message at its original location at a later point in time, the message will still be available in this message list. Of course, the collection of entire messages must be done judiciously, because a large amount of space could be consumed.

In such a manner, the communications of the corporation—e-mail, transcripted telephone conversations, and other communications—can be analyzed in a repeatable, systematic, and automated process and can create business metadata immediately useful to the compliance endeavor.

### 14.4.2 Periodic Audits

Once the auditing has been done as described, the output can be used in a periodic audit as required by the rules of compliance. Figure 14.5 shows that the auditor can use the results of the communications screening as a basis for compliance.

### 14.4.3 Creating a Historical Collection

The output from the screen process can be collected over time, thereby increasing its usefulness to the compliance effort. It can be used as a control for periodic monitoring and tracking for the program. Figure 14.6 shows the historical library that can be collected.

The historical library has many uses, but its primary value is in allowing the user to look back in time at issues that are today unknown. The organization can use the historical audit to answer questions over time; something that it is decidedly not prepared to do today.

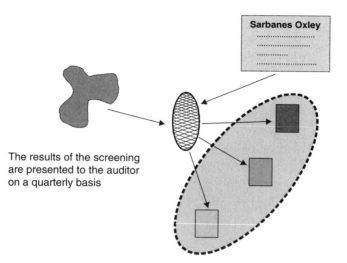

**Figure 14.5** Screening Results Presented Quarterly.

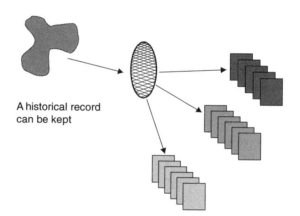

**Figure 14.6** Keeping a Historical Library for Tracking.

# 14.5 Using Data Profiling for Compliance

Data profiling can assist in compliance in areas such as ongoing financial auditing and fraud detection. Like the historic collection of communications data, it can be considered a control in monitoring the financial health of the organization and in permitting advance detection of suspicious activity.

Data profiling runs the data through an automated process and provides statistics for each column in a database table. In Chapter 10 we discussed data profiling and its important role in business metadata creation. To review, data profiling information for each column includes:

✦ Minimum Value

✦ Maximum Value

✦ Percent Distinct (100% in a given column is unique and indicates a Primary Key)

✦ Defined Datatype

✦ Actual Datatype (as opposed to what was defined in the database)

✦ Most Common Pattern (numbers, alpha characters, special characters, punctuation)

✦ Percent Null

Figure 14.7 shows some of this column profile data:

| | Attribute | # Distinc | # Record | Distinct Ratio | Documented | Inferred Data Typ | Data Type Flag | Documen | Inferred N | Inferred Min Value | Inferred Max Value |
|---|---|---|---|---|---|---|---|---|---|---|---|
| 1 | op_oper_nbr | 19058 | 19066 | 0.9996 | CHAR(6) | INTEGER | Incompatible | Null OK | Not Null | 21000 | 498441 |
| 2 | om_name1 | 16824 | 19066 | 0.8824 | CHAR(20) | VARCHAR(20, 0) | Convertible | Null OK | Not Null | "C" PUNCH RANCH | ZZZ RESVERED |
| 3 | om_name2 | 3712 | 19066 | 0.1947 | CHAR(20) | VARCHAR(20, 0) | Convertible | Null OK | Null OK | "BUDDY" AND BARBARA | ZOILA |
| 4 | om_auth_rep | 6453 | 19066 | 0.3385 | CHAR(20) | VARCHAR(20, 0) | Convertible | Null OK | Null OK | % RUSS MILLER | ZWICKER, ELDON |
| 5 | om_c_o_name | 5778 | 19066 | 0.3031 | CHAR(20) | VARCHAR(20, 0) | Convertible | Null OK | Null OK | #414 | ZX LAND & CATTLE |
| 6 | om_prnt_appl | 2 | 19066 | 0.0001 | CHAR(1) | CHAR(1) | Identical | Null OK | Not Null | N | Y |
| 7 | om_prefer_cd | 3 | 19066 | 0.0002 | CHAR(2) | SMALLINT | Incompatible | Null OK | Not Null | 3 | 15 |
| 8 | om_adr_stret | 12456 | 19066 | 0.6533 | CHAR(20) | VARCHAR(20, 0) | Convertible | Null OK | Null OK | # 25 LAFAYETTE LOOP | YOST ROUTE |
| 9 | om_adr_city | 2435 | 19066 | 0.1277 | CHAR(20) | VARCHAR(20, 0) | Convertible | Null OK | Null OK | ..... | ZZZ RESERVED |
| 10 | om_adr_st | 45 | 19066 | 0.0024 | CHAR(2) | CHAR(2) | Identical | Null OK | Not Null | AK | WY |
| 11 | om_adr_zipa | 2783 | 19066 | 0.1460 | CHAR(5) | INTEGER | Incompatible | Null OK | Not Null | 0 | 99999 |
| 12 | om_adr_zipb | 770 | 19066 | 0.0404 | CHAR(4) | SMALLINT | Incompatible | Null OK | Null OK | 0 | 9999 |
| 13 | om_phone | 10363 | 19066 | 0.5435 | CHAR(12) | VARCHAR(12, 0) | Convertible | Null OK | Null OK | (200)3662012 | ~ |
| 14 | om_eff_dt | 1697 | 19066 | 0.0890 | CHAR(8) | INTEGER | Incompatible | Null OK | Not Null | 1011992 | 12311999 |
| 15 | om_exp_dt | 1282 | 19066 | 0.0672 | CHAR(8) | INTEGER | Incompatible | Null OK | Not Null | 1011996 | 12312010 |
| 16 | om_pl_retnd | 2 | 19066 | 0.0001 | CHAR(1) | CHAR(1) | Identical | Null OK | Not Null | N | Y |
| 17 | om_undef_1 | 481 | 19066 | 0.0252 | CHAR(6) | VARCHAR(6, 0) | Convertible | Null OK | Null OK | ' | YUMA |
| 18 | om_undef_2 | 394 | 19066 | 0.0207 | CHAR(6) | VARCHAR(6, 0) | Convertible | Null OK | Null OK | #4531 | YES |
| 19 | om_undef_3 | 439 | 19066 | 0.0230 | CHAR(6) | VARCHAR(6, 0) | Convertible | Null OK | Null OK | &14546 | ~ |
| 20 | om_perm_prt | 2534 | 19066 | 0.1329 | CHAR(8) | DATETIME YEAR T | Convertible | Null OK | Null OK | 1979-01-22 00:00:00.00 | 2000-10-31 00:00:00.00 |
| 21 | om_base_lse | 497 | 19066 | 0.0261 | CHAR(8) | DATETIME YEAR T | Convertible | Null OK | Null OK | 1995-02-28 00:00:00.00 | 2000-01-02 00:00:00.00 |
| 22 | om_graz_nbr | 20 | 19066 | 0.0010 | CHAR(2) | SMALLINT | Incompatible | Null OK | Null OK | 1 | 98 |
| 23 | om_appl_prt | 1098 | 19066 | 0.0576 | CHAR(8) | DATETIME YEAR T | Convertible | Null OK | Null OK | 1900-01-04 00:00:00.00 | 2000-10-27 00:00:00.00 |
| 24 | om_bill_cnt | 101 | 19066 | 0.0053 | CHAR(2) | SMALLINT | Incompatible | Null OK | Null OK | 0 | 99 |
| 25 | om_perm_hol | 1 | 19066 | 0.0001 | CHAR(1) | CHAR(1) | Identical | Null OK | Null OK | Y | Y |
| 26 | om_chg_dt | 0 | 19066 | 0.0 | CHAR(8) | | | Null OK | Null OK | | |
| 27 | state | 10 | 19066 | 0.0005 | CHAR(2) | CHAR(2) | Identical | Null OK | Not Null | AZ | WY |
| 28 | office | 63 | 19066 | 0.0033 | CHAR(3) | SMALLINT | Incompatible | Null OK | Not Null | 10 | 690 |

**Figure 14.7**  Column Profile Data.

Note the columns entitled "Inferred Min Value" and "Inferred Max Value". The data in these columns can be used for financial compliance to spot outliers: values on either end (minimum or maximum value) that may indicate abnormality. Domain profiling can also be helpful in spotting counts of outliers or other unexpected values. Tools can be used to set thresholds and automatically alert the business if such values are found.

Is this type of metadata *business metadata*? Chapter 10 pointed out the pluses and minuses of profiling data. Perhaps the distinction is made in how it is presented to the business. Raw profiling data, usually represented in tabular format (like that shown in Figures 14.7), is not very useful, and it is difficult for the business to interpret its significance. Profiling data must be presented in business language: What does this mean to the business? For example, graphs showing number of occurrences over time of abnormal data, with the business rule beside it interpreting what the data means, communicate clearly and precisely what the abnormality means to the business. See Figure 14.8.

Figure 14.8 could be further enhanced by stating the rule violation or tacit assumption (such as: "Amount shown represents $1000's; most orders are under $5000. Although not impossible, it is extremely rare to have a single transaction amount exceed $14,000"). It is therefore not enough to perform data profiling or even to perform it on a periodic basis. It must be directly tied to the business and the delivery mechanism designed to expose business issues clearly in the language of the business.

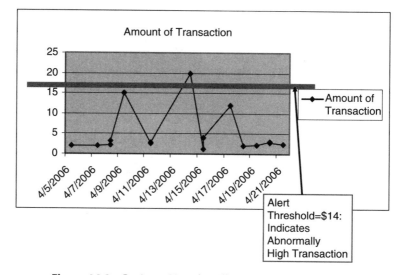

**Figure 14.8**    Business Metadata Illustrates Noncompliance.

## 14.6 Summary

The world of compliance is divided into two segments: financial compliance and communications compliance. Communications compliance includes:

✦ E-mails

✦ Reports

✦ Articles

✦ Transcripted telephone conversations

There are different regulations that are of concern, and they are generally related to the type of business an industry conducts. Common regulations include Sarbanes-Oxley, Basel II, HIPAA, and the Patriot Act.

In order to conduct a corporate communications compliance audit, the text is passed against a screen that consists of the words and phrases that the compliance is sensitive to. Words can be divided into different classes of compliance concern, based on their criticality. The details of what is stored concerning a given message or document can be dictated by the class.

Data profiling can help create business metadata related to outliers and other abnormalities. It can be performed on a periodic basis to create a historical record, and it can be mined over time. Results should be presented to the business in a form that easily communicates the critical factors needed to determine compliance or noncompliance.

## 14.7 Reference

✦ Wikipedia. "Sarbanes-Oxley Act." http://en.wikipedia.org/wiki/Sarbanes-Oxley_Act

# Knowledge Management and Business Metadata

CHAPTER 15

## 15.1 Introduction

In Chapters 8 and 9, we discussed business metadata capture and delivery, borrowing from the realm of knowledge management. In this chapter, we discuss the intersection of business metadata and knowledge management. First, we explore the discipline of knowledge management and next, we discuss its intersection with business metadata. We also discuss issues such as the role of business metadata and tacit knowledge, and intellectual capital. Lastly, we discuss the impact of business metadata on social issues such as the graying of the workforce and collaboration. We will draw from topics covered in other chapters, notably Chapters 4, 6, 7, and 8, which cover business metadata capture and delivery.

# 15.2 What Is Knowledge Management (KM)?

The entry for knowledge management in Wikipedia is very comprehensive and descriptive, and therefore we include it in its entirety.

> **Knowledge Management** (KM) refers to a range of practices used by organizations to identify, create, represent, and distribute <u>knowledge</u> for reuse, awareness, and learning across the organization.
>
> Knowledge management programs are typically tied to organizational objectives and are intended to lead to the achievement of specific outcomes such as shared intelligence, improved performance, competitive advantage, or higher levels of innovation.
>
> <u>Knowledge transfer</u> (one aspect of knowledge management) has always existed in one form or another, for example, through on-the-job peer discussions, formal apprenticeship, corporate libraries, professional training, and mentoring programs. However, since the late twentieth century—additional technology has been applied to this task, such as <u>knowledge bases</u>, <u>expert systems</u>, and <u>knowledge repositories</u>.
>
> Knowledge management programs attempt to manage the process of creation or identification, accumulation, and application of knowledge or <u>intellectual capital</u> across an organization. Knowledge management, therefore, attempts to bring under one set of practices various strands of thought and practice relating to:
>
> + intellectual capital and the <u>knowledge worker</u> in the <u>knowledge economy</u>;
> + the idea of the <u>learning organization</u>;
> + various *enabling organizational practices* such as <u>Communities of Practice</u> and corporate <u>Yellow Pages directories</u> for accessing key personnel and expertise;
> + various *enabling technologies* such as knowledge bases and expert systems, help desks, corporate <u>intranets</u> and <u>extranets</u>, <u>Content Management</u>, <u>wikis</u>, and <u>Document Management</u>.
>
> While knowledge management programs are closely related to <u>organizational learning</u> initiatives, knowledge management may be distinguished from organizational learning by its greater focus on the management of specific knowledge assets and its development and cultivation of the channels through which knowledge flows.

The emergence of knowledge management has generated new organizational roles and responsibilities, an early example of which was the <u>chief knowledge officer</u>. In recent years, the practice of <u>personal knowledge management</u> (PKM) has arisen in which individuals apply knowledge management practice to themselves, their role in the organization, and their career development.

While it has been applied to all industrial sectors, and increasingly to government, knowledge management is a continually evolving discipline, with a wide range of contributions and a wide range of views on what represents good practice in knowledge management (Wikipedia, 2006}

### 15.2.1 Why Is Knowledge Management Important?

In Chapter 4, we demonstrated that the lack of ability to find information when it is needed critically cripples an organization and costs money—big money. Nancy Dixon, has noted that companies "need to find ways to keep from continually reinventing the wheel" (Dixon, 2000, p. 1]. Later in this chapter we talk about social issues that knowledge management can help alleviate, such as the graying of the workforce and the expense of employee exodus. In Chapter 4 we discussed the fact that the business economy is increasingly becoming centered around information—hence the popularity of the term *knowledge worker*, referred to in the Wikipedia article, which is very descriptive of what most office workers do. To no small degree, a company's success today depends on its ability to manage information and use corporate knowledge to gain the greatest benefit.

## 15.3 The Intersection of Business Metadata and Knowledge Management

As we have observed throughout this book, business metadata not only delivers context to businesspeople directly (as opposed to technical people) but is also created by businesspeople. Therefore, knowledge management can be considered an intrinsic part of business metadata, and knowledge management is built into its core. Business metadata is:

+ Involved in the creation and maintenance of the corporate knowledge base

+ Involved with the capture and dissemination of information and knowledge from and to businesspeople

Not only do business metadata and knowledge management intersect, but they are by definition intertwined. Both have the same overarching purpose: to provide value to the organization by identifying, creating, representing, and distributing knowledge for reuse, awareness, and learning [rephrased from the Wikipedia reference quoted above]. *Business metadata also constitutes a chunk of the business knowledge that knowledge management is supposed to manage!*

### 15.3.1 Knowledge Management Generates Business Metadata Artifacts

The main difference between knowledge management and business metadata is that knowledge management concerns itself with the processes behind the generation and maintenance of knowledge, whereas business metadata captures the artifacts from these processes. Knowledge management is process-oriented, and business metadata is data-oriented, but just as process and data are related, they have a synergistic and symbiotic relationship. They are two sides of the same coin (see Figure 15.1).

Because knowledge management is process-centric and business metadata is data-centric, we can understand this symbiotic relationship better if we see it in its broader context: the classic relationship between process and data. See Figure 15.2, which is essentially the same as Figure 15.1, except it replaces the names.

Processes, in order to be useful to the organization over time and beyond the process itself, must leave artifacts (data) behind. Data, owing to its persistence and the fact that it outlives the process itself (the process being by nature bound in time), adds longevity to the process and makes the results of the process valuable to the business over time. Additionally, business metadata can also make the knowledge management processes repeatable and can feed the process by providing parameters to a report program. It can

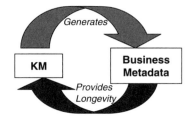

**Figure 15.1**   Business Metadata and Knowledge Management.

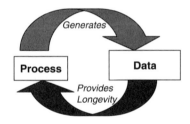

**Figure 15.2**   Process and Data.

allow metrics to be created for the process and can therefore facilitate process improvement.

Business metadata can partner with knowledge management to the extent that the knowledge management initiatives can articulate knowledge artifacts. These artifacts can be stored as business metadata and disseminated to business users when and where they can be helpful.

The interesting aspect of this relationship is business metadata's later use to supply context for data throughout the organization. But business metadata also has context: for example, the knowledge management process that created it or is using it. Therefore, it could be said that knowledge management provides the meta-metadata for business metadata!

We need to emphasize, however, that knowledge management is separate from business metadata. Not all business metadata is generated from knowledge management, as business metadata may come from other sources such as the transformation of technical metadata. Moreover, knowledge management does things other than generate business metadata. None of these considerations, however, discount the symbiotic nature of business metadata and knowledge management, as discussed earlier.

### 15.3.2   *Knowledge Management Example: Corporate Dictionary*

In Chapter 6, we used a corporate dictionary as an example of a business metadata capture project. The goal of the corporation profiled in that chapter was to create a corporate dictionary that would be authored by the business-people themselves. This is a great example of a knowledge management project that generates business metadata. The dictionary project created dictionary entries, which are knowledge components or building blocks (artifacts). This is business metadata because dictionary definitions can be used throughout the technical environment to enhance understanding and add context to data. See Chapter 8 for examples of business metadata delivery (or as knowledge management folks say, dissemination.)

# 15.4    Business Metadata and Tacit Knowledge

The relationship between knowledge management and business metadata becomes a little weak and tenuous when the discussion turns to tacit knowledge, however. Tacit knowledge does not easily lend itself to articulation and transformation into business metadata. Here's part of Wikipedia's formal definition of tacit knowledge:

> Tacit knowledge consists often of habits and culture that we do not recognize in ourselves. In the field of <u>knowledge management</u> the concept of tacit knowledge refers to a knowledge which is only known to you and hard to share with someone else, which is the opposite of the concept of <u>explicit knowledge</u>. (Wikipedia, "Tacit Knowledge," 2006)

Later, the same article states that tacit knowledge "involves learning and skill but not in a way that can be written down."

Business metadata is the result of articulating knowledge so that it can be disseminated to a user; it is stored as data, usually in a DBMS (but can also be stored in groupware like wikis). Since tacit knowledge typically isn't written down, it cannot be stored as business metadata unless it is made explicit knowledge. The knowledge management field is highly concerned with the transmission of tacit knowledge in face-to-face interactions. Nancy Dixon states that one of the three myths of knowledge sharing is that "technology can replace face-to-face [interactions]" (Dixon, 2000, p. 5). So there appears to be a facet of knowledge management that cannot be articulated as business metadata.

## 15.4.1    Making Tacit Knowledge Explicit

Tacit knowledge is therefore "know-how." It is the ability to just *know* how to do something, perform a job, or notice when something does not look quite right—without being able to explain it. Perhaps one of the biggest challenges for knowledge management and the attempt to capture business metadata is to get expert employees to be able to express tacit knowledge; if it can be articulated, it can be put in a business metadata knowledge base.

Sometimes just the act of socialization can drive out tacit knowledge, concretize it, and create the necessary artifacts to add to a knowledge base. The nice thing about collaboration and groupware is their ability to create an audit trail of the socialization process, so that you can actually see where the ideas came from, as they were incubated, in the process of creation. However, some tacit knowledge requires face-to-face interaction. Sometimes the act of explaining one's job to someone else, and the rationale used, can make tacit knowledge too explicit. In the face-to-face case, it is critical that the notes that are taken can be made useful at a later time. These notes become business metadata.

The process, therefore, of how junior employees learn the job—mentoring—should be considered fertile ground for business metadata capture.

### 15.4.1.1   Note-Taking as Asset-Producing

What currently happens to the notes a junior employee takes in mentoring? Usually, these notes are cryptic at best and are lost in the morass of an employee's desk. They are certainly not seen as anything of potential value to the corporation.

Notes are usually very sloppy, not in proper sentences, and unintelligible to anyone other than the note-taker—and sometimes the notes don't even make sense to the note-taker! Notes are also very difficult to organize. If they are supposed to be made available afterward, someone should review them, selecting the salient points and putting them in a format that can be understood. This task usually requires rewriting.

Business metadata management, therefore, involves a process. Note-taking should perhaps be elevated as an important skill. In many methodologies, note-taking is mandatory for meetings. For example, in CMMI,[1] meeting minutes are used as indirect evidence that certain category process areas are being followed. CMMI consists of processes to measure levels of project maturity; notes are considered critical for monitoring and control, in order to reach Level 2, called a "managed process". Notes are instrumental in the following areas:

✦ Fostering stakeholder involvement

✦ Risk monitoring and management

✦ Regular communication of the status of project work

✦ Evidence of identifying issues and deviations from the project plan

✦ Evidence of conducting activities such as milestone reviews and verification activities such as peer reviews

In the mentoring scenario, perhaps the senior employee should go over the junior employee's notes, marking those points of special attention; the two together can perhaps form a knowledge artifact and post it in the corporate knowledge base. In order for this to be done universally throughout the organization,

---

[1]CMMI stands for Capability Maturity Model Integration, which was created by the Software Engineering Institute (SEI); the full set of models were released by SEI in January 2002. It is a very detailed process improvement framework consisting of guidance and best practices for software engineering projects.

however, it must be sanctioned by the company and may require training. The important point here, however, is that mentoring can create vital knowledge artifacts, but people must be encouraged and possibly trained to do so.

In addition, the artifacts themselves have to be managed. They must be placed in a location where all who might find them valuable can access them; even more importantly, the people have to know that they are there. Delivering business metadata artifacts also takes planning and possibly some training. Part of the orientation of new employees can include introduction to the knowledge base.

Notes are therefore very important business metadata, but they need to be well written and managed if they are to be useful to the enterprise.

### 15.4.2 The Knowledge-Sharing Environment: Nurturing Tacit Knowledge Transfer

The discipline of knowledge management focuses on the environment of knowledge sharing and methods of knowledge transfer, with heavy (and sometimes exclusive) focus on face-to-face interactions. Understanding tacit knowledge transfer can lead to innovation, which is the premise of von Krogh, Ichijo, and Nonaka's book, *Enabling Knowledge Creation*. Even though it may not be possible to write the tacit knowledge itself down, the factors that nurture its transfer can be written down. These factors can not only be written and recorded as business metadata, but they can be measured and these metrics will become business metadata. This business metadata can then be used to help the business improve its knowledge-sharing strategy.

## 15.5 Building the Corporate Knowledge Base

In Chapter 6, we defined the corporate knowledge base as everything the organization collectively knows pertaining to its business. Adelman and O'Neil describe it this way:

> It's both organizational knowledge as well as industry knowledge. It's the ability to apply skills to complex situations, it's the cognitive knowledge gained through training and experience, it's the system understanding of cause and effects, it's knowing how the business runs, it's knowing how to avoid the minefields, it's the knowledge of how to find information; who knows it and where to get it. It's been said that the power is not knowing all things yourself but knowing where to find the information. (Adelman and O'Neil, 2007)

We have been using the term *knowledge base* in an abstract fashion; Wikipedia defines it in database terms:

> A **knowledge base** (or **knowledgebase**; abbreviated **KB**, **kb** or Δ) is a special kind of *database* for *knowledge management*. It provides the means for the computerized collection, organization, and *retrieval* of *knowledge*. (Wikipedia, "Knowledge Base," November 25, 2006)

When the knowledge base moves from being abstract and amorphous, out of people's heads, and into an articulated form stored in a database, it becomes business metadata.

Chapter 6 discussed in detail some ideas and techniques for encouraging people to give form to their ideas and share them, whether it is in a wiki or a knowledge-oriented database. Business metadata is required to record the corporate knowledge base and to make it accessible and organized so that it can be useful.

Chapter 6, along with Chapter 4, brought to the forefront several principles for building the corporate knowledge base:

+ The organization must have a plan for encouraging employees to share what they know; sometimes public relations approaches are helpful.

+ A technology must be used that fits into employees' existing workflow and is easy to use.

+ A technology must be used that allows the data to be accessible and repurposed from other applications throughout the enterprise.

The main emphasis of the knowledge management discipline is on the social dynamics and techniques of encouraging knowledge sharing between individuals. The corporate knowledge base, as it becomes represented in a database or other retrievable technology, is business metadata.

# 15.6  Knowledge Management in Practice

Nancy Dixon, in her book *Common Knowledge*, highlights a technique that she calls serial transfer. She notes that each member of a small group or team makes observations concerning an activity: on the environment, on what worked and what didn't, and so on.

> Serial Transfer is a process that moves the unique knowledge that each individual has constructed into a group or public space so that the knowledge can be integrated and made sense of by the whole team. (Dixon, 2000, p. 35)

Serial transfer is a debrief meeting or "postmortem" in which the team can socialize the ideas and come up with insights that the group makes from various individual contributions. Here are Dixon's observations on the socialization factor:

> But the transfer process is more complex than just team members reporting out their knowledge so that others in the group are aware of it. Individual team members are able to use what others have said to reinterpret how they themselves understand the situation. In the Haiti example, the soldier who "knew" that he had not seen many dogs in the village now "knows" that in a new way. The fact has not changed, but the way that fact relates to other facts has changed. This integration of ideas spawns the reconsideration of cause and effect, it produces the if/then that leads to new team action, it identifies discrepancies in the perception of what occurred, and it develops new generalizations that may guide future action. It is in this important sense that a transfer of knowledge has occurred, from individual knowing to group knowing. (Dixon, 2000, p. 35)

The dog example she refers to is part of a story relating to a U.S. Army disarmament of a rebel town in Haiti in 1994. At their debrief meeting, the first soldier noticed that there were few dogs; the second noticed that the people were fearful of the soldiers' police dogs. This led to a suggestion that the next time the soldiers should take dogs with them.

In Chapter 6, we discussed this phenomenon as "socialization." Groups are often smarter than individuals because of this socialization factor. Business metadata is concerned with the socialization phenomenon, so that it can be captured as explicit knowledge in a knowledge base, and organized and made available for future use in similar situations.

It doesn't matter whether these socialization "debrief" meetings are face-to-face or online. The main point is to capture what was learned, and the various people's comments too, so that both can be used in subsequent situations.

As we discussed in Chapter 8, information that is not easily accessible is not very useful to the organization. Business metadata, therefore, can support knowledge management by

- ✦ Facilitating knowledge capture through technologies like wikis or collaboration/groupware (Chapter 6)

- ✦ Facilitating knowledge dissemination by using technologies that allow the information to be accessed when and where it is most likely to be needed (Chapter 8)

- ✦ Providing for organization of the metadata by categorization schemes, controlled vocabularies, taxonomies, and ontology so that information can be easily found.

# 15.7 Knowledge Management and Social Issues

### 15.7.1 Graying of the Workforce

In 2006, approximately 75 million people born between 1946 and 1964, turned 60 years old (see Segel, 2006). As noted at the beginning of this chapter, the main type of worker in the knowledge economy is the knowledge worker. Obviously, then, if a large percentage of the workforce retires at once, the result will be an incredible brain drain. This is precisely what is about to occur as the "baby-boomer" generation hits retirement age. K.C. Jones, quoting IBM, describes the ramifications of this event as follows: "The aging population will be one of the major social and <u>business</u> issues of the 21<sup>st</sup> Century."

IBM has recognized the importance of the shifting population demographics by setting up a special division to help its clients figure out their best strategies to cope with it.

Here's how another article puts it:

> When aging workers start retiring, the shift will likely result in serious shortages of specific skilled positions such as machinists and engineers and, perhaps more importantly, a loss of intellectual capital and institutional memory. ... Pretty soon, tens of millions of those boomers are going to walk out the door, taking with them a wealth of knowledge that can't easily be replaced. (Sun Executive Board Room, 2004)

Obviously, knowledge management is interested in the capture of business knowledge, and in no time in our history has this capture been needed more than now. All of the techniques discussed in this book are required to assist in this massive knowledge capture exercise. These techniques include:

✦ Brainstorming sessions (and adequate note-taking)

✦ Employee mentoring (and good note-taking)

✦ Wikis

✦ Blogs

✦ Employee-authored dictionaries, encyclopedias, and knowledge artifact libraries

✦ Social networking

✦ Cultural emphasis on knowledge sharing

✦ Groupware and collaboration software

All of these techniques involve business metadata in some way, even cultural emphasis. As discussed earlier in this chapter, the enabling factors that encourage knowledge sharing can be measured, and not only are these enabling factors themselves business metadata, but they generate metrics which is also business metadata. Business metadata, partnered with knowledge management, can play a huge role in assisting the enterprise in capturing some of the intellectual capital before it walks out the door.

### 15.7.2 The Effect of Socialization on Knowledge

Knowledge socialization, described in Chapter 6 as the way people share knowledge about a topic, actually increases the quality and value of the knowledge itself, as well as making the group as a whole smarter. This effect can be summarized as follows:

- ✦ Knowledge evolves, based on one idea being added onto others that have gone before.

- ✦ A group is usually smarter than any one individual, even an expert.

- ✦ Socialization, therefore, not only helps make the group smarter, but also grows the knowledge, which can enable the individual to find the knowledge later (therefore helping the individual to be smarter).

As a corporate asset-building vehicle, socialization can be very powerful. It can not only help assuage the graying-of-the-workforce brain drain, but it can help grow knowledge in the corporation, create a reusable business metadata knowledge base, and also make everyone smarter in the process, both as a group and by using a readily available knowledge resource. This sounds like something important that every enterprise should be doing!

# 15.8 Summary

This chapter has built on several previous chapters in this book to bring all the ideas together from the perspective of knowledge management. We discovered that business metadata not only intersects the field of knowledge management, but that the two are actually inextricably intertwined.

This linkage is due to the symbiotic relationship between process and data: both are required for the enterprise to succeed, and both need each other.

We discussed the role of business metadata and tacit knowledge, and at first glance it appears that business metadata cannot help capture what cannot be articulated. However, business metadata could perhaps aid two aspects of tacit knowledge:

+ During the mentoring process, with good note-taking, some tacit knowledge can actually be captured.

+ Business metadata can record the factors that knowledge management has determined facilitate tacit knowledge sharing, and these factors can be turned into metrics to help the business track its progress.

Lastly, we discussed the impact of business metadata on social issues like the graying of the workforce, and we noted the importance of knowledge socialization. Knowledge management and business metadata are too important to ignore and should be incorporated into every organization's strategic plans.

# 15.9 References

+ Adelman, Sid, and O'Neil, Bonnie. "Capturing Intellectual Capital in Metadata." *DM Review,* February, 2007. http://www.dmreview.com/editorial/dmreview/print_action.cfm?articleId = 1075079

+ Dixon, Nancy. *Common Knowledge.* Cambridge, MA: Harvard Business School Press, 2000.

+ Jones, K.C. "Big Blue Offers Solutions for Graying Workforce." TechWeb, September 28, 2005. http://www.techweb.com/wire/ebiz/171201471.

+ Segel, Jonathan A. "Time Is on Their Side." *HR Magazine*, February 2006. http://findarticles.com/p/articles/mi_m3495/is_2_51/ai_n16101872

+ Sun Executive Boardroom. "How to Deal with a Graying Workforce." January, 2004. http://www.sun.com/br/0104_ezine/man_graying.html

+ Von Krogh, Georg, et al. Enabling Knowledge Creation. Oxford: Oxford University Press, 2000.

+ Wikipedia. "Knowledge Base." Referenced on November 26, 2006, http://en.wikipedia.org/wiki/Knowledge_base

+ Wikipedia. "Knowledge Management." Referenced on November 25, 2006, http://en.wikipedia.org/wiki/Knowledge_management

+ Wikipedia. "Tacit Knowledge." Referenced on November 25, 2006, http://en.wikipedia.org/wiki/Tacit_knowledge

# In Summary

## 16.1 Introduction

This chapter ties together the main topics of the present book, looking mainly at the value that business metadata brings to the business and the major industry trends that focus on facilitating both the capture and dissemination of business metadata. Like most things of value, the capture and dissemination of business metadata require discipline. As we have learned in this book, both are important to the business metadata equation.

The essence of business metadata is reducing or eliminating the barriers of communication between the human and the computer, so that the data conveyed from reports, data warehouses, and information systems in general can be crystal clear and can facilitate business actions and decision making. This chapter reviews these barriers. The book has explored all kinds of mitigation strategies to circumvent these barriers.

This chapter discusses several topics we have learned from implementation of business metadata:

✦ Use of the business rules approach to manage business change

✦ Virtual knowledge sharing through groupware

✦ Enterprise search, and how business metadata can facilitate finding documents faster

In an attempt to forecast the future for business metadata, four industry trends become evident:

✦ Metadata delivery, including innovative portal vendors offering new vehicles for users to integrate and share information, like enterprise "mashups"

✦ Semantic integration and discovery: tools that enable you to detect what treasures are lurking underneath your data

✦ Compliance, serving as a heavy business driver toward better data understanding

✦ A leap in unstructured data mining and content management in general, with more and more reasons to utilize them, such as compliance efforts as mentioned above.

In addition, a few resources are listed concerning conferences and Web sites specializing in some of the areas we have labeled "business metadata."

## 16.2 The Importance of Business Metadata

Business metadata emphasizes the most important aspect of IT: making computers and information technology useful to the businesspeople themselves; not indirectly, but directly. Business metadata is about clarification and meaning; it is about enhancing reports and one-dimensional data with background information, allowing data to be turned into information and the information to be turned into wisdom.

Business metadata has been with us in many forms throughout the years of IT history; what is different now is our intentionality surrounding it. Business metadata management should be practiced by all IT shops and should be brought out into the business itself. Businesspeople need to be empowered to create their own business metadata. One of the obstacles businesspeople have had in the past has been the technologies available for creating business metadata. In the past, IT was limited in the development of applications to create and integrate business metadata. Today, folksonomies, wikis, blogs, portal technologies, groupware in general, and enterprise mashups are some of the technologies that are making business metadata more accessible to businesspeople with limited IT resource requirements.

We are living in an exciting era of new technologies; it is likely that after this book is published, yet more technologies will become available that will enable businesspeople to create their own business metadata and share it with others. That is the key; the true power of business metadata is for businesspersons themselves to create their own business metadata, but they have to open it up and enable others to share it.

# 16.3  Business Metadata and Metadata Initiatives

Business metadata is often ignored when an organization launches a metadata initiative. There are a number of factors behind its neglect:

- ✦ Technical metadata is more accessible.

- ✦ Business metadata is not well understood. (Hopefully, this book will help rectify this failing!)

- ✦ Tool vendors concentrate on technical metadata.

- ✦ IT staff are the main consumers of technical metadata, so this is what they focus on.

- ✦ Technical metadata helps the IT shop handle some of their biggest problems, like impact analysis.

Perhaps the largest barrier that business metadata presents is its capture. It is extremely difficult to capture what is in businesspeoples' heads. Part of the problem is getting them to recognize that sharing business metadata can have significant financial value for the enterprise as a whole. Some organizational cultures are downright hostile concerning information sharing between departments, some political barriers exist between organizations, and some actually provide disincentives concerning the sharing of information (or business metadata). However, sharing information can be enormously valuable, as we saw especially in the discussion of Surowiecki's book, *The Wisdom of Crowds*, in Chapter 6. There is indeed strength in the "collective" mentality. Considering the value that business metadata can bring to an enterprise, we hope resistance is futile.

# 16.4   The Essence of Business Metadata

The interest in semantic technologies is very interesting and encouraging; the fact that we need to focus on transferring meaning between computers is a critical part of getting computers to be really useful. Semantic technology, however, has not come full circle yet. It enables knowledge to be coded in such a way as to encase meaning. Semantic technology is very powerful, because it enables the computer to "know" certain things, and new knowledge can be inferred, or actually created, based on what is already known. However, what it doesn't provide (yet) is the round trip—it doesn't communicate this knowledge very well back to the user. Instead, a programmer is required to act as an interpreter, and an interface is required to interpret the inferred knowledge back to the user, especially business users. I don't know many business users that can readily understand OWL or RDF. Open-source software is presently available from Stanford University and others, which creates a (somewhat) user-friendly application environment, but the semantic technology discipline doesn't presently focus on the human factor. Their main focus at the moment is on the computer understandability problem.

### 16.4.1   The Human to Computer Communication Problem

The communication problem, from human to computer and then back again, is a huge area of both concern and promise. Let's revisit several figures from Chapter 10 to review this problem.

The first communication barrier is that involving human to human (Figure 16.1). As we can see by the illustration, there is an inherent problem in sharing basic semantics between humans.

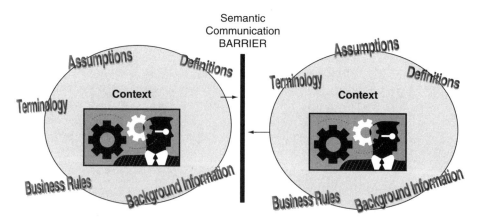

**Figure 16.1**   Human to Human Communication Barrier.

If there is a semantic gap between humans, obviously a very large gap exists between human and computer. Requirements get in the way; it is like the child's game of telephone. It is even worse than what is shown in Figure 16.2 because usually a chain of humans is involved. The businessperson tells the requirements analyst what their requirements are; then the requirements analyst tells the programmer; next, the programmer writes the code; and then the programmer tells the tester what to test for. An as we know from Figure 16.1, a semantic gap exists between each pair of humans. It's amazing we get anything right at all!

Computer to computer data sharing is very problematic. How do we know that the semantics embedded in one system are the same as the semantics in any other system? The fact is, we don't, and the probability is nil, especially since we do such a poor job of documenting these semantics (see Figure 16.3).

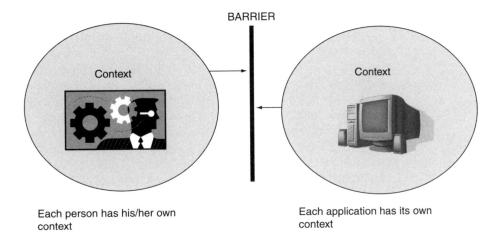

**Figure 16.2**   Human/Computer Communication Barrier.

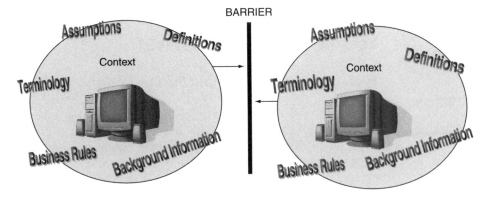

**Figure 16.3**   Computer to Computer Communication Barrier.

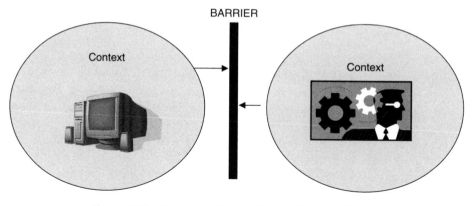

**Figure 16.4** Computer Back to Human Semantic Barrier.

Lastly, there's the computer back to human interaction, shown in Figure 16.4. It looks the same as Figure 16.2 but it is really not, in this context.

Business metadata mainly addresses the fourth gap, computer to human, but it also addresses the others tangentially. The main thrust of business metadata is about adding context to data that is housed in computer applications and about helping businesspeople make sense of their data. The Roach Motel analogy comes to mind here: You can get data into a system all you want, but if you can't get it out, then what good is it? This observation applies especially to understanding the data. For decades we have focused on building more and more sophisticated applications for capturing and tracking corporate data. However, you can put lots and lots of data into your corporate applications, like ERP, financial applications, CRM, you name it, any application that runs your business, but if the data coming out doesn't make sense, including reports and graphs, then the data is not very useful. All the effort, time, and expense needed to build and populate these systems are wasted. Business metadata addresses this problem.

# 16.5 Lessons Learned in the Field

## 16.5.1 Business Rules and Business Change

The business rules community has been in existence for almost 20 years, as we discussed in Chapter 13. It represents perhaps the first concentrated effort in business metadata: Its primary concern was in bridging the gap between businesspeople and the computer, allowing for businesspeople to express their business rules in such a way as to permit them to change the rules on their own and to overthrow the tyranny of IT when it comes to responding to business and market change. This is not an attempt to say that IT personnel are not doing their job; to the contrary, IT people are working harder today than they were 50 years ago. IT has the daunting challenges to respond in a manner that is faster and better all at the same time. In today's global economy and fast-paced environment, he who hesitates loses. The faster an enterprise can respond to shifting market forces, the better its chances are of staying alive.

Business rules represent a different paradigm of building applications. The business rules approach requires a different infrastructure than traditional applications, and as such there is a barrier of entry, as there is for business metadata in general. Traditional applications require architecture to be in place, which in turn requires planning. As in the business rules approach, however, the end result empowers businesspeople.

### 16.5.2 Virtual Knowledge Sharing via Groupware

Groupware has created new ways for employees within a company to collaborate. Groupware can set up virtual ways of sharing information and turning data into information. In one project, the use of groupware enabled the virtual team, spread out all over the country including Alaska, to exchange ideas that resulted in fewer face-to-face meetings and even enabled the meeting, when it did take place, to get out early!

Groupware is an example of business metadata. It provides a vehicle for businesspeople to share information and to provide extra information about data; to comment on existing data (comment threads concerning reports, for example); as well as to create new knowledge or add onto someone else's entry, as in the use of wikis.

### 16.5.3 Enterprise Search

In Chapter 4, we examined the whole problem of searching for information; it is often frustrating, and business metadata can greatly improve the search experience and increase the odds of finding what you are looking for faster. Business metadata can be in the form of categorization schemes such as taxonomies, but can also be as simple as good descriptive file names. Some interesting Web trends are setting the stage for new ways of sharing tags and categorizing information such as folksonomies, manifested in sites such as del.icio.us and flickr. Del.icio.us allows you to tag Web sites and share your tags with others, and it also takes advantage of other people's tags to find similar information. Flickr is another example of a folksonomy; you share your pictures online, and you tag them different things, based on your own way of understanding the world. Both are creative examples of business metadata.

# 16.6   What Does the Future Hold?

### 16.6.1   Metadata Delivery

As we saw in Chapter 8, new products that allow businesspeople to create their own portal applications can facilitate the sharing of business metadata. This very exciting trend should be expected to continue, with more powerful tools for businesspeople to build their own mini-applications and do so faster, better, and cheaper than in the past.

### 16.6.2   Semantic Integration and Discovery

Integration and sorting out the semantics between two or more systems is not as easily accomplished, but even in this complex area, new tools are on the horizon that will help discover hidden semantics in structured and unstructured data, exposing to us the often hidden business metadata. These tools uncover "nuggets of meaning" in the underlying data through both top-down and bottom-up processes.

In addition, new tools now on the market can help ferret out and determine by sophisticated semantic matching underlying connections between fields, and even parts of fields. For example, laws are on the books that restrict sensitive data from being released to third parties. Sometimes sensitive data can be released inadvertently because there is an underlying connection between that data and other, seemingly innocuous data. These tools can reveal these hidden connections, protecting your company from fines and jail terms.

### 16.6.3   Compliance

As the previous example concerning sensitive data illustrates, the compliance issue for major government agencies and corporations is not going away any time soon. It is a fact of life that must be faced and surmounted. Business metadata can assist companies in fighting fraud and in tracing customer interactions by understanding the trail of events in a new way. Business metadata can provide traceability by utilizing the trail of unstructured metadata surrounding these events: the e-mails, correspondence, presentations, and other unstructured data that before would have gone unnoticed. In addition, as businesspeople get used to sharing information, they will (hopefully) document the results of interactions with customers and other external entities more often, which will also facilitate traceability of business communications more completely.

### 16.6.4 Content Management and Unstructured Data Mining

Managing unstructured data has become a hot area of interest in recent years, mainly because there is so much out there that is so underutilized. Making sense of the vast quantity of documents, e-mails, and the like, and, most importantly, tying it to the structured world will become more and more important with time. In addition, delivering unstructured content on demand such as video clips and audio files is also becoming possible due to advances in technology. Such data carries with it metadata, and of course, business metadata.

## 16.7 Resources

Business metadata is beginning to attract more attention at conferences. Each year at the International DAMA (Data Administrative Management Association) Conference a few presentations are made on business metadata. Interestingly enough, more and more articles are mentioning its importance, and in 2006, most of the applicants for the International DAMA Metadata Award demonstrated implementation for business metadata capture and dissemination, in addition to the usual technical metadata techniques.

To our knowledge, this is the first general business or IT book to appear on this subject. Past works have mentioned it, but none really concentrated on it to any great degree. Most recent authors on metadata acknowledge the existence of business metadata but have not focused on it. However, there are many articles and vendor white papers on the subject.

Conferences and communities of interest specializing in various aspects of business metadata include the following:

- ✦ Dictionaries: *The Dictionary Society of North America:* http://polyglot. lss.wisc.edu/dsna/

- ✦ Portals and Collaboration

    - ✦ Collaborative Technologies Conference, renamed Enterprise 2.0 http://www.enterprise2conf.com/

    - ✦ Portals, Collaboration, and Content Conference http://www.enterprise2conf.com/

- ✦ Semantics: Semantic Technologies Conference: www.semantic-conference. com/

- ✦ Business Rules Community: online resource for business rules http:// www.brcommunity.com/index.php

Business metadata is becoming a more recognized component of the data warehouse. In (Data Warehouse) DW 2.0™, metadata is a recognized component, and its subtypes are business and technical.

# 16.8 **Summary**

This chapter has reviewed the main topics covered by the book and has attempted to make the case for the importance of business metadata to the future of computing. It is imperative that business users begin to see that their on-the-job discoveries and revelations concerning how they can better perform their jobs can benefit others. It is also crucial that they begin to share these revelations with their colleagues. In addition, technologists need to be alert to opportunities and new avenues to facilitate interaction between businesspeople in the sharing of this information. This means setting up metadata infrastructure (see Chapter 9) and creating new knowledge collaboration and dissemination methods that will reach out to ever more businesspeople in the places where they most need clarity.

New technological advancements are on the horizon that will continue to facilitate business collaboration. However, the real challenge is in harnessing these technologies in such a way as to create business wisdom. This will take architecture and engineering; it will not happen by itself. To a great extent it is in the creative applications of these technologies that the power will be gained. It is hoped that this book will stimulate your creativity and assist you in that great adventure we all have before us.

# Appendix

## Metadata System of Record Example

**Table 1**  Metadata object system of record

| Meta Object | Strategic Modeling Tool | Tactical Modeling Tool | DBMS Tool | Data Integration Tool | Reporting Tool |
|---|---|---|---|---|---|
| Entity Name | C | | | | |
| Entity Type | C | | | | |
| Entity Definition | C | U | | | |
| Entity Scope | C | | | | |
| Entity Active Ind | C | U | | | |
| Entity Logical Business Rule | C | U | | U | |
| Logical Application Name | C | | | | |
| Entity Synonym Name | C | | | | |
| Logical Attribute | C | | | | |
| Logical Attribute Definition | C | U | | | |
| Attribute Logical Business Rule | C | U | | U | |
| Attribute Logical FK Ind | C | U | | | |
| Attribute Business Area | C | U | | | |
| Logical Business Function | C | U | | | |
| Data Subject Area | C | | | | |
| Physical Column Name | | | C | U | |
| Physical Column Data Type | | | C | U | |
| Physical Column Length | | | C | U | |
| Physical Column Precision | | | C | U | |

*(Cont.)*

**Table 1** Metadata object system of record (continued)

| Meta Object | Strategic Modeling Tool | Tactical Modeling Tool | DBMS Tool | Data Integration Tool | Reporting Tool |
|---|---|---|---|---|---|
| Physical Column Decimal places | | | | | |
| Physical Column Default Value | C | U | | | |
| Physical Column Nullable Ind | C | U | | | |
| Physical Column Comment | C | U | | | |
| Physical Column Primary Key Ind | C | U | | | |
| Physical Column Foreign Key Ind | C | U | | | |
| Table Name | C | U | | | |
| Table Owner | C | U | | | |
| Table Type | C | U | | | |
| Table Comments | C | U | | | |
| Physical Table Name | | | C | | |
| Physical Column Name | | | C | | |
| Physical View Name | | | C | | |
| Physical Database Name | | | C | | |
| Physical Schema Name | | | C | | |
| ETL Object Name | | | | C | |
| Source Table | | | | R | |
| Source Column | | | | R | |
| Target Table | | | | R | |
| Target Column | | | | R | |
| ETL Job Name | | | | C | |
| ETL Transformation Rule | | | | C | |
| ETL Job Run Date | | | | C | |
| ETL Job Execution Time | | | | C | |
| ETL Job Row Count | | | | C | |
| ETL Job Status | | | | C | |
| Report Name | | | | | C |
| Report Element Name | | | | | R |
| Report Table Name | | | | | R |
| Report Database Name | | | | | R |
| Report DB Sequence | | | | | R |
| Report Element Business Rule | | | | | C |

# Metadata Usage Matrix Example

The following table summarizes the metadata objects and the anticipated usage of each object in the following functions:

**Table 1**   Summary of metadata objects usage

| Source – Metadata Object | Data Lineage | Impact Analysis | Definition and or Glossary |
|---|---|---|---|
| Entity Name | Y | Y | Y |
| Entity Type | Y | Y | Y |
| Entity Definition | Y | Y | Y |
| Entity Scope | Y | Y | Y |
| Entity Container | Y | Y | Y |
| Entity Active Ind | Y | Y | Y |
| Entity Logical Business Rule | Y | Y | Y |
| Logical Application Name | Y | Y | Y |
| Entity Synonym Name | Y | Y | Y |
| Logical Attribute | Y | Y | Y |
| Logical Attribute Definition | Y | Y | Y |
| Attribute Logical Business Rule | Y | Y | Y |
| Attribute Logical FK Ind | Y | Y | |
| Attribute Business Area | Y | Y | Y |
| Logical Business Function | | | Y |
| Data Subject Area | | | Y |
| Physical Column Name | Y | Y | Y |
| Physical Column Data Type | Y | Y | Y |
| Physical Column Length | Y | Y | Y |
| Physical Column Precision | Y | Y | Y |
| Physical Column Decimal Places | Y | Y | Y |
| Physical Column Default Value | Y | Y | |
| Physical Column Nullable Ind | Y | Y | |

**Table 1**  Summary of metadata objects usage (continued)

| Source – Metadata Object | Data Lineage | Impact Analysis | Definition and or Glossary |
|---|:---:|:---:|:---:|
| Physical Column Comment | Y | Y | Y |
| Physical Column Primary Key Ind | Y | Y | Y |
| Physical Column Foreign Key Ind | Y | Y | Y |
| Table Name | Y | Y | Y |
| Table Owner | Y | Y | Y |
| Table Type | Y | Y | Y |
| Table Comments | Y | Y | Y |
| Physical Table Name | Y | Y | |
| Physical Column Name | Y | Y | |
| Physical View Name | Y | Y | |
| Physical Database Name | Y | Y | Y |
| Physical Schema Name | Y | Y | Y |
| ETL Object Name | Y | Y | Y |
| Source Table | Y | Y | Y |
| Source Column | Y | Y | |
| Target Table | Y | Y | |
| Target Column | Y | Y | |
| ETL Job Name | Y | Y | |
| ETL Transformation Rule | Y | Y | |
| ETL Job Run Date | Y | Y | |
| ETL Job Execution Time | Y | Y | |
| ETL Job Row Count | Y | Y | |
| ETL Job Status | Y | Y | |
| Report Name | Y | Y | |
| Report Element Name | Y | Y | |
| Report Table Name | Y | Y | |
| Report Database Name | Y | Y | |
| Report DB Sequence | Y | Y | |
| Report Element Business Rule | | | Y |

# Index